AN AMERICAN HERO

AN
AMERICAN HERO

THE RED ADAIR STORY

An Authorized Biography
by Philip Singerman

LITTLE, BROWN AND COMPANY

BOSTON   TORONTO   LONDON

First American Edition

Library of Congress Cataloging-in-Publication Data

Singerman, Philip.
    An American hero : the Red Adair story : an authorized biography /
by Philip Singerman. — 1st U.S. ed.
        p.   cm.
    ISBN 0-316-79281-0
    1. Adair, Red.   2. Fire fighters — United States — Biography.
3. Oil wells — Fires and fire prevention.   4. Gas wells — Fires and
fire prevention.   1. Title
TH9118.A33S56   1990
628.9'2'092 — dc20
    [B]   921   89-77162
                                                        CIP

10 9 8 7 6 5 4

BP
*Published simultaneously in Canada
by Little, Brown & Company (Canada) Limited*

Printed in the United States of America

For Marcia
Philip Singerman

In memory of Myron M. Kinley
Red Adair

CONTENTS

ACKNOWLEDGMENTS

I would like to thank the many people who were so generous with their time, their stories, and their expertise, all of which were invaluable to me as I researched and wrote this book. My thanks to Red's family: his wife, Kemmie, his son, Jimmy, his grandson, Paul Wayne, his sisters, Faye and May, and especially his daughter, Robyn, whose years of dedication and persistence finally made possible the telling of her father's story; Red's men: Raymond Henry, Richard Hatteberg, Brian Krause, Danny Clayton, and Gregg Spedale; his old friends Jerry Morton, Squirt Baker, Doug Henderson, Wiley Hodgens, John Mecom, Jr., and Betty and Lea DeMontrond; Joy Hamilton, Red's first secretary, and Paula Pearce, who coordinates things around his office now; Bob Eslinger, drilling instructor for the Chevron Oil Company, who taught me so much about the way an oil rig works; Ron Thomas of Hall Houston Oil Company, who kindly got me out on an offshore rig in the Gulf of Mexico; Neil Watson, news editor of *The Press and Journal* in Aberdeen, Scotland, who helped me gather information about the Piper Alpha disaster; to my friends Alan and Carolyn Luce and Bill Geary, who were always there to help while I was putting the book together; a special thanks, as well, to my agent, Ned Leavitt, for his patience and diplomacy, and to my editors Fredi Friedman and Colleen Mohyde at Little, Brown and Kathy Rooney at Bloomsbury; and of course, my heartfelt thanks to Red himself, whose motto, "Nothing is impossible," stayed with me during the two and a half years I worked on the story of his life.

Philip Singerman
1989

To all the men who lived and died in the oil patch: this book is for you.

To the late Robert Arthur and Sam Weisbord: you have my deepest respect and appreciation for believing in this project and introducing my daughter to Irene Webb and Ned Leavitt. Without Irene, Ned, their staff, and our editors, Kathy Rooney, Fredi Friedman, and Colleen Mohyde, we could never have made it. And of course, my sincere thanks to Phil Singerman, with whom we shared many heartfelt moments.

To my son, Jimmy, his wife, Candy, my daughter, Robyn, and my grandchildren, Paul Wayne and Sunny: thank you for sharing your lives with me and your memories, some of them quite painful, with Phil.

To my wife, Kemmie, who was there when no one else was and who never stopped believing in me: always remember, I'd do it all over again!

Red Adair
1989

PREFACE

Down in Texas, they tell this story about Red Adair. It seems a Texan died and came face to face with St. Peter. Now this Texan was a big shot, a real mover and shaker, and a Lone Star chauvinist to boot. St. Peter, who was sick and tired of hearing what a great place Texas was, decided to put him quickly in his place.

"Look over there," St. Peter said to the Texan. "You see those lush, rolling hills covered with flowers, and that beautiful forest beyond it? You have anything as pretty as that in Texas?"

"Sure do," the Texan replied. "As a matter of fact, we got a place just like that up near Tyler."

"Well, take a look over yonder," said St. Peter. "See that sparkling river and those bubbling rapids with fish jumping around in them? You have anything like that in Texas?"

"Sure do," said the old boy. "Up north of Austin we got a place that looks every bit as inviting as that there river of yours."

About this time, St. Peter was getting a bit annoyed, so he snapped his fingers and pointed over his shoulder where the fires of hell were raging. "What about that?" he asked. "You have anything the equal of that down in Texas?"

The old boy took a long look at the inferno, at the flames shooting hundreds of feet into the air and the boiling lava surging around the fire's base. "No sir, we surely don't," he said. "But we got the only son of a bitch who can put it out."

AN AMERICAN HERO

CHAPTER ONE

Drilling a well's a gamble. The payoff can be real big, or you can go broke in a hurry. The payoff can be terrible when men's lives are lost. You can take every precaution, but you never know when something will let go. It can happen any time. It can happen any place. Sure as hell, it'll happen again, but then that's the romance of oil.

Red Adair

THE NORTH SEA — 1988

First came the scream of escaping gas — a piercing, paralyzing scream, the scream of a thousand nightmares, as terrifying as the roar of an angry jungle cat six feet from your tent. It was a scream that turned the world around it into nothing but sound, ripping through a man's nervous system, riveting him to his boots, pinning him to his mattress, sucking the breath from his lungs. Hear it once and you'll never rest easy on a drilling rig again — if you're lucky enough to be alive for another chance.

There were 229 men on Occidental Petroleum's Piper Alpha production platform in the North Sea on the night of July 6, 1988, and none of them knew the source of the screaming gas. It might have been a faulty valve in the wellhead module. It was from this location on the floor of the platform, known as module A, that thirty-six wells snaked their way down into a vast, bulbous, undersea hydrocarbon formation, reaching depths more than five miles below the water's surface. Equipment was constantly being changed, cleaned, and adjusted at the wellheads, and that, coupled with the large quantity of oil — at peak, more than 300,000 barrels a day — mixed with voluminous amounts of gas, made module A the most dangerous location on the platform.

The screaming gas might have come from a crack in a pipe

between the separation module, module B, where chemical processes separated the gas and oil, and module C, the gas compression module. In module C two huge compressors, powered by Rolls-Royce RB211 engines, similar to those used on jumbo jets, raised the 5,000-pound-per-square-inch surface pressure of the gas to over 15,000 pounds per square inch, a level necessary to propel the gas through a subsea pipe to shore. Perhaps a fissure in one of the high-pressure vessels in the gas compression module was the cause, or maybe it was a leak in the piping between module C and the twin gas turbines in module D, the platform power generation module that also housed the rig's control room. No one would ever know for sure. But every man on the platform — from flight personnel on the helideck, to roustabouts on the drilling floor, to cooks in the galley — even those who had never heard it before, understood instantly what the scream meant and what could follow.

These men knew the sound of the North Sea wind that howled up to 100 miles an hour through the drilling derrick atop the platform. They knew the sound of eighty-foot waves crashing against the tubular steel production jacket, a 14,000-ton skeleton of beams and braces rising out of the water, on which the platform rested. They knew the thudding rotor sound of helicopters taking off and landing on the platform, as well as the pulsing drone of diesel engines from work boats that came alongside. All of these were familiar to the men, part of the rhythm of life offshore, as were the sounds of Piper herself.

Piper Alpha had been put in place 120 miles northeast of Aberdeen, Scotland, in 1975, in water 474 feet deep. Massive pilings were sunk 380 feet into the ocean floor on top of which the production jacket was anchored. The 495-foot production jacket had been built on shore and was towed to the drilling site on a 500-foot barge, where it was tipped into the water by barge-mounted cranes. Then, giant steel buoyancy bottles, welded to the jacket's legs, were slowly filled with water, sinking the jacket. As it sank, tugboats cabled to its legs maneuvered the jacket onto the pilings. On top of the production jacket, which stuck out of the water about one hundred feet, a steel deck-support frame was welded. On this frame were placed a number of large rectangular boxes — Piper's modules — each a subdivision enclosing a distinct platform function.

If you looked at a cutaway of Piper Alpha from the side, you would see a bottom row of four modules — wellhead, oil and gas separation, gas compression, and platform power generation — sitting directly on the deck-support frame. Above these four were the drilling derrick, a crane, and modules for storage, pressure tanks, platform filtration, and exhaust. High over module D, the power generation module, were stacked two accommodation modules that served as quarters for Piper's crew. In addition to sleeping and dining facilities, these modules had game rooms, a library, space for watching movies and television, and the rig's administrative offices. Piper Alpha had two rotating crews, each spending seven days offshore on the rig followed by seven days in port. On the platform, a crew was divided into two twelve-hour shifts, so at any given time approximately half the men on board could be found in the accommodation modules.

When the platform was first assembled, all the modules were constructed of steel except for the accommodation modules, which were made of wood and fiberglass, much like ones used in the Gulf of Mexico. The British government had given Occidental Petroleum a dispensation to use the wood and fiberglass modules temporarily with the understanding that steel enclosures with fire-protection walls would eventually be installed. One of the original modules had, in fact, been replaced by a steel construction, but one of the old accommodation modules still remained on board.

Above the accommodation modules, 180 feet off the water, was the platform's helideck with twin helipads. Diagonally across the rig from the helideck, at the corner nearest the drilling derrick, two 100-foot flare booms stuck out over the water like long skeletal snouts. These booms supported two pipes, through which the platform's excess gas flowed. This gas was continuously burned off, or "flared," using burners at the ends of the pipes, the flames coloring the sea below them a burnt orange, as though the rig was sitting in a perpetual sunset.

At a distance, especially in the umbral twilight of a subarctic summer night, the platform looked like a gigantic, multilegged, fire-breathing monster rising up out of the waves. Surrounded as it was by nothing but hundreds of square miles of cold, dark sea, it appeared formidable and thrilling in its isolation. From the top of its derrick to the bottom of its pilings, it stood 1,120 feet tall and weighed more than 34,000 tons. But it was an old monster. Buffeted for thirteen years by the most corrosive weather conditions on earth, it creaked and groaned, and when all its wells were pumping it shuddered like an old freighter under full power. The vibration was most pronounced in the wooden accommodation module, where newcomers, curled in their bunks, sometimes wondered whether the rig was about to self-destruct. Even veterans of the rig were wary, remembering a gas leak in 1984 that killed no one, but blew a door off module C.

The pay was good, however, and there was a mystique to working offshore, as though a man led a double life: calm and mundane at home with his family, tough and dangerous out on the platform where he was cut off from the rest of the world and catastrophe was always a heartbeat away. So the men accepted the volatile nature of the rig filled with pressurized oil and gas, and they worked and ate and slept in tune with its shakes and moans, the old hands saying to the new, "Forget it, laddie, dance to it, it ain't nothing but the music of old Piper."

The screaming gas was something else altogether. It was the shriek of the devil, freezing every man to his bones faster than a March dip in the North Sea, compressing a lifetime of noise into a microsecond. It was 9:30 P.M. — the night shift was at work, the day shift at rest — when the screaming came. There was enough time to realize what it was, enough time for a man to quickly say a prayer, before a spark from a piece of electrical apparatus, a dropped tool, or a welding torch hit the gas and the first explosion blew a corner of the rig by modules C and D to bits. The control room was destroyed, all communication lines obliterated, and the platform's power-generating system demolished. The only light on Piper Alpha now was from the fire, enveloping the blown-up portion of the platform and spreading, obscuring forever the number of men killed instantly by the blast.

Steel beams and pieces of equipment hurtled through the air as a series of additional explosions tore through modules A and B, igniting a number of the platform's wells. The rig trembled and convulsed, and the accommodation modules, now engulfed in flames, shifted so that the three-inch-thick steel fire doors at all the exits were jammed shut. Inside the accommodation modules, where more than a hundred men were now trapped in darkness, the air began to fill with billows of thick smoke. There were screams and curses and cries for help as the men waited for orders to evacuate the rig.

Discipline on an offshore production platform is very strict — stricter, in fact, than on most military installations. There are no alcoholic beverages on board — not even a single cold beer to wash away the grit of a twelve-hour shift — and if you do drugs of any kind, get in a fight, get caught sleeping on the job, or disobey a superior's command, you're through. No court-martial, no appeal, no second chance. Take the next helicopter to shore and don't come back.

Workers on the platform are constantly reminded to follow orders and adhere to specific offshore directives. They are cautioned, for example, to avoid jumping into the water at all costs, because even in summer the North Sea is so cold a man floating in it would remain conscious for just a few minutes. At Aberdeen's famous Offshore Survival Centre, where many rig workers are trained, the men learn that plunging into water from great heights is like plunging from a rooftop onto concrete. If you don't do it right, the impact will result in irreparable spinal injury, and water gushing up your nose will sever one of the vagus nerves, causing instant death. At the school, men learn to jump properly by pinching their noses and clenching their buttocks, but they practice from a platform ten feet high, not from a swaying flare boom one hundred feet above the waves, or a helideck eighty feet higher than that.

The man in charge of a production platform, the offshore installation manager, is in total control, the absolute authority, with even greater jurisdiction than the captain of a ship. He can lock a man up, authorize helicopters to land or tell them not to land, tell ships to come in or not come in, and shut the rig down if he deems it necessary. On Piper Alpha, the installation manager was named Colin Seaton. The men on board had been trained to remain where they were within the accommodation module in the event of an emergency because that was the safest place for them to stay. They had been instructed to wait for a public address announcement by Colin Seaton, who would tell them whether to evacuate to their lifeboat stations or ascend to the helideck to be airlifted to safety. But somewhere in the inferno Colin Seaton was already lying dead and the public address system no longer existed. The men in the accommodation modules, and any others on the platform expecting to be told what to do, were waiting for orders that would never come. The men who made it through the Piper Alpha disaster that July night lived by disregarding the urge to wait for instructions. They were saved by their own initiative, or by pure chance, not by any preplanned procedures. As the fire intensified and large portions of the platform turned red hot, blistering men's feet right through their boots, scorching their faces, burning the skin from their hands, each survivor made a personal, split-second decision to jump into the water and take his chances rather than stay on board the platform and fry.

In his darkened cabin, a sleeping man cried out as the first explosion lifted him from his bunk. He was a roustabout, a general helper on the drilling deck, thirty-eight years old with a wife and two kids, and as he groped about in the smoky gloom two of his friends rushed into his room.

"The rig's on fire," they yelled. "We've got to get out of here." The three of them dashed frantically from door to door, but all exits were blocked by flames.

"We're dead men, mates," the roustabout said, when suddenly the deck collapsed and the floor in front of them split apart, revealing, as if by magic, a clear opening to the sea. It was seventy feet straight down but the men didn't hesitate for an instant. They jumped, hit the water and remained conscious, and began swimming away from the rig.

In one of the accommodation modules three wellhead specialists were watching a movie in the recreation area when large chunks of steel crashed through the roof and ripped a gaping hole in the floor, showering them with dust and large slivers of wood. It was as though a meteorite had passed through the room, the men later thought, but when it happened they never paused to reflect. They immediately raced down some stairs to a supply station, grabbed some warm clothing and climbed through a hatchway to the pipe deck. Flash fires blocked their way and explosions sounded all around them, but at least the air was fresher than in the accommodation module. Then, miraculously, there was a momentary lull in the ferocity of the flames, and without pause they went over the side, a hundred feet down to the water.

An experienced rigger, fifty years old, stood for several minutes in a stairwell with a group of men who refused to move. He left them and dashed into the reception area located in one of the accommodation modules, only to find another group huddled together in panic. "I am not going to sit down and burn to death," he told himself. His only avenue of escape was in the direction of the flames, but he took it, burning himself badly in the process. He managed to reach the drilling deck and, along with three other men already there, climbed down one of the platform legs and jumped into the waves.

Several members of the drilling crew at work when the blast

struck the platform crawled out onto one of the flare booms. All but one of them jumped into the water. The man who didn't jump had seen, in the glow of the fire, a number of men standing on the helideck. They were galley workers getting some air after their shift, strolling around the helideck when Piper caught fire, and they had little or no survival training. The driller saw the flames rising toward these men and realized they would soon be cut off from any means of escape except for leaping 180 feet to the sea. He crawled back off the flare boom, ran across the platform and shouted to the men above him. "There's a way off," he cried. "There's a way off. Follow me. We can jump off the flare boom. It's your best chance to make it." But the galley workers on the helideck had decided not to budge until a helicopter came for them and refused to listen to the driller. He dashed back to the flare boom, inhaling smoke and blistering his face on the way, dangled for a moment above the water, and let go. He lived.

So did others: the divers who check the wellheads on the ocean floor and who, unlike the galley workers, leaped from the helideck; two valve menders, working in the gas compression module itself, who somehow were blown clear of the fire in the first explosion and found themselves on a deck forty feet above the waves. Some men lucky enough to be working on a lower level of the rig climbed down knotted ropes they found hanging almost to the water line. An instrument technician on the northern corner of the platform, not far from where the first blast struck, had no time to go over the side of the rig. He jumped instead right through the railings, struck none of them, and kept himself alive in the water thinking about his wife and children.

The men who did reach the water would surely have died had Piper Alpha been alone in that part of the North Sea that night, for the waves soon filled with jagged debris that clobbered the swimmers and tore at their flesh, and the water itself, in the vicinity of the rig, was so hot it began to bubble. In places where boiling oil poured from the platform, fires broke out on top of the ocean and survivors had to keep ducking below the surface to keep from being scalded. Moreover, from the instant of the first explosion the only form of communication possible from the platform to the rest of the world was the waving of men's arms. Even their shouts were futile in the roar of the fire.

But within a couple of miles of Piper Alpha were the *Silver Pit* and the *Sandhaven*, two fishing trawlers converted to work boats, on duty to help Piper with undersea work. Both heard the first explosion, saw the flames, and within minutes launched fast, inflatable rescue dinghies that converged on the stricken rig and began picking survivors from the sea. Mayday calls went out from the boats as well, and rescue helicopters scrambled from the northern Scottish coastal towns of Kinloss and Lossiemouth. The helicopters were airborne within a minute of the Mayday call and, though some eighty miles away, their crews could see the flames from Piper Alpha immediately.

In addition, the multiservice vessel, *Tharos*, also assisting Piper in undersea work, was only a quarter of a mile away. Essentially, the *Tharos* was a huge, twin-hulled, self-propelled work barge with a deck area as big as two and a half football fields mounted on eight large stabilizing columns, four attached to each submerged hull. With her cranes and booms, her steel enclosures and towers, her walkways and helideck all crammed onto a rectangular platform, she looked like an overcrowded industrial park floating high out of the water on a bunch of smokestacks.

The *Tharos* was, however, a carefully designed, highly sophisticated support machine with accommodation for 300 men. She was a fire-fighting vessel capable of pumping 40,000 gallons of water per minute across 240 horizontal feet. She had a fully equipped, eighty-eight-bed hospital with facilities for treating shock, hypothermia, and burns. She had a machine shop, compression and decompression chambers for a team of divers, remote-controlled submarines equipped with video cameras for underwater surveillance, and four 3,000-horsepower computer-controlled thrusters — two in each hull — that stabilized her automatically according to conditions at sea. She was semisubmersible, the variable ballast in her hulls allowing her to be raised or lowered in the water, and her hydraulic gangway could link her securely to any North Sea production platform. In short, she could perform just about any task imaginable related to servicing or assisting an offshore oil rig. But, for all her technical prowess, there was no way she was going to get close enough to Piper Alpha to help the men left on board.

When the first explosion hit Piper, alarms on the *Tharos* went off and she immediately began to approach the rig, but neither she, nor the helicopters, nor the supply boats were able to do anything but pull people from the waves. All of them tried to board Piper, but the fire, within twenty minutes of the first scream of gas, was simply too hot.

Place yourself now in the cab of the pedestal crane of the *Tharos*, high above its deck, almost as high as the accommodation modules of Piper Alpha. There is a man in the cab, the crane operator. His vantage point affords him a panoramic view of the action in the water and on the rig, which seems to be unfolding before him in slow motion. He will remember what he sees for the rest of his life. There are men standing on the helideck, the galley workers, but the crane operator can't quite reach them with his crane. If he could reach them he could pluck them off the platform, but there is no way for him to do this because the *Tharos* is slowly pulling back, away from the men on the helideck, who are now on fire. The *Tharos* is spraying water on Piper Alpha, but even 40,000 gallons per minute is like spitting on a burning barn. The crane operator can see the galley workers screaming. He can't hear them — the noise of the gas makes that impossible — but he can see their mouths. It seems to him that he is like a man stretching out to someone drowning, someone whose hand he can't reach.

His gaze shifts to the swells below him, where he sees men swimming to the *Tharos*. Other men cling to debris. Others grab lines dangled from hovering helicopters. Some are sitting in dinghies, some are still underneath the platform, waving in the boiling sea. In one dinghy are nine men: a three-man rescue team and six survivors from Piper Alpha they have just picked up. The crane operator sees the dinghy move in close to the rig, right into the boiling water coated with oil, and pick up two more survivors. Then an explosion, larger even than the first, rocks the platform, and the dinghy underneath it disappears, the galley workers and the helideck disappear, and there is nothing but a wall of fire from the top of the rig to the sea. The giant steel legs on one side of the platform buckle, the entire rig tilts nearly forty-five degrees, and the accommodation modules, with more than one hundred screaming men inside, slide from their moorings like pats of butter down a canted skillet and drop into the waves. Whether the men drown or burn to death will never be known.

The *Tharos* pulls back farther, away from the unbelievable heat, as do the supply boats and the helicopters. Not that any further rescue is even possible. The crane operator stares in horror at Piper Alpha. Through the conflagration he can see that almost all of the platform is gone. Clearly, there is no one on the rig or in the flaming water beneath it who is left alive.

CHAPTER TWO

HOUSTON — 1988

It was almost 6:00 P.M. on July 6, and Red Adair had been rumbling around in his condominium like a restless old bear for over an hour, ever since he'd come home from his office. The condo was huge, more than 8,000 square feet in size, with three bedroom suites, a sunken living room, an indoor swimming pool with a bar, a gym, and a spacious deck overlooking a tree-lined lake. Adair was by himself, but his presence alone seemed to fill the place. He wandered from room to room, at seventy-three still moving with quick, sure-footed steps, bobbing his head slightly and rolling his shoulders like a prizefighter as he walked.

With a cold beer in his hand, he went into his study, sat behind his desk, and stared at the coat rack with the fire chief's hat hanging from it, at the dozens of awards on the wall and on the shelves — plaques, diplomas, honorary memberships in civic organizations, citations from state and local governments, even commendations from heads of state — all given to him for putting out oil-well fires, saving countless lives and hundreds of millions of dollars in revenue and equipment all over the world. He took a sip of beer and grunted. It wasn't that he didn't appreciate the recognition, but all that was in the past, and though Red Adair loved the past for its memories and the stories he could tell, he was a man who lived for the action of the present and the anticipation of the future.

In the mid-1980s the bottom had fallen out of the American petroleum business due to the glut of foreign oil on the world market. Wildcatters all but vanished from the oil patch, and even the major petroleum companies stopped drilling new wells. Drilling rigs were stacked by the dozens along the highways of Oklahoma, Texas, and Louisiana, and harbors from Brownsville to Biloxi were clogged with offshore drilling equipment. In Texas, petroleum engineers were working as bartenders, houses and yachts had been sold for half the price they'd brought five years before, and oil-field hands moved on to Florida to work in construction while they waited for the situation to improve.

Red Adair himself had seen little action for months, for a couple of years actually, and his spirits had ebbed as low as the industry he had served for nearly half a century. Of course, he could simply have packed it in. He certainly didn't need the money. For many years Adair had been extremely well paid for his work, often netting hundreds of thousands of dollars for a single job and occasionally earning over a million. While men he knew in the business had dabbled in high-risk ventures during the height of the mid-70s oil boom, Adair remained conservative. He had made and lost a fortune more than once in oil-patch boom-and-bust cycles and wasn't about to get bitten by the same dog again. Now, he was a millionaire many times over. "I'm heavily invested in cash," he would say when asked where his money was.

He could have put his feet up and done nothing, or played golf, or gone boating or fishing with his wife, Kemmie Lou. He did have a new boat, although it was a fifty-foot Scarab speedboat with three 420-cubic-inch Chevy engines, not exactly a senior citizen's special. About the only thing that could touch it on the water, other than an all-out racing machine, was something souped up by the DEA to chase drug runners. "See, that's the reason Mamma and Daddy can't go fishing together," Red's son Jimmy would say. "Mamma, she goes out on the water and fishes, and Daddy . . . well, you ever try catching any fish when you're trolling at seventy miles an hour?"

Two years earlier, when Adair had a minor heart attack, his doctor had suggested retirement. Then he saw the look on Red's face and said, "Well, at least try not to get too close to a real hot well fire." Adair would never tell anyone, but maybe it was the specter of retirement looming over him like the threat of an incurable disease that had him depressed. There were rumors in the oil patch, started by rivals in Houston who had once worked for Red, that he had in fact retired. They spread like an oily film across windblown water: Red's through, the rumors went. He can't work anymore, and the men he has under him can't cut it without him.

All of it was untrue, but with the lull in the oil patch what could Red do to disprove the lies? He thrived on hard work, on the rush of facing off against a burning well and the challenge of defeating it, and had spent a lifetime proving himself by doing something, not talking about it. Now he had been forced to do the one thing that drove him to distraction quicker than anything else. He had to sit and wait patiently for things to change instead of being able to change things himself.

He was hell around the office. He snapped at the secretaries, jumped at his men, found fault with inconsequential details around his warehouse, and then, being a kind, good-natured man at heart, felt bad about making someone miserable and bought him a new car or gave him a Rolex watch, only to begin the cycle all over again in a few days. Truth be told, he never belonged in any office at all, even in the best of times. The only place he'd ever felt comfortable was outdoors, on a job, in the midst of turmoil and chaos and crisis in the jungles of Sumatra, or the mountains of Colombia, or the West Texas plains, when his ass was on the line and fifty or sixty men looked to him for guidance near a raging, blowing well.

He took his beer, moved into the living room, and sat on the couch. His hair, once a deep, rich red, was laced with gray on top and turned completely white along the sides. His face was battered from the heat of burning wells and extremes of weather, and exposure to corrosive gas had left his eyes rimmed permanently red. Around him were artifacts from some of the exotic places he'd worked: a circular, carved teak coffee table with carved seats that slid out from underneath it and a rectangular traveling food basket made of woven bamboo, both from China; two cloisonné birds and two Buddhas from Nepal; a polished brass heater from Iraq; and, on the wall, a brass tray, three feet across, made in Iran. The last time he worked in Iran, he had been forced to leave a burning well when rebel forces moved in to attack the location. Later, the CIA had shown him a rebel hit list with "Texas Oilwell Firefighter" scribbled near the top. There were wells on fire in Iran even as he sat sipping his beer, but United States intelligence agents had advised him to let them burn, at least for the time being. Adair, who had been through a dozen or more revolutions in various parts of the world and never spent a day in jail, paid the agents heed, much as he would have enjoyed the work.

He ambled into the kitchen and took one of Kemmie's tuna casseroles out of the floor-to-ceiling Zero King refrigerator. In the floor-to-ceiling freezer next to the refrigerator were trays of similar casseroles, trays of her specially prepared meat loaf, meat balls and spaghetti, and veal parmigiana. There were also a half dozen of her homemade cakes — walnut, banana, and German chocolate — that were famous throughout the oil patch. She had brought the food to

Houston for Red on her last visit several weeks earlier from her home on Lake LBJ, northwest of Austin.

They had been living like that for twenty years. He had a place in Houston not far from his office, near his buddies from the early days in the oil patch and his childhood in Houston Heights. He kept another place on Clear Lake, east of Houston, where his boat was moored and where, in years past, when he was a championship powerboat racer, he could carouse with the boat-racing crowd. Kemmie had her home in the Texas hill country out where it was peaceful and quiet, where she could fish, play poker with her friends, go out to eat in relative anonymity at the local hamburger joint, and entertain her grandchildren.

In the early 1960s Red had bought her a rustic cabin in the woods on the lake, where she spent her weekends. Gradually, she began staying for longer and longer periods of time until the lake house, as they called it, became her home and Houston, where she'd lived her whole life, became a place she visited from time to time. Red was away so often on jobs anyway — as many as 200 days a year in busy times — that she saw him as often as when she'd lived in the big city.

Of course there was all kinds of gossip about the arrangement. People said there was another woman who drove Kemmie away. People said she was an alcoholic who left to take the cure and never returned. People said she was a drug addict and Red sent her away, or that he was a drug addict and she left him. Neither she nor Red paid any attention to the stories, which were totally preposterous. The real reasons had to do with Kemmie's decision, after twenty-five years of complete devotion to her husband and children, to live a lifestyle that suited her, away from the headlines, the glitter, the society luncheons where the women sat around comparing jewelry and designer clothes, and away, too, from the frenetic pace Red loved and the constant tension that seemed to surround him like an electrical charge. The mistake people sometimes made (often paying dearly for it) was assuming Kemmie's absence from Houston signified a lack of influence with Red or a lack of interest on her part in what went on inside his company.

Now Red picked up the phone and dialed Kemmie's number, although they'd spoken to each other twice already that day. "Whatcha up to?" he said, when she answered the phone.

"I'm reading a book," she answered. "What are you doing?"

"I'm eating tuna fish casserole."

"I bet it's good," she said. She had moved from the first lake house to a larger one after a few years, to accommodate the kids and the kids' friends and all their friends who always wanted to come up to the woods and visit, but two years ago had settled into a more manageable condominium on Lake LBJ. She was sitting now on the lowest of the condo's three levels, in the den. Outside the sliding glass door she could see her boat, a small fishing dory, hanging in its rack, level with the deck, which doubled as a dock. Beyond the dock a speedboat pulling a skier turned hard and accelerated across the lake, kicking up a sheet of water that broke into a million sparkles of silver and blue. She thought suddenly of the time, two years before, when she and Red had gone off together on a fishing trip. They had a big boat then, a sixty-two-foot Hatteras, and they had taken it across the Gulf of Mexico, through the Straits of Florida and on over to Chub Cay. Red had never cared much for fishing, but she knew if he got into the really big stuff, if maybe he could hang a marlin, he'd love it. He never hung a marlin, though she prayed he would, but he did get into it, did enjoy himself, so much so that he even forgot to call the office, which had never happened in all the years he'd been in business for himself. One afternoon, he hooked a big wahoo, and when it arched into the air it brought with it a sheet of water that dissolved, like the speedboat's wake, into droplets filled with sunlight. Red had fought the wahoo and fought it, and in the end, before he could land it, a shark came and bit off all but the wahoo's head. That night they'd drunk wine under the Bahamian stars and held each other the way they had when he courted her forty-six years before. It hadn't mattered to him that he lost the fish, and she'd thought that maybe the day would come when he'd realize he'd won enough battles and deserved to rest.

"Something's gonna happen pretty quick," he said. "A big job. I can feel it in my bones."

"Your bones almost always know," she said, and she wasn't kidding. His instincts about impending jobs were so acute she sometimes thought he had a sixth sense, plugged into the bowels of the earth, that vibrated when an oil well was about to blow. Sometimes, when they were younger, weeks would go by without a job. She'd fret while he'd go out with his pals. Then one day he'd wake up and say, "I got this feeling, Kemmie," and sure as a rainstorm's wet they'd catch a job, or, more likely, get three or four at once.

"Well," he said, "I guess I'll eat some more of this tuna. And I'll probably take a ride up there this weekend, so I'll see you in a couple of days."

"Well, fine," she said, although it would be almost two months before she saw him again.

No sooner did Red set the phone down than it rang and he picked it up again. "Hey, Daddy, you got the TV on?" asked his daughter Robyn. She was the younger of his two children, vice president of his company and a feisty, aggressive woman of forty-three with a temperament not unlike his own. She was calling from her house several blocks away.

"No, I'm not watching TV," he said. "I was just sittin' here talkin' to your mamma and eating some of her food."

"You better turn the TV on, Daddy," she told him. "I just saw a news bulletin about an Occidental rig blowing up in the North Sea."

Dr. Armand Hammer, ninety-year-old chairman of Occidental Petroleum Company, sat in the study of his home in Westwood, California. It had been several hours since he received the news about Piper Alpha and he was still stunned. As soon as word of the explosion reached California, Leon Daniels, Occidental's worldwide drilling manager, left from corporate headquarters in Bakersfield for Aberdeen, Scotland, on a company jet. Until Daniels reported back, Hammer would not know the exact extent of the catastrophe, but he already knew that loss of life was great. The destruction of the rig, while certainly not happy news, would have been taken in his stride. It was part of the risk of running an oil company, and in any case, the equipment was insured. The fact that so many men died, however, was devastating to Hammer, a physician and humanitarian as well as the founder of a major petroleum corporation. First reports indicated that 66 survivors had been rescued from the North Sea, which would mean that 166 had been killed. Hammer held on to a small measure of hope that more men might be found floating alive in the water, but he knew, too, that all rescue craft had pulled back because of the severity of the fire. In terms of men lost, Piper Alpha was by far the worst oil-well disaster in history, and all Hammer could think about was how men's lives could be spared in the oil fields in the future.

Something must be done to prevent this from happening again, he was thinking when his telephone rang. "Dr. Hammer, this is Red Adair," said the voice on the other end of the line. Though the two men had known each other for many years and regarded one another as good friends, Red still insisted on addressing Hammer formally out of a deep respect for the older man's accomplishments. The respect, however, was mutual. For decades, Hammer had known of Red's exploits fighting well fires, his resourcefulness and ability always to get the job done. "You don't ever have to worry about whether Red Adair knows what he's doing, which you can't truly say about that many men," Hammer would tell people. "He's a man who absolutely understands his work." Then, in the late 1970s, Hammer had watched as Red designed the multiservice vessel *Tharos* for Occidental and saw firsthand the extent of Adair's inventive genius. When India's first major offshore oil installation, Bomba High, caught fire in 1982, and Indira Gandhi asked Hammer to recommend someone to help control the well, Hammer told her there was only one man to consider, his friend, Red Adair.

Now, hearing Red's voice for the first time in over a year, Armand Hammer felt comforted. There was something reassuring, even calming, about the sound of the Texan's drawl. "Red, how are you?" Hammer asked.

"Well, Dr. Hammer, I'm fine," Red said, "but I just this minute saw the news on TV about Piper Alpha. Dr. Hammer, I'm calling to tell you that if I can be of any help in dealing with it, you know you can count on me."

"Red, I can't tell you how much I appreciate you calling me to say that," Hammer said. "Really, I can't. The whole thing is just terrible, Red, a nightmare. You know about all the men? Was that on TV?" The cadence of Hammer's voice had slowed since Adair had last talked to him, but the precision of his words, tinged ever so slightly with an eastern European accent, remained unchanged.

"No, uh-uh," Adair answered. "How bad is it? How many men were lost?"

"We don't know for certain yet, but there were quite a number. More than a hundred gone. More than a hundred and fifty, maybe," said Hammer. "Leon Daniels is on his way to Aberdeen right now. Until I hear from him, I don't even know whether there's anything left of Piper for you to work on. If there is, if some of the rig's still standing, then the quicker you could get over there the better."

"Soon as I put this phone down, Dr. Hammer, my men and I will get ready to go."

"Good," replied Hammer. "I'll alert my people in Bakersfield and call you back as soon as Daniels calls me. And thanks, Red. Thanks very much."

"We'll do our best for you, Dr. Hammer, you know that," Adair said.

"If I know anything, I know that, Red," Hammer told him.

THE NORTH ATLANTIC — JULY 7, 1988

The fire and smoke were in front of Red again, up on the movie screen, in the first-class cabin of the British Airways jet winging through the night to London. It was an aerial picture, relayed from a BBC helicopter circling a good ways off from the rig, but he could tell, even from the distant shot, that the majority of the platform had disappeared. At first, Leon Daniels hadn't thought that any of the platform would be standing by daylight, but when, on the morning of the seventh, a section of it still remained, they'd called Adair from Bakersfield and in several hours he'd been on his way.

The media had been everywhere, from the moment they'd gotten word he was on the job. They were at his condo, interviewing him while he packed. They trailed the Chevy Suburban he and his men rode in to the airport and followed them from the parking lot to the gate. There weren't any that he knew of on the plane, but for sure the airport in London would be swarming with reporters when they landed.

"The whole world is watching this one," he thought. "The whole world is watching to see what we can do." He settled back in the wide leather seat, feeling a rush of emotions. He had spent a lot of time in the North Sea over the years. He felt very close to the friendly, hardworking people in that part of the world, not far from where his own ancestors had lived, and regarded them almost as kinfolk. He felt deep sadness for the families of the lost men. He felt, too, a sense of excitement, of anticipation, *because* the whole world was watching — *because* the TV networks and newspapers and magazines would be covering the story of Piper Alpha in such detail. Up against what was already being spoken of as the worst wild-well disaster in history, he was about to show everyone that Red Adair and his men could take care of business.

He looked across the aisle at the two men with him. In the seat on the aisle was Brian Krause, at thirty-two the youngest of his four senior firefighters. Krause was a lean, handsome man, a go-getter who always found work to do around the company when he wasn't out in the field on a fire or blowout. What he lacked in experience he made up for in intelligence and dedication. Red only had to tell Krause once how to handle a particular situation for the instruction to stick. Furthermore, Krause had great reflexes, was quick on his feet, and could squeeze surefootedly into tight spaces. Red liked having Brian with him on a job. There was something about him, about his enthusiasm, that reminded Red of himself, when he was young.

Beside Krause, asleep next to the window, sat Raymond Henry, forty-three. Henry was a huge man. He stood six-two and weighed 280 pounds, most of it muscle. The gold Rolex on his wrist looked like a tiny charm. With his dark hair, thick moustache, and heavy-lidded eyes, his ostrich-skin cowboy boots and diamond studded belt buckle, he looked like a cross between a Mexican gunfighter and a grizzly bear. Gentle and kind among friends, he was fearless in a fight or on a job. So unruffled was he around a blowing well that the Saudis nicknamed him "the man with no nerves." His family had lived a block from the house where Red and Kemmie raised their children, and Raymond, one of Jimmy's closest friends, had pretty much grown up in Adair's home. At twelve he began running errands for Red (this was out in the country, and Raymond, who looked old enough to drive at ten, had no trouble handling a car) and joined Red's company for good when he finished high school. Raymond was especially adept at dealing with an offshore rig since he had worked on them in every corner of the globe for nearly twenty-five years.

"Yeah," Red thought, "we'll show 'em. No doubt about that." A hand touched his shoulder and he jumped slightly. It was one of the flight attendants, a young, attractive woman with dark, serious eyes. She had been listening while Red and his men watched the news clips on the plane's movie screen and discussed what they might encounter on the burning rig. Though Leon Daniels had told Red a portion of the rig was still standing, he could see from the BBC's pictures that what was left of Piper was tilted at a precarious angle. This would make boarding the platform extremely treacherous. Red knew, too, that that deck would be littered with pieces of exploded structural steel and hunks of drilling equipment, and that all of the debris and the deck itself would be covered with hot oil.

"I tell you what, Raymond," he had said. "Working on that's gonna be like dumping a couple of hundred wrecked cars on the side of a mountain, having a freezing rain fall on it for a day or two, and then trying to ice-skate from the top to the bottom with a pregnant pig on your back. And if that old North Sea wind gets to blowing . . . ummm hmmm . . . we'll be earning our bread and butter on this one, don't you forget it."

Red also had no way of knowing yet how many of Piper's thirty-six wells were on fire and whether Piper Alpha's remains were such a twisted mass of scrap iron that getting to the wellheads, extinguishing the fires, and capping the wellheads would be possible. If not, a relief well would have to be drilled by the crew of a drill ship from a position a few hundred yards from Piper Alpha. The relief well would angle down under the sea where, far below the surface, it would intersect P1, one of Piper's main producing wells. Once completed, the relief well would divert the flow of oil and gas from the platform and allow the rig's wells to be controlled, but the process would take months and cost millions of dollars, and meanwhile millions of barrels of oil would pour into the North Sea, causing massive pollution.

The flight attendant had moved from behind Red's seat and was sitting across from him, on the arm of the chair in front of the one in which Brian Krause now slept. "Mr. Adair," she said. "Could I ask you something please?"

"Why sure, honey," Red said. "Ask away. Anything you want. 'Course, if you're gonna ask me out in London, I gotta tell you we're about to be pretty busy up in the North Sea."

"Well," she replied, smiling, "that wasn't it. It's that I was watching the fire up there on the news, the fire you're going to try to put out, and I was wondering, are you ever afraid?"

Red swallowed once and pursed his lips slightly, narrowing his eyes and looking at the movie screen, which was now blank. "No," he said softly. "Never afraid, just very careful."

After forty-eight years in the oil fields, hauling equipment, working on drilling rigs, stopping blowouts before they could ignite or extinguishing them when they did, Red Adair was well aware of the power of fear. He had come away from jobs with footprints on his coveralls left by men who literally ran over him as they fled in terror from a wild well. He had seen countless men of action — tough, ornery, oil-patch brawlers — rendered immobile as granite blocks by the fury of a well fire, unable even to draw a breath, and watched others run in panic straight into the flames rather than to safety. In all that time, Adair never felt fear himself.

People questioned him about it constantly. "Weren't you just a little bit scared on that one, Red?" they'd ask, after he'd successfully fought a blaze that had turned hundreds of tons of functioning machinery into steel spaghetti, or capped a poison gas well that had killed half the crew that tried to stop the blowout before he got there.

"Uh-uh," he'd answer.

"Why not?" they'd ask, hoping to discover the secret of Adair's consummate coolness under the most extreme pressure imaginable. (Maybe hoping, too, that some of the cool would rub off.) The question made no sense to him. It was like asking a great major-league hitter why he's not afraid of a ninety-five-mile-an-hour fastball, or a skilled neurosurgeon how he has the audacity to invade the skull of a living human being.

In fact, Adair was uncomfortable talking about his bravery, and as quickly as he could he'd change the subject, maybe describing a new safety device he'd designed for a wellhead or laughing about how much everyone partied after the fire they'd been fighting was out. Folks who knew him well and were around him at times like that noticed that, when pressed to describe his exploits, Red almost always spoke about himself in the second person, as though the man who dared look straight into the mouth of hell was somehow distinct from the guy sitting with them in a bar, drinking beer and swapping jokes.

"You don't fear your job," Red would say. "You respect it. You know your equipment and your men, and you don't trust anybody but yourself." There was no bravado in his reply. He was merely telling the truth. The few times he'd gotten into trouble on jobs were when he'd relied on someone else; the few times he'd been hurt were when his back was turned and another man made a mistake. Red learned quickly from those experiences and early on began paying absolute attention to detail, leaving nothing under his control to chance, and he always made sure he left himself an escape route, his hind door, he called it. "You don't ever go in someplace," he'd say, "before you figure out how the hell you're gonna get your ass back out. Then you just go on about your work, try to do it right, and don't worry." The bravery, the solitary combat against some of the most awesome of natural forces, were not subjects for idle conversation. Who could understand the feelings of tranquillity and ease he experienced in places that terrified other men so badly they'd remember them later in dreams and wake drenched in cold sweat?

"Did I ask the wrong question?" said the flight attendant. "I didn't mean to intrude . . . you looked so thoughtful. I guess it's the fire."

"It's a bad one," Red said. "One of the worst. And I'm not sure until I see it, what-all we can do."

"Well, good luck, Mr. Adair," she said.

"Thank you, honey," he said. "We're gonna need it." He closed his eyes, remembering, then, another flight across the Atlantic to another job, twenty-seven years before. The whole world had been watching that one, too. It had been a job that changed his life, bringing his fame far beyond the oil fields. Lulled by the low roar of the jet's engines, he drifted back in time until he could smell the hot metal of the blown-up rig and feel its heat spreading from his neck to his face. "There was fear there, too," he thought. "You could taste it."

CHAPTER THREE

ALGERIA — 1961

When the car, a Citroen DS19, came within 1,500 feet of the burning gas well, the roar was so loud it set the floorboards thrumming like a bass guitar. The hood began dancing on its hinges, and the windshield, peppered by driven sand, threatened to pop loose from its seals. Even with the windows rolled up you had to shout to make yourself heard, though at that moment no one in the car was saying a thing.

In front of them were the twisted remains of a drilling rig, jutting here and there from the dunes, melted and blown into grotesque shapes like the wreck of a spaceship on the moon. At the center of the mess, raging from the wellhead, was an 800-foot column of fire so intense that at its apex it was creating its own weather system, spawning gale-force winds, sending sandstorms laced with rocks howling across the desert. A bushel or so of these rocks, combined perhaps with some metal debris from the rig, had caught a ton-and-a-half supply truck broadside. The Citroen passed the truck where it rested at a forty-five-degree angle in a ditch, its roof shredded, the driver's door hanging by a filament of hinge, as though it had been mortared. No doubt about it, the men in the car with Red Adair were scared.

Two French scientists, experts in the area of oil and gas exploration, sat in the back seat. The director of North African operations for Phillips Petroleum was driving. His company was in consort with the French government on this drilling project, which had turned into the nightmare soon to be known as The Devil's Cigarette Lighter. All three men were oil field veterans. They had worked in Algeria off and on since oil and gas were discovered there in 1956, first at Edjeleh near the Libyan border, then 40 miles west at Tiguentourine, and finally 200 miles to the north at Hassi Messaoud, an enormous oil reservoir beneath the towering Saharan sand dunes of the Great Eastern Erg that was also the largest natural gas field in the world.

These men had been around wells that had blown out. They had witnessed the rupture of massive well-pressure control valves, the disintegration of drilling rigs, and the great geysers of gas and oil that spewed into the air. They had also watched (though from a great distance) wild wells that caught fire, but never had they seen one as terrifying, as seemingly uncontrollable as this. It was in a gas field just south of Hassi Messaoud, near a remote desert outpost called Gassi Touil. The burning well was the second one put into production there, hence it had been named GT-2. As the Citroen crept toward it, the sonic waves emanating from the well caused the car to pitch and yaw, gently at first, but soon with enough force to threaten the sedan's hydropneumatic suspension system. The man at the wheel braked hard and glanced over at Red with alarm. Sitting in the passenger seat beside the driver, Red could sense the fear around him, almost as though it were another palpable presence that had entered the car.

But there, in east central Algeria, just as everywhere else he worked, Red Adair ignored the cloud of fear that surrounded him. He focused instead on the pillar of flame fed by 550 million cubic feet of gas a day, a fire so hot it had melted the nearby desert sand, turning it to glass, a fire so bright that two months later when John Glenn became the first American astronaut to orbit the earth, he would see it from 200 miles out in space.

"Closer," Adair hollered, flicking an index finger in the direction of the well as though he were casting for trout.

"Jesus Christ, Red," screamed the oil man, gripping the steering wheel that was now humming in tune with the floorboards, "we can see the bastard from right here just fine."

"I want a closer look," Adair yelled. "I want to know what I'm dealing with." Once again he cast his finger, this time letting it hang in the air and turning, as he did, to look straight at the oil man.

Adair is a short man, actually, five-foot-six, though you'd never think so unless you saw him standing next to someone much taller. The index finger he shook was connected to a heavy, gnarled hand covered with scars and calluses, the hand to a thick, sinewy wrist, the wrist to a forearm bulging with muscles and wrapped with prominent veins. His shoulders stretched the seams of his sport shirt nearly to bursting, and his massive head, topped by neatly combed, dark red hair, sat on a bulky, corded, wrestler's neck.

As a young man, Adair had been a superb baseball player and championship swimmer. Weighing only 145 pounds, he had been an all-city halfback as a high-school freshman football player in Houston, using his quickness and remarkable balance to evade 200-pound tacklers or bounce off them while remaining on his feet. He was forty-six when he first looked up at The Devil's Cigarette Lighter, considerably thicker through the waist and fuller of face than in his playing days, but he still possessed a premier athlete's easy grace and self-assurance, even as he sat in that trembling car on a scorching desert afternoon. Two hours earlier, while driving south from Algiers, the Citroen had passed through Hassi Messaoud, the campsite where Allied soldiers had met up with the French army during the North African campaign in World War II, joining forces to fight the Germans. The significance of that place was not lost on Adair. "Doing a job like this, fighting a well fire of this proportion, is just like mounting an invasion," he would say on more than one occasion. "You form a battle plan, gather your men and equipment, and attack. You have only one thought in mind: you will do whatever it takes to win."

For a while, when he was a teenager, Red Adair was a semipro boxer. He fought about once a month and was paid eight dollars if he won, two dollars if he lost. This was at the height of the Depression when eight dollars was a considerable sum, more in fact than Adair made in a week from his job in a drugstore. He never lost a fight. Once, when he was seventeen, he was matched against a 210-pound Cajun dockworker known as Short-neck Ladue who was ten years older than Adair and outweighed him by nearly seventy pounds. This discrepancy was not unusual. Adair was consistently pitted against much larger opponents by a promoter who packed a tiny, stifling, smoke-filled arena on the outskirts of Houston with people who paid a quarter to watch the little guy with cobra-quick hands whip one heavyweight after another.

At the beginning of the fourth round, Short-neck caught Red with a right hook that flattened him, breaking his jaw in two places. The crowd was silent. Slowly, Adair rose to his hands and knees, and as he did he heard someone at ringside say, "He's through, this time the little fella's through."

"I ain't through," Adair said, though all that came out of his mouth was a spurt of blood and a noise that sounded like the low growl of an angry dog.

He stood and shook his head to clear his vision. The referee asked, "Can you go on?" and Red nodded. He crossed the ring, chin thrust sideways at an angle that gave his face a most horrible, crazed warp and leaped at the startled Cajun. With three quick punches he knocked Short-neck down, cutting him badly below the left eye. Twice more he floored the big man, drawing blood each time, until finally the referee stopped the fight.

Adair's jaw was still wired together and all he'd eaten since the fight was soup when Short-neck came to see him at the drugstore ten days later. Red had lost a lot of weight and there were still two or three purple blotches on his face. Short-neck had stitches under both eyes and on his forehead just below the hairline. He sat at the counter behind which Adair was mixing ice cream sodas. Short-neck folded his arms on the counter and waited until Red was done and had delivered the sodas to two young women in sunbonnets.

"Why'd you get up?" Short-neck asked him. "That's the hardest I ever hit a man. There's no way you shoulda got up." It was a hot August afternoon. A small electric fan droned on the far end of the counter. Dust from a car passing by on the gravel street filtered through the drugstore's screen door and hung in a shaft of sunlight above the two young women whose spoons clinked against their ice-cream soda glasses. No one else was in the store.

"I needed the eight bucks," Adair said through clamped teeth.

The Cajun nodded, but he knew it was more than the money. "You got the eyes," he said. "I seen 'em burnin' when you come across that ring. They burnin' now, sayin' you mean business. Ain't but a few men really mean business. You gonna turn pro?"

Adair shrugged. Pop Adams, his old football and boxing coach who once helped train Jack Dempsey, had asked him the same question, but Red wasn't sure. Before he fought the Cajun, he knocked a man out who went into convulsions. The man's skin turned blue and his breath rasped like the gearbox of an overloaded truck. The man recovered, but Red kept seeing his face in his dreams. As good a fighter as he was, somehow boxing for a living didn't feel right, and even at seventeen Adair had learned to listen to his instincts.

"Well," said Short-neck, "that was some good fight anyhow." He offered his hand and Adair shook it. "I'll see you around," the Cajun said, but Adair never saw him again. Two years later he heard the man had been stabbed to death with a broken whiskey bottle by an irate barmaid in a Mexican whorehouse. By then, Red had quit boxing and gone to work for the Southern Pacific Railroad.

Now, thirty years later, with his mouth set in a thin hard line, he stared at the man from Phillips Petroleum at the wheel of the Citroen. The oilman saw those same eyes, narrowed to slits no wider

27

than the weather creases around them, burning at him, pulling him and the shaking car and the whole damn desert for that matter, into an orbit of confidence he'd never before experienced. He put the car in gear and slowly advanced toward the well. The scientists in the back seat began talking rapidly to one another, gesturing as they spoke. Adair couldn't hear them and wouldn't have known what they were saying if he could, but when he turned around he could see they were both sweating profusely. Were it not for Red's presence, the two of them would have bailed out of the car and dashed back down the dirt road away from the well.

In a way, their trepidation was understandable. They had been at Gassi Touil on November 3, when GT-2 came into production with such force it exploded the safety devices on the wellhead and sent a column of gas thirteen inches thick into the air. For two and a half days after that, the French drilling crew did its best to control the well when suddenly, early on the morning of November 6, there was an earth-shaking eruption that sounded like a pair of jet fighter planes taking off together from your living room. A half-mile of five-inch-diameter drill-pipe casing, weighing twenty-five tons, catapulted up through the wellhead and rained down in forty-foot sections, sending every rig hand, engineer, and technician on the job running for his life. Within an hour the call, well known by this time in oil fields around the world, was made to the Phillips Petroleum offices in Bartlesville, Oklahoma, and from there relayed on to Houston: "Get Red Adair and get him quick."

This urgency, of course, was completely normal. When anyone needed Red, he needed him immediately, if not sooner. Moreover, it seemed that oil and gas wells tended to come loose in groups of three or more, as though there were some diabolical hydrocarbon conspiracy at work designed to drive Adair crazy. He could sit in his office every day for a month and the phone wouldn't ring once. He'd shuffle through stacks of paperwork, growl incomprehensible orders to his staff, and pace from room to room like a caged panther, causing more tension than a squadron of ex-wives at an all-male group therapy session.

Finally, when everyone else was on the brink of mayhem, Red would disappear. He'd go out on his boat, go drinking with some friends, or catch a job and be off working on some remote location. "If anybody calls, don't tell 'em I'm out of town," he'd say to Joy Hamilton, his secretary, on his way out the door.

"Yeah, but boss," Joy would say. "What if you're in South America or something?"

"Hell, South America ain't that far away," Red would tell her with a grin. "Just say I'll be right back and give me a call. Let me worry about the rest." Sure enough, as soon as Red would leave, the phone would ring. And ring, and ring. Nine different oil companies would need to talk to him at the same time. The oil men would be in a state of near panic. Joy and the rest of Red's office staff would be frantic. Red . . . well, Red would be gone.

When the message from North Africa arrived at the Red Adair company office in Houston, Red was as calm as the bottom of an ice-covered pond. He was sitting next to the pilot in a small, twin-engine airplane, leased by an independent oil producer who was flying Adair to a well fire in West Texas, not far from the town of Ft. Stockton. In his lap was an 8½-by-11-inch pad of lined paper on which he'd sketched a facsimile of an oil well, complete with valves and lengths of drill-pipe casing that overlapped and decreased in diameter, like sections of a long telescope, the deeper they went. Based on information given to him by the rig operator, Red was calculating the approximate pressures he thought he'd encounter once he put out the fire and began capping the oil-spewing well. He showed no signs of fatigue, although two days earlier he'd returned from a job in the jungles of Brazil, the second one he'd done there in eight weeks. This was also the second time in less than two months that Adair had traveled to Ft. Stockton. The first time he'd been summoned to handle a blowout for Mobil Oil that had killed five men and injured seventy-two others.

"There's some mean wells out in West Texas," Red said to the pilot. "Umm-hmm. Wells out there, they're just like the women. You don't pay real careful attention to 'em, they'll come to see you and make you pay with your life. One way or the other you're gonna pay."

The pilot stuck a plug of Beechnut in his mouth and gave Adair a doleful grin. He had been married once to a rodeo barrel racer from Odessa who stuck a .44 in his ear when he came home early one morning smelling of another woman's perfume. She pulled the trigger, too, but the gun was empty. "That click sounded like an atom bomb, lemme tell you," the pilot was saying, when he was interrupted by the radio. It was the fixed base operator of the small airport they'd just left behind.

"Hey Red, this is Andrau Airport," the man said. "I got Joy on the phone here. Phillips just called in from Oklahoma and they got a well blowin' out over in North Africa. She wants to know what you want to do."

Joy Hamilton, a tall, pretty woman, then in her midtwenties, was a country girl from Henderson, Texas, who hadn't known what a visa was the first time she made international travel arrangements for Adair and his crew. But Joy was smart and she learned fast, and by 1961, two years after she'd come to work for Red, she had developed a network of bartenders, waitresses, hotel managers, cops, filling station attendants, coast guard and army officers, and all manner of foreign political and military officials who were constantly being pressed into service in what became a worldwide tracking and courier service designed to find Adair or his men and give them vital information. Not long before The Devil's Cigarette Lighter erupted, she had managed to locate one of Red's firefighters just as he was climbing into bed in a Parisian brothel, even though she didn't speak a word of French.

"Joy, how the hell did you find me?" the shocked firefighter asked.

"Well, honey, I know how hard you been working, so I just asked the telephone operator to connect me to the best whorehouse in town."

As a matter of fact, the last time Adair was in Ft. Stockton she called the local sheriff there, who went out to the location to get Red because all the phone lines had been blown up along with the well. Humble Oil had a bad blowout near Corpus Christi, and since Red was almost finished in Ft. Stockton he decided to go. The problem was that Hurricane Carla, in full force, made flying into Corpus Christi impossible. The sheriff, however, was an admirer of Red's, so he drove him, at 110 miles an hour, all the way to Humble's well, waited while Red took care of the blowout in the middle of the hurricane, and then drove Adair back to Ft. Stockton to complete the job for Mobil.

"Andrau, this is Red Adair," Red said. "This plane belongs to another oil company, and I don't guess they'd be too happy if I took it to Africa for a Phillips job. You tell Joy I'm gonna fly on in to Ft. Stockton and to have Boots and Coots get ready to fly over to North Africa and check out that well. Tell her I'll talk to them tonight and get everything lined up."

The next morning, Adair's two top assistants, Asgar "Boots" Hansen and Edward "Coots" Matthews, flew to Paris and then on to

Algeria. In Ft. Stockton, Red shot out the fire with a charge of explosives and capped the well — that is, he subdued the uncontrolled flow of oil, or blowout, by maneuvering a heavy-duty valve over the pipe at the top of the wellbore, or "hole." The job was straightforward, with no unforeseen complications, and Red was through with it in a day and a half. He was back in Houston when the telegram arrived from his two men, three days after they'd left for North Africa.

"It's a simple pumping job," they cabled. "Will take three days to rig up. No problem." Rigging up involved the attachment of a series of valves to what was left of GT-2's wellhead and the stringing of pipe from these valves to the giant diesel pumps used to pump drilling fluid, or mud, as it's usually called, into the well. Boots and Coots had been well trained by Red and, in spite of the heat, the noise, and the blowing sand, could probably have handled the job under ordinary circumstances. But GT-2 was no ordinary well and would soon provide Adair's men with considerably more excitement than they'd bargained for.

There was plenty of drilling mud, mixed and stored in large cylindrical tanks, on the GT-2 location, just as there is on the site of any petroleum well. The reason for this is that drilling mud performs three essential tasks in a well. It is run down into the hole, where it cools the rotating drill bit. It then circulates back to the surface, bringing with it the drill bit's cuttings and all sorts of impurities from the bottom of the well. Back on the surface, the mud travels by pipe and trough through a number of tanks, tubs, and metal chambers equipped with a variety of screens where the cuttings and any extraneous chemicals are removed. This journey through shale shakers, desilters, desanders, and degassers is critical, because the mud is reused, descending into the hole to begin the cooling and cleaning cycle once again, and it must return to the well in the same state as when it was first mixed. Furthermore, the flow of drilling mud must be continuous, because its third function is that of a counterbalance, equalizing with its weight the upward pressure of the oil or gas in the well. If the flow of mud is interrupted — if there is loss of circulation — the only thing between the drilling rig and its crew on the surface, and oil or gas forcing its way skyward at five or seven or ten thousand pounds of pressure per square inch, is a stack of valves called blowout preventers. In theory, they can halt the flow, as long as the well pressure is less than their seals can stand, and as long as someone operates the preventers in time. More often than not, especially on modern drilling rigs, someone on the rig gets the blowout preventers closed and they hold, but rig hands have been known to fall asleep on the job, and sometimes, as with GT-2, the surge is just too great for containment by the valves. When that happens, the results are catastrophic and the telephone in Red Adair's office starts to ring.

On January 10, 1901, at Spindletop, four miles south of Beaumont, Texas, a drilling crew directed by a mining engineer named Anthony Lucas brought in a gusher that blew oil two hundred feet above the sixty-foot derrick they had erected. The Lucas well, dug with the relatively new rotary drill bit, produced 84,000 barrels of oil a day and signaled the advent of the age of petroleum as we know it. In the years shortly following Spindletop, drilling mud was exactly that: huge chunks of clay carved out of river beds in Texas, Arkansas, and Louisiana. This clay was hauled by truck to open pits dug near the drilling rigs, where it was stomped and pulverized by horses or oxen driven round and round by the well hands. Water was added to obtain a consistency that seemed right, and the mud was pumped into the well. Sometimes the weight of the mud controlled the well pressure and sometimes it didn't, in which case the well came loose, but since well control was in its infancy, this dice roll was accepted as a simple hardship of drilling for oil.

Modern well drilling is much less of a gamble. Men are employed by rig operators to monitor existing well pressure and, with sophisticated measuring devices, anticipate pressures that will be encountered the deeper the well is drilled. This information is relayed to a mud engineer, the "mud man," who alters the consistency of the mud accordingly and constantly checks the properties of the mud as it comes to the surface. The drilling mud these men deal with is a mixture of barite, clay, water, and chemical additives. Its weight, expressed in pounds per gallon, can be precisely regulated by adding more or less barite — barium sulfate, $BaSO_4$ — a naturally occurring mineral with a specific gravity of 4.2, slightly more than four times the weight of water, which tips the scales at 8.3 pounds per gallon. Eight- or nine-pound drilling mud is considered light, eighteen- or twenty-pound mud is heavy, and there have been times when Adair and his men have even used twenty-five-pound mud, three times heavier than water, to control a well.

Heavier mud, containing larger quantities of barite, is considerably more expensive than light mud, so an oil company obviously tries to get away with the lightest-weight mud possible when drilling a well. On occasion, this frugality has cost an oil producer millions of dollars and a number of lives. Sometimes, even after his well blew out, the rig operator would argue with Red about what mud weight should be used to gain control of the flow. The operator's concern, in addition to the cost of the mud, is that pumping very heavy drilling fluid downhole might damage the petroleum-bearing zone — the formation — deep underground and prevent further production. Often, the oil company would have two or three or even a half dozen mud engineers on the payroll, some with graduate degrees, all of whose careers were devoted to the analysis, improvement, and use of drilling mud and its interaction with petroleum formations. More than once these engineers were at odds with Adair, who in nearly fifty years fighting wild wells has never lost one of his men, and whose only concern has always been to get the job done safely and as fast as possible.

Nobody knows more about how to use the mud than Red. "I was over in Louisiana fifteen, maybe twenty years back, down in the swamp, in the bay, at the edge of the Gulf of Mexico (where the saltwater mosquitoes are so big you'd need a transfusion if more than one of them bit you). It was July or August, I don't remember which. Anyway, it was hotter'n hell, but we still had to keep our slicker suits on so those mosquitoes didn't eat us alive. This was at a well that was on fire, and brother, you could take a walk up near that well with your dinner in your hand and when you came back your food would be cooked. That's how hot it was."

He worked sixteen hours a day for five days straight, finally got that fire put out, and was just about to pump in when the company man — the man in charge of the location — came up to him with a young engineer. "Company man says, 'Red, I hear you're gonna pump eighteen-pound mud, why's that?' I told him, 'I'm gonna pump eighteen-pound mud because that's what it's gonna take to control the son of a bitch.' This young engineer says, 'Well, we don't want you to pump eighteen-pound mud down our well. Our calculations tell us all you need is thirteen-pound mud.' He says if you use eighteen-pound mud it'll damage the formation and ruin the chances of reentering the well for future production. I said eighteen-pound mud wasn't gonna hurt nothing in that hole, but that engineer wasn't about to listen to anything but his own voice so I turned to the company man and I said, 'OK buddy, I'll pump thirteen-pound mud, but just don't forget you're gonna have to pay me for another blowout if that well cuts loose again.' He says, 'Why's that?' and I said, 'Because you want to use a lighter-weight mud than I do, so if there's another problem then it's another job.'

"We pumped in what they wanted and it held for a while, but I wasn't halfway to Houston before that well came to see 'em again. I turned around and went on back and they had to pay me to do the thing over again, and while I'm working that same young engineer comes up to me and says, 'Red, we did all these calculations and computations and we were sure thirteen-pound mud would do the trick. How'd you know it wouldn't?' I said, 'Son, I could feel it.' He says, 'What do you mean you could feel it?' I said, 'You hang around these wells for twenty, thirty years and you work right up in close to 'em where the mud comes up to your chest and the gas burns the skin right off your neck and you'll know what I mean.'"

No one, in any case, was arguing about mud weight with Boots and Coots on the morning of November 12, 1961, while they got ready to pump into GT-2. In fact, there were men on the location who wondered whether there *was* mud heavy enough to counteract the power of the giant gas well that set up sonic vibrations that people five miles away could feel through the soles of their shoes. Boots and Coots had been toiling since dawn, trying to get the final lengths of pipe connected from the mud pumps to the well before the searing desert sun made the sand too hot for them to work. In the din, they checked and rechecked the pipe joints, following the meticulous instructions Red had drummed into them on job after job since the day each had gone to work for him.

Boots and Coots, eight and ten years younger than Red respectively, were a couple of good old boys from Houston who had been hired by Red in the mid-1950s when both of them were out of work. That, and the fact that neither one minded a bottle of good whiskey or a pretty woman, was where any apparent similarity between them ended.

Boots was only a little taller than Red, stockily built, with an outthrust jaw and a pugnacious nature to go along with it, although no one who knew him could ever remember him getting into a fight. He thought nothing of bellowing a string of curses at some oil field worker he didn't even know, like the time over in Hackberry, Louisiana when Red pulled up to the site of a burning well in a pickup truck just in time to hear Boots scream, "You worthless, Coonass, son of a bitch," at a man astride a stalled Caterpillar bulldozer. The bulldozer operator was a small, wiry Cajun with long sideburns who lived back in the swamp and took no umbrage at being called a Coon-ass, inasmuch as every man he was born and raised with used the term to refer to one another. But, though poor and diminutive, he took great pride in his value as a human being and would allow no man to call him a worthless son of a bitch.

He was off the bulldozer with a two-foot wrench cocked behind his ear faster than Boots could clear his throat and spit in the mud, and were it not for Adair's own quickness of foot and tongue he would surely have buried the wrench in Boots's head. "Let him be," Red said to the furious Cat skinner. "He don't mean nothing by it."

"What he means gonna get him dead," the man replied, but Adair could see his rage had faded. He stood between the two men, facing the Cajun.

"Get in the truck," he said to Boots without turning. "Don't mind him," he said to the Cajun. "You're a good worker. Get back on the Cat and haul that iron away from the well." Adair waved an arm in the direction of a pile of iron debris fifty yards away.

"If it wasn't you between us it'd be his ass I was haulin' away, you know that," the Cajun said.

Red nodded and patted the man on the back. "I appreciate it," he said. He made a mental note to see to it there was something extra in the Cat skinner's pay envelope that week.

Coots was a completely different man. He was a tall, lean, easy-going cowboy who loved horses and golf, listened very well, and spoke only when necessary. Boots would sometimes act impulsively and insist, if Red weren't around, that things only be done his way. Coots, on the other hand, was methodical, remembering everything Red taught him. When he was in charge, he was open to other men's ideas and so would benefit from the advice of savvy oil-field hands or even a youngster with a good plan. When Coots did speak, folks almost always paid attention because he was a man who had no aversion to backing up his words with his fists. In a dark alley, faced by a couple of knife-wielding thugs, Coots was a man you'd like by your side.

Two years before The Devil's Cigarette Lighter he had been with Red in a fancy Houston nightclub. A wealthy oil man — a wildcat-ter who had made and lost a fortune four or five times and was meaner than a mule whip — sat at a nearby table with his wife, his bodyguard and the bodyguard's girlfriend. Red was telling Coots a joke when he saw the wildcatter slap his wife hard, then slap her again. The woman raised her arms to protect herself and screamed as the wildcatter moved to strike her once more. Adair sprang from his chair and grabbed the oil man's arm, cuffing him across the head as he did. Red's back was to the oil man's bodyguard, a giant man who rose to protect his boss. The man had a blackjack in his hand and was about to level Red, who never saw him coming, when Coots knocked the bodyguard cold with one punch. The oil man looked at his friend stretched out on the floor and said, "Hold it Red! I got no beef with you." Red told the oil man they'd sure have a beef if he saw him hit a lady again, even if it was the man's wife, and went back to his table with Coots, where the two of them ordered one more drink and watched the wildcatter drag his bodyguard from the club.

But Boots loved boats and so did Red, and Adair actually spent more of his free time with him than with Coots, who was basically a loner. The relationship between Red and Boots was a mystery to Red's wife, Kemmie, a fiercely loyal and protective woman who saw Boots as divisive and mean-spirited. She cautioned her husband, but to no avail.

Boots and Coots had started out running errands for Red, hauling equipment to jobs, cleaning and fixing things around the shop, and finally following him into the oil patch. In spite of any shortcomings either one had, Red instinctively felt they both possessed the rare boldness needed to confront a wild well. Neither of them, he believed, would run on him in a pinch, and neither did. By late 1961, both men were skilled enough at well control to work without Red's direct supervision, though it was standard company procedure for them to call him every night if possible to discuss what had taken place during the day on the job. Telephone contact was not possible from Gassi Touil, but even if it had been, what happened there could not have been avoided.

Adair's men were just about ready to begin pumping drilling mud into the hole. They had made a final check of connections at the wellhead and returned to where the pumping trucks were positioned a hundred yards from the well when sand, whipped from the desert floor to the speed of a tornado by the blowout, struck nearby metal equipment. Since GT-2 blew out, this had probably happened a hundred times with no disastrous results, but this time static electricity was produced right next to the flow. With a blinding flash and a noise that onlookers likened to a never-ending clap of thunder taking place inside their heads, the gas exploded and The Devil's Cigarette Lighter rocketed skyward. Boots and Coots dove for cover behind Adair-designed corrugated metal heat shields rigged up as a safety measure for just such a freak occurrence. They stared at one another, motionless, as smoke from the fire, mixed with swirling sand, blotted out the sun, and pieces of steel shrieked through the air. Had they stayed by the wellhead a minute longer, they would have been broiled alive by the biggest, most violent conflagration yet recorded in the history of the petroleum industry.

CHAPTER FOUR

"The well caught fire," said the man on the phone.

"Was anybody hurt?" Red asked him.

"No casualties," said the man, whose name was Belknap. He was talking to Adair from his office at Phillips Petroleum in Bartlesville, Oklahoma. "You better go on over there, Red," he said. "There's nobody can deal with it now but you."

"Yeah," said Red. "I'll leave as soon as possible. But you're sure nobody got hurt?"

"I'm sure," said Belknap. "Made a helluva mess, but nobody hurt. At least not yet."

Ten minutes before, Adair had come through the intersection of Kirby and Westheimer in Houston in his brand new Lincoln, two weeks old, 175 miles on the odometer. Someone cut Red off and when he jammed on the brakes they locked. The Lincoln did a quick three-sixty through the intersection, caught a piece of curb, and turned 180 degrees, skidding ass-backwards into the parking lot of a Cadillac dealership where it came to rest, without a scratch on it, six inches from the plate-glass showroom window. Behind the window stood an ashen-faced salesman, his eyes bugging out of his head. Red climbed from his car and strode inside. "You see that Lincoln?" he asked. The salesman, who was trembling slightly, nodded. All he could see was the Lincoln, two and a half tons of it in bright red, directly in front of him. He hadn't taken his eyes off the car, and watched it now as though he were not really sure it had stopped moving.

"Brakes locked up on me," Red said. "Can't be having that kind of thing happen to you. I want to trade it in for this Cadillac you got sitting here on the floor."

"Yes sir," said the salesman. "How many miles on the Lincoln?"

"About two hundred," Red said.

"Well, I'm sure we can work something out, Mr. . . . . ?"

"Adair," Red said. "Red Adair. Look, do me a favor, will you?

Here's the keys to the Lincoln. Take all my stuff out of it and put it in the Caddy and change my plates. You got a phone I can use? I have to call my office."

"You're Red Adair?" said the salesman. "I should have known. Red Lincoln . . . Red Adair . . . of course, use the phone over there in the sales manager's office." The man scurried off to organize the car switch while Red sat down and called Joy Hamilton, who patched his call through to Oklahoma.

The news about GT-2 did not really surprise Red. As usual when his men were on a job without him, he had worried about Boots and Coots, even though he knew they were skilled at their work. He was like a father who knows his son is a good driver but frets anyway when the boy takes the family car out alone at night. This time, though, his fretting had taken on an added dimension, since the night before he had dreamed about the well, waking with a start when he saw it in flames. It was 4:00 A.M., but Red switched on his reading light and reached for the pad of paper and pen he always kept on the night table beside him. For over an hour he scribbled notes, drew diagrams of valves and fittings and lengths of pipe, imagining how the well might be controlled. He tried to sleep some more but only tossed and turned, so finally, at 5:30, he got up, did his exercises, showered, and ate breakfast, expecting a call about GT-2 at any second. Before he left the house, he made certain that his packed suitcase and equipment bag were in the trunk of his car.

As soon as he finished talking to Belknap, Adair got Joy back on the line and had her make plane reservations to Paris, where he would meet with officials from the French government and representatives from Phillips Petroleum before continuing on to North Africa. Then, moving quickly, he was out in the parking lot, where the plates were already on the Cadillac and a small crowd had gathered, asking him questions, wondering about what job he was off to now. "Can't talk with you now, fellas," he said, friendly but serious, checking the automobile's trunk to make sure all his stuff was there. "Gotta hurry, gotta hurry . . . leaving for Africa tonight . . . you never know what you'll find over there, but it'll be hot, yes sir, you can bet on that . . . but here, thanks for helping me out." Reaching into the trunk of his new car, he pulled out a small carton, opened it, and gave every man standing there a Zippo lighter with a blazing oil well stamped on one side and the words "Red Adair Company, Wild Well Control" below it. Before anyone could say more than "Thanks, Red, and good luck," he'd slammed the Caddy's trunk, hopped into the driver's seat, and started the engine, hollering out the window to the salesman, "Send the bill to my office," as he jammed the car into gear and spun the wheels out of the parking lot, back onto Westheimer, his senses crackling, running on pure adrenaline, ready to operate for weeks now on no more than four hours of sleep a night.

On November 16, 1961, Red met in Paris with representatives of the French government and Phillips Petroleum. The Frenchmen spoke somberly, their pallor contrasting sharply with Adair's ruddy, weatherbeaten skin. Aware that these men were under great strain, Red paid careful attention not only to what they said, but to the way they talked, how they related to one another, and how they sat in their chairs. In order to get the job done at Gassi Touil, he would need their absolute cooperation, and he wanted to be sure he knew what kind of men he was dealing with. Within minutes he was certain they'd give him total control at GT-2, for it was obvious to him they were desperate and had no idea at all about what to do.

At the time, gas was selling for three dollars per thousand cubic feet. The burning well was consuming 550 million cubic feet of gas a day, which translated into more than a million and half dollars a day in potential revenue going up into the sky. The French, though, had considerably more on their minds at that moment than lost revenue from burning gas. The bloody Algerian Revolution, fought since 1954, was in its final stages. Negotiations, known as the "Evian Talks," were underway to end hostilities and bring independence to the Algerians, but the country was still wracked by bombings, kidnappings, and terrorists' assassinations. As always in situations like these, petroleum wells and pipelines were particularly vulnerable to attack, and GT-2, already dubbed The Devil's Cigarette Lighter by the world's press, would make a prime target for publicity-hungry guerillas.

"Naturally, we will do everything in our power to protect you and your men, Mr. Adair," a senior French official said. "But you must realize the situation in Algeria these days is . . . shall we say, volatile. It may become rather wild, even for a man like you."

Adair smiled at the Frenchman and scratched his head. He always made it his business to learn as much as possible about the customs and traditions of every country where he worked so that he would blend in and not offend anyone. A student of history, he knew things had been pretty wild in Algeria for centuries, ever since successive invasions of Phoenicians, Romans, Vandals, and Byzantines tried to wrest the land from the fierce, bellicose Berber tribesmen. It was those tribesmen for whom the Barbary Coast was named and from whom the word *barbarian* derives. Eventually, in the seventh century, the Sword of Islam prevailed over the Berbers, who were defeated, converted to Islam, and driven into the North African mountains where they live to this day. The conquering Arabs settled along the fertile coastal strip — the Tell — and on the plains to the south.

In subsequent centuries, the fortified city of Algiers became a haven for pirates who plundered merchant ships in the southern Mediterranean. Inland, all manner of European cutthroats and desperados seeking refuge took more and more territory by force from the natives. Finally, in the middle of the nineteenth century, control of Algeria was assumed by France, who shipped thousands of undesirables to the country as colonists, or *colons*, as they were called. The *colons* received subsidies from the French government, and many developed large, prosperous farms. The Muslims lived poorly and primitively with about a 90 percent illiteracy rate, separated from the Europeans by a gulf of mutual suspicion, setting the stage for political and military insurrection that began in earnest after World War II.

In November of 1957, a year and a half after oil was first discovered in Algeria, a party of oil prospectors and their military escort were ambushed near Timimoun by rebels, and sixteen men were killed. French paratroopers were flown in and forty or so rebels were killed in the following week, and on December 10, 1957, the "Saharan Front" of the rebellious Armée de Liberation Nationale (the ALN) was declared by the French to have been eliminated. The declaration did not prevent the rebels from blowing up rail lines between the oil fields and the coast and further terrorizing various outposts of the burgeoning petroleum industry in the Algerian desert.

What happened next in Algeria confirmed Red Adair's rather sardonic view of political factions of every stripe, to all of whom he maintained a neutral, friendly demeanor while secretly not trusting any. In November 1958 General Charles de Gaulle returned to power. With 80 percent of the French electorate voting in favor of his new constitution, the Fourth Republic in France was over and de Gaulle's Fifth Republic began. The Europeans in Algeria, who had played no small role in de Gaulle's victory, expected him to support their pro-French, anti-independence position. De Gaulle, sensing the ultimate futility of the cause of the vastly outnumbered European minority and commanding a war-weary French army, did just the opposite. Soon after his election, he affirmed a policy of Algerian self-determination, which in essence signaled the end of French rule. In short order, European military and civilian dissidents formed the Secret Army Organization — the OAS — and mounted a terrorist campaign of their own, bombing, shooting, and burning with a vengeance. In May 1961 alone, there were 222 plastique-bomb attacks by the OAS, who also managed to murder the police chief of Algiers, burn down a number of schools, and set fire to farms throughout the Algerian countryside. In the oil fields, rebel ALN terrorism was replaced by rebel OAS terrorism with much the same results, only this time the French soldiers who were called in found themselves shooting other Frenchmen instead of Arabs and Berbers.

"Gentlemen," said Red Adair to the men in Paris, "it sounds to me like what you got over there in Algeria is a bunch of folks with different points of view running around shootin' at each other, which isn't a whole lot different than what went on in Texas in the good old days. Now, Texas shaking free of Mexico is one thing, but I'm not about to take sides in this battle 'cause I'm going to have enough on my mind fighting that well. The thing is, it sure would be comforting to know I'm not gonna get a wake-up call from a bomb under my bunk while I'm over there."

"Mr. Adair," said the senior French official, "GT-2 is surrounded by French soldiers. There are checkpoints monitoring everyone and everything coming into the area and leaving it. You will be as safe as one can reasonably hope to be in times like this."

"Well, I hope so," said Red. "These revolutions have a nasty way of catching innocent people in the crossfire."

Adair was remembering a trip he had made to Venezuela four years earlier, after putting out an oil-well fire in the mountains not far from the Colombian border. It had been treacherous terrain, at the base of a rocky canyon covered with dense undergrowth and infested with poisonous snakes. He had spent Christmas in the mud, nursing a bad cold, while he capped the well. Now he was about to miss being home for New Year's as well because of erratic airline services out of Caracas. "What the hell," he thought, and settled in for a relaxing New Year's Eve in Caracas before flying home.

Unfortunately for him, his plans were disrupted by a group of young military officers who were protesting the repressive rule of the Venezuelan dictator, Marcos Perez Jimenez, and chose the precise moment Red slipped into a hot, muscle-soothing bath to attack

the presidential palace. Hearing gunfire in the street outside his hotel, Red leaped from the tub and dashed naked across the room
where he crouched next to the window and peered out, only to feel
the concussion of a mortar striking an automobile below. "Oh, shit,"
Adair said aloud, and quickly dressed and packed his bags. By the
time he got down to the lobby he was in the midst of a full-scale
uprising and wound up spending two weeks trapped inside the hotel
listening to machine guns and grenades going off while drinking
brandy with the hotel manager and a farm-machinery salesman from
Kansas City. Finally, under cover of darkness, the hotel manager's
mistress whisked Adair to the airport, where he left for the States,
not far ahead of Jimenez, who relinquished control of the country to
a junta and fled to Miami.

He remembered Venezuela again, five days after his meeting with
the French in Paris, as he lay in bed in his hotel in Algiers listening
to sporadic explosions taking place in various parts of the city. He
had sent Boots and Coots back to the States to begin rounding up
equipment to fight the fire and the following day would make the
300-mile drive to Gassi Touil.

"Tell whoever's driving your car down to the well not to stop if he
sees something laying in the road," Coots had told him. "What these
bastards are doin' is shootin' somebody and putting the body on the
highway. If you stop, they'll nail your ass, too."

"'Course they may pick you off even if you don't stop," added
Boots.

The next morning, under a flawless Mediterranean sky, Red, the
French scientists, and the Phillips man drove south in the Citroen.
It was painted the color of the desert sand and bore no government
markings or oil-company insignias. The streets were quiet in
Algiers, the air calm, though scented slightly with the smoke of
smoldering buildings. They crossed the fertile Tell, where the
weather was much like that of southern California, traversed the
very dry high plateaus and the even drier Saharan Atlas Mountains,
then dropped down into the Sahara Desert itself with its mammoth,
shifting sand dunes that altered the landscape from one day to the
next, even along the principal highways. Only the Berber camel
men, controllers of the Saharan caravan routes for thousands of
years, traveled this territory with impunity. For anyone else, a trip
of even a few miles without clearly painted markers to guide him, a
good supply of water, and a two-way radio was a dangerous and
often fatal excursion. Here, in eastern Algeria, midday desert

temperatures soared well over one hundred degrees, even in winter, although, in the clear dry air, the loss of heat at night was rapid.

The Citroen made the journey to Gassi Touil without incident, stopping only at the French army checkpoints at an encampment eight miles from GT-2. This was the place where General Eisenhower met with other allied commanders during the North African campaign of World War II and seemed to Red the likely spot for him to set up his own base of operation. The men stopped at the camp only momentarily, however, since Red was anxious to see GT-2 close up as soon as possible.

At 500 feet from the well, the paint on the Citroen began popping like a pot of boiling oatmeal and the tires caught fire. "For God's sake, Red, we're going to fry if we get any closer," the oil man shouted. Adair held up his hand and the car stopped. He folded his enormous arms and pursed his lips. For a moment he remained motionless, studying the flames towering above him. So great was this fire that it seemed as though the inferno had been unleashed from the center of the earth itself and directed toward the heavens. Adair's muscles tensed as he glared at it, taking its measure. All thoughts of terrorists' bombs, of snipers and midnight arsonists, disappeared as he sized up what now was his personal enemy. Then he gestured with a thumb pointed over his shoulder for the oil man to pull back.

"Can you do it?" the man screamed, as he gunned the steaming, shuddering remains of the car away from the blazing well. "Can you put it out?"

"I can do it," Adair replied, "I'll kill the son of a bitch."

The French officials had indeed turned the show over to him without reservation, saying, "Whatever you need, Red, whatever it takes for you to put it out and cap it, just say the word and you'll have it." Given command, Adair responded without hesitation, leaping now from the car and walking by himself back toward the fire. He came so close his shoe soles began to melt and smoke curled from the cuffs of his pants. Around him was rubble, junk, devastation, but already he could see a battle plan taking shape. Positions of attack appeared before his eyes, places for bunkers where his fire monitors would go, bulldozer paths, pipelines, all clearly laid out in a grid inside his head. He marched back toward the Citroen, sat down on the paint-bare hood, and grinned through the cracked windshield at the men in the car.

"What the hell's so funny?" the oil man shouted at him out the window.

"It's Thanksgiving," Adair told him. "Seems like every time a big holiday rolls around I'm off in some God-forsaken place instead of back in Houston, but I'm thankful anyway, 'cause I've been here in Algeria for a whole day now and I haven't been shot at yet."

The first thing they needed at Gassi Touil, Adair told the French scientists, was water: not to put out the fire — Red would do that with his specially designed explosives — but to cool down the surrounding desert and provide a continuous soaking for Adair and his men when they made their final assault on the burning well. That there was no water in the immediate vicinity was regarded by Red as only a minor stumbling block. Throughout his career he battled against what seemed to others overwhelming obstacles, confronting the monumental the same way he dealt with 220-pound defensive linemen when he was a 145-pound halfback: if he couldn't outrun them he outsmarted them. Furthermore, Red Adair, the short guy, was born with a willingness to think big.

When he was nineteen, he designed a levering device that enabled him to unload coal from railroad cars faster than men who outweighed him by a hundred pounds. It was made out of scrap lumber and cost him nothing. When he was faced with the problems of fighting oil well fires in the North Sea forty-five years later, he designed the *Tharos*, which cost over 100 million dollars. To Red, this was a mere detail that gave him no more pause than building the lever for free. He simply saw all obstacles — men, weather, fires — as hurdles in a race he would win either by jumping over them or knocking them down. "I never in my life was concerned with the cost or size of something when I had a job to do," he said. "All I ever thought about was getting that job done."

At Gassi Touil Red directed an extensive search that eventually turned up water five miles from GT-2, deep beneath the desert. Water wells were dug there, and the water was piped overland to three reservoirs, each the size of a football field and ten feet deep, built a mile from the fire. The reservoirs were lined with polyethylene sheets to keep the water from seeping back into the sand, and powerful pumps, designed, like everything else on the site, by Red, were shipped in. The pumps were capable of hurling 40,000 gallons of water a minute a distance of 300–400 feet, but the whole operation took more than a month to complete.

For days Red surveyed the area, measuring, calculating, and sketching, working day and night out on the hot sand or hunched over a rough wooden table in the primitive barracks-type living quarters of the camp at Gassi Touil. He ordered eight brand new D-8 Caterpillar bulldozers, tons of pipe in various diameters, and large quantities of tin sheet metal from which the crew at the site would fashion heat shields enabling Adair and his assault team to approach the fire. He ordered pumps from England and Germany; welding equipment, fire nozzles, and wellhead valves from the United States; and two thousand pounds of solidified nitroglycerin from France, which was delivered by a French army detachment accompanied by heavy artillery. The explosives, with which he would attempt to blow out the fire, were kept in the camp under twenty-four-hour guard. Saboteurs had already blown up two other unguarded wells in the desert, and before Adair was finished in North Africa they would attack a couple more. Even Red himself had to account for every stick of explosive he used once he began fashioning his charges.

In all, Adair ordered more than $4 million worth of equipment. He designed an expanded version of the camp — the base of his operation — which was complete with a small field hospital. Closer to the well, he drew up plans for a machine shop, facilities for welders and mechanics, and the network of pipes and hoses needed to saturate the ground around the well. It would be months before all of this was delivered to Gassi Touil and assembled, before Adair would actually be able to make his move against The Devil's Cigarette Lighter. In the meantime, other jobs awaited him, but before he left the desert he called a meeting of everyone involved in the job at GT-2.

It was late at night. Outside, the desert wind blew cold and the well fire, eight miles away, lit up the sky, while in the meeting room of the camp the noise coming from the well shook the wooden plank floor and caused the lights to sway. Adair surveyed the men before him. There were French soldiers, engineers, and medical personnel. There were Germans — remnants of Rommel's North African troops who had disappeared into the desert at the end of the Second World War — who would operate the cranes and bulldozers. There were Algerian Arabs and Berbers working as welders, mechanics, machinists, and wellhead specialists. Each group had been assigned a vital role by Red in a carefully orchestrated plan to make these men all dependent on one another.

"Men," Adair said to them, "we have an important job to do here, and I want you to realize that there's no way in hell we're going to get it done unless everyone works together. Tomorrow morning, I have to leave for another fire in Bolivia. The equipment and material you need is on its way, and I have no doubt in my mind whatsoever that you all know what to do with it once it gets here. What I'm asking each one of you to do, 'cause this is what concerns me, is put aside your differences. Don't let 'em stand in the way of what we have to do to put this son of a bitch out and get the well capped."

Adair paused. He turned his back on the men and threw open the door at one end of the barracks. The deafening roar of the well rushed with the wind into the room. "Listen to that bastard," he said, his back still to the men. "Look at it out there." He turned again and faced the group who watched him in absolute silence. "Are we going to get it?" he shouted.

Each in his own language, yet in unison, every man in the room shouted back at him, "Yes!" Later on, Adair would have trouble at GT-2, but not from a single man who was in the room that night.

Red's life, which for him had crept slowly for several months, moved now on greased rails. No sooner had he put out the well fire in Bolivia than he was called to another one in Nigeria, where he spent another New Year's away from home. From Nigeria he flew back to Paris for another meeting with Phillips Petroleum and the French government. There he learned that construction at Gassi Touil was proceeding on schedule, but that explosives had been disappearing from the compound in spite of the intense security. "We can only hope," said a French official, "that after all your men have done there, some terrorist group doesn't come and blow it up, or use the explosives on another well. But in any case, Mr. Adair, be assured we are doing everything we can to catch whoever is stealing your nitroglycerin."

"Good," Red said. He would have liked to go directly to North Africa to see if he could catch the thief himself, but first he had to travel to Houston to pick up several of the water pumps he had designed specifically for GT-2.

There was another reason Red felt compelled to return to Houston. His daughter, Robyn, was due to deliver her first child sometime in mid-February 1962. As a child, Robyn, or Bobbie, as both Red and Kemmie called her, had been shy and quiet, but once she became a teenager, she blossomed into a socially active girl with a large circle of friends. Like both her parents, she had a keen mind, and though Red still lived in a world where women stayed home, cooked, cleaned, took care of the kids, and looked pretty, he was eager for his daughter to graduate from high school and go on to college. When she announced she was quitting high school to get married, Red was distressed. The man Robyn was marrying, a pipefitter named Gene Moore, though quite intelligent, seemed too young to him and Kemmie, and besides, Red still thought of Bobbie as his baby girl. Nevertheless, he did nothing to stop her because secretly Red believed the marriage would never last and he felt it more important to support Robyn than alienate her. Now, though not quite eighteen, she was about to become a mother and Red wanted very much to be at her side.

Torn between love for his family and devotion to his work, he waited in Houston as long as he could, but on January 17 Red told Robyn he had to leave. "I have to go, Bobbie," he said, "I have to see how they're doing on the well. I've been gone from it too long already."

"Daddy, you better not go," Robyn said to him, "'cause I'm fixin' to have this baby." There was a hint of desperation in her voice since she knew in her heart Red had made up his mind to leave. It wasn't that he didn't care about her, or her mamma or brother, but he had been so poor when he was young, and had fought so hard to get where he was, that his work came before everything else.

"Hell, Bobbie," he said to her, "that baby's not coming so quick. I'll bet you a hundred dollars . . . no, I'll bet you five hundred dollars I'm back in Houston before you deliver."

Adair lost the bet. On January 21, as he stood beneath the withering desert sun checking a shipment of high-pressure pipe, an army officer handed him a telegram. "Congratulations," it read. "You are now a grandfather. Your grandson, Paul Wayne, born January 20th. Baby and mother doing fine."

They put a picture of Robyn and the baby on the front pages of the Houston press with a little story about how grandpa was off fighting the world's biggest well fire. Wire services picked up the story, there were calls from papers around the country and overseas, and suddenly the family began to realize that The Devil's Cigarette Lighter was going to change things for them forever. Adair had only been in business for himself for two and a half years, and though he was making a good living and had won great respect and acclaim within the oil industry, he was not an internationally renowned figure, but the time was right for a man like him to become one.

In the United States, national pride had not fully recovered from the blow dealt by the disastrous Bay of Pigs invasion of Cuba in April 1961 and President John Kennedy's ineffectual meeting with

Soviet premier Nikita Khrushchev in Vienna two months later. It wouldn't be until the fall of 1962 that Kennedy redeemed himself by calling Khrushchev's bluff during the Cuban Missile Crisis. Meanwhile, in western Europe, spirits weren't much higher. The East Germans had recently constructed the Berlin Wall to halt the flow of East Europeans to West Berlin, a flow that in early August of 1961 numbered six thousand a day. In Algeria itself, the OAS had stepped up its terrorist activities, burning dozens of public buildings in a scorched-earth policy and launching a series of bazooka attacks on squads of police in their attempt to thwart de Gaulle's move toward Algerian independence.

In the midst of all this international hostility and gloom came Red Adair, exactly what the free world, what the *whole* world, for that matter, was looking for: a lone-wolf, Texas-tough, oil-patch cowboy with no political agenda, no speeches to make, no CIA or KGB to brief him, about to have a showdown with the fire of the Devil himself, armed with nothing but a high-pressure hose and a ton of dynamite. No matter which side of the ideological fence you were on, you had to be rooting for Red Adair.

"Mamma, things are about to get crazy," Robyn said to her mother.

"Bobbie, things around here have *always* been crazy, only now everybody's gonna be watching."

Red, in any case, had no time to celebrate his grandson's birth, for the cable about Robyn's baby was followed two hours later by another from Sun Oil Company, who wanted him on a fire in Fort St. John, British Columbia. From the forty-below-zero January weather of Canada, Red returned to Texas to put out two more fires, then rushed up to Michigan for another, then, in rapid succession, dealt with wild wells in Texas, Louisiana, and finally Texas once again, all within a month of Paul Wayne's birth.

On February 20, 1962, while Adair readied his equipment for still another job, this time in El Campo, Texas, John Glenn became the first American astronaut to orbit the earth. Several days after Glenn's return, Red received a call from him. "Just wanted to let you know I could see that burning well in North Africa all the way up in space, Red," Glenn told him. "It must be some humdinger."

"It sure is, John," Red said, "but I'll tell you, if we can do half the job you just did, then that Devil's Cigarette Lighter doesn't have a chance."

"That's kind of you to say so," Glenn responded, "but Red, I'd rather fly in space than fight one of those wild wells any day, believe me."

"I'll bet you a case of cognac it's that little mayor who's been stealing my explosives," Red said to the colonel.

"The mayor of Hassi Larrocque? But Monsieur Adair, he is a respected man," said the colonel. "He has always been very cooperative with us."

It was mid-April 1962, Red had returned once again to North Africa, and he was sitting in the mess hall of the barracks at Gassi Touil talking to the man in charge of the French army detachment at GT-2. Hassi Larrocque was the tiny town not far from the well, and the mayor was the political leader who ran it.

"He may be respected," Red said to the colonel, "but he's a shifty bastard, and he's been comin' and goin' in this camp since we started. I'm telling you, he's the one. Maybe being so cooperative is that guy's problem. I mean, what's he gonna do once you guys pull out of Algeria? Maybe he's afraid the new people running the country'll string him up, or maybe he's just runnin' it down the middle and tryin' to make a few extra bucks. But he looks at me funny, and he looks at you funny too. Haven't you noticed that?"

"Well, to tell you the truth, Monsieur Adair, I am not going to take your bet, because I, too, have wondered about this respected man. We will watch him very carefully."

"Good idea," said Red, who was reasonably certain the colonel had suspected the mayor all along, otherwise the prudent officer would never have so bluntly accused the man.

By this time the drilling camp of thirty men had grown to a small town of three hundred. Adair wanted the missing nitroglycerin situation solved as soon as possible since even though the camp was protected by a detachment of French troops, the additional personnel and furious last-minute preparations for his assault on the well would make it easier for saboteurs to slip into the camp. As always, Red was most concerned about the safety of the men working for him, and he didn't want any innocent people blown up.

The camp itself looked nothing like the desolate outpost Adair had surveyed five months earlier. Now, near the expanded barracks, mechanics worked over the dozens of diesel engines that powered the generators on site, and welders joined sections of pipe and finished work on the sixty-five-foot-long steel boom that was then fitted onto the front of one of the bulldozers. Over each of the dozers, sitting

like a rectangular suit of armor, was a tin enclosure that would protect the driver and any other occupants from the well fire's heat when
the time came to advance.

The three reservoirs were full now. At first the water in them had
been brackish, but the hot desert sun had turned them into clear,
sparkling lakes. Beside them stood giant pumps, ready to force water
at enormous pressure through the 10¾-inch lines snaking their way
toward the well. In addition, Algerian drilling crews worked around
the clock digging three relief wells. These wells, drilled at angles
from separate locations in the desert, would tap into the main well
bore of GT-2. Once Red had the fire put out and the main well was
capped, drilling mud would be pumped into it through these relief
wells in order to achieve the hydrostatic balance necessary to stop
the flow of gas.

"Except for those missing explosives, things don't look too bad,"
Red said. It was late at night, the colonel had left the barracks' mess
hall, and Red was sipping a beer, studying the sketch of the water-
cooled steel hook he designed that was now attached to the end of
the sixty-five-foot boom. This hook would be used to tear the old
drilling rig apart and pull it away from the wellhead. For two reasons, this had to be done before Red attempted to blow out the fire.
When he made his assault on the well and set his explosive charge,
the area needed to be free of debris. This would lessen the chances
of Red or other members of his assault team being tripped by a stray
piece of scrap metal, or the electrical lines leading from the charge
to the detonator becoming tangled. The other reason was that when
the charge went off, anything near the wellhead would become
shrapnel.

"Yeah, things look pretty good," Red said. "We'll start clearing the
old rig away first thing in the morning." With him now at the table
were Boots, Coots, and Charlie Tolar. Tolar, the fullback for the old
Houston Oilers of the American Football League, had been after
Red to take him on as an employee in the offseason, and Red, an
avid booster of his hometown team, had finally agreed to hire
Charlie. Two days earlier Tolar had flown to North Africa, spent a
sleepless night in his hotel room in Algiers listening to gunfire
outside, then driven to Gassi Touil, where Adair handed him a set
of his famous fire-engine red coveralls and told Charlie to walk up to
the wellhead with him to check out the lay of the land.

"Walk on up *next* to that sumbitch?" Tolar shouted. He and Red
had been buddies for some time now, and Charlie figured Red finally

hired him because they were built about the same — short, stocky, and hard to knock down — but until that afternoon he had no idea how serious the deal would turn out to be. Being tackled by a linebacker was one thing, getting cheek to jowl with that monster of a fire coming out of the ground was something else altogether. He looked at Red and could see he wasn't fooling.

"Here," Red said to him. "Grab this piece of tin. It'll help shield you from the heat."

Tolar took the rectangular tin shield, about three feet square with a handle on one side, and started walking. "What the hell," he thought. "Red's going up there, too, and he don't want to die no more'n I do, so I'll follow him. He's made it back every time so far."

A hundred yards from the fire Tolar's boots began to smoke and his face felt as though it were being pressed squarely into a barbecue pit. Adair, up ahead of him, was still walking like he was out for a stroll on the beach. They had their ears packed with cotton soaked in vaseline to provide a tighter seal — Red's standard means of protection when working near a blowing well — and could only communicate by hand signals. This vaseline-soaked cotton, Red had found, worked even better than standard plastic earplugs. For Tolar, the noise seemed to center itself in his mouth, where his teeth were trying their best to shake their way out of his gums. It seemed, too, that his fingernails were working loose from their beds. "Noise torture," he thought. "You never read about that in spy novels. If I ever write one I'll put in noise torture for sure." Then Adair stopped. He turned and smiled at Charlie and motioned with his head back toward the reservoirs.

Red had taken the walk to check on the positioning of some of the demolished drilling rig, but it had also been a test of Tolar's courage. Now Red knew he could trust Charlie to follow his directions when it came time to blow out the fire. He would use Tolar, who was extremely strong and could run swiftly, to help Coots lay out the electrical lines from the well to the bunker where the detonator would be placed.

"You did real good today, Charlie," Red told him. "Have another beer." Tolar's hands were still shaking uncontrollably, and he kept running his tongue around in his mouth, prodding his teeth to see whether any had loosened up. He waved off the beer. He had already observed Adair's work habits on two smaller jobs. Red was more than willing to sit around drinking beer, talking with the guys and kidding the barmaids once the day was over, but before dawn the next day he'd be dressed and ready to start work again. It was understood that every man on the job had better be ready with him.

"I'm going to bed, Red," Tolar said.

The clearing away of the old drilling rig went smoothly. While the bulldozer equipped with the boom and hook pulled pieces of the rig from around the wellhead, other dozers, with nozzles protruding from small square openings in their tin enclosures like cannons sticking out of advancing tanks, kept steady streams of water on the men and equipment that had moved to a staging area one hundred feet from the well. Since all communication was by hand signal, the drivers of the dozers sat with their backs to the burning well, working always in reverse, while navigators, facing the blaze, directed their movements. The deluge from the hoses was so heavy that when Red came within fifty feet of the wellhead he felt cool. When he moved even closer to the giant flame, he was actually cold from the combination of the soaking spray and the draft created by the fire.

Shivering and wet, Red crouched near the damaged pipe and looked up at the flame shooting skyward from it. His eyes and nose ran unremittingly from the intensity of the noise, his stomach vibrated like a tuning fork, and it seemed as though his chest were pinned beneath one of the dozers. Still, he felt completely calm. He saw where he would set his explosive charge, the way he would shape it so its force would be directed precisely to the point just above the opening of the well pipe in order to extinguish the flame. He saw, too, where he could direct the powerful hoses to drive the fire up and away from the wellhead so that he could place his charge right at the flame's base. It would be tricky. The charge would have to be wrapped perfectly so that once it was in place the heat of the fire wouldn't set it off and blow him and his assault team into a million pieces, but Adair was confident it could be done.

He had planned his invasion carefully, delegating responsibility, equipping his army, clearing the battlefield. Now he would have to be patient as well, because it was obvious to him that in addition to all the other factors he had considered in attacking The Devil's Cigarette Lighter, timing was critical in extinguishing the blaze. Between the moment he put the fire out (and there was no doubt in his mind that he would) and the time he capped the well, an uncontrollable jet of the most volatile gas imaginable would spew from the wellhead. If the wind were wrong, the gas would blow over the 300-man crew spread out all the way from the area of the well to the camp eight miles away. That possibility had to be avoided at all costs. Those who only knew of Red Adair often thought of him as a daredevil, but those who worked with him knew different; Red was extremely careful and would never jeopardize the safety of his men. So until the wind was right, Red would wait to kill The Devil's Cigarette Lighter. It was like putting the final pieces into a complicated puzzle, pieces that were clear and distinct to him as he knelt there by himself.

Somehow it had always been like that for him, even when he stood ankle deep in crude oil on the floor of a Texas drilling rig that could blow up at any second, or was enveloped in a cloud of deadly hydrogen sulfide gas next to a wild well in northern Canada where it was forty degrees below zero and a man stuck to any piece of metal he touched. At times like that, when men who were otherwise made of steel turned to jelly, Red Adair remained steadfast, serene, as though dealing with a wild well was the most natural thing in the world for him, as though he'd been born to do it.

> *RED*
>
> A lot of guys would get up so far to the wellhead and they just couldn't take the heat and noise. Many's the time I'd begin walking up on a well starting out with a group of ten guys and pretty soon I'd look around and there'd be five left. I'd go on some more and look around and maybe there'd be one with me. A lot of times I'd look back and there'd be no one with me and I'd say, "Well, it's just me now, but this is it. I've got to go up there and see what's going on." It didn't bother me. In fact, I kind of liked it that way. Just me and the well. Me against the unknown. You look back and everyone else is way back yonder and you're the Lone Ranger. *You* go in there. So I'd keep walking, not knowing exactly what was happening at the wellhead or on the floor of the drilling rig 'cause you *never* know until you're there and I'd say, "I will defeat it, whatever it is. I will win." But that's a lonely walk, boy, you better believe it.

Red Adair had a nitro headache. He'd been working nonstop for ten hours shaping the charges he would use to blow out The Devil's Cigarette Lighter, molding the explosives into loaves like a baker kneading bread, and now it felt as though one of the loaves had already gone off inside his skull. "Ain't nothin' you can do about it," he told Charlie Tolar, who watched attentively nearby. "Aspirin's useless, and I've tried damn near everything else known to man. I've rubbed crushed ice on my forehead. I've used raisins and horseradish leaves. I've even tried rubbing in whiskey. All that does is waste good booze. Not a remedy will blunt it because once you get that nitro on your hands you're sure as hell gonna wipe 'em on your fore-head and brother, you don't know the meaning of the word headache until you've had a nitro headache. Only consolation I have this time is knowing that little mayor's got a worse one than me."

Adair had been right about the local mayor. Two days earlier he'd been caught smuggling two sticks of nitro out of the camp in his pants pockets and, during vigorous interrogation, confessed to being part of a band of saboteurs who had been terrorizing the country-side. He was taken away by a squad of French soldiers and Adair never saw him again, although the colonel spoke obliquely to Red once about the politician. "Monsieur Adair, it appears we both won the wager you proposed," the colonel said. "My men discovered some quite respectable cognac along with what was left of the stolen nitro-glycerin, enough in fact for both of us."

In spite of his excruciating headache, Red kept on working through the night, because finally the wind had begun to die and conditions appeared almost right for him to make his move. He had gathered his men together and informed them that in a few hours the assault on the well fire would begin. Each man was reminded of his task and impressed with the importance of obeying only the hand signals of Red, or his lieutenants Boots and Coots.

At 3:00 A.M., in the eerie glow of the towering blaze, the crew manning the water hoses advanced and began cooling down the area around the well. They cooled for six hours while the wind abated and Adair finished molding the charges, which he packed into a drum custom-made almost twice as big as the fifty-five-gallon drums he ordinarily used. Inside that drum a smaller drum was placed, filled with 750 pounds of solidified nitroglycerin. Next, dry, non-explosive chemical was packed around the entire charge in order to knock out any small ground fires that might start as a result of the explosion — fires that might reignite the well fire.

In the morning, with the wind gone, Red mounted the explosives on his water-cooled hook at the end of the fifty-foot boom of the bulldozer. He hopped into the dozer's seat, and, with Boots directing him, drove straight for the wellhead. He was the point man now, spearheading the attack he had so painstakingly engineered. Mean-while, Coots and Charlie Tolar unspooled the electrical lines, making certain no line snagged or broke. What with the dozer bucking and shaking like an enraged bull from the well's noise, the boom swinging to and fro with enough nitro dangling off its end to make brick dust of a fifteen-story apartment house, and the fire so hot the charge could go off any old time without the benefit of an electrical impulse, the last thing Adair needed was a broken connection between the drum of explosives and the detonator. When he hit that plunger, he wanted results.

Working from the dozer's cab, Red positioned the boom as close to the base of the flame as possible. Then he leaped from the seat and, running low to the ground and as fast as any tailback Charlie Tolar had ever seen, scooted up under the fire, signaled to Boots, who'd jumped into the dozer, to bring the boom down just a touch, and pulled the barrel of nitro right in where he wanted it by hand. He took a deep breath, squinted through the downpour created by a dozen hoses trained on the well, and sprinted for the bunker a hundred yards away. Coots and Tolar could see him coming and made room, because it was clear from the look in Red's eye he was going to dive straight for the detonator, which he did, his hands curled like two claws outstretched to grab the plunger. Without breaking stride, he pushed down on it as though he wanted to shove it right through the desert floor. Only the charge didn't explode. Red looked up. His equipment was still in place and the monstrous flame still roared above it, mocking him, he thought. "Son of a bitch!" he said, and plunged again, and this time the device worked, going off with such a mighty blast that the bulldozer jumped three feet off the ground. Through the enormous cloud of dust, filled with rocks and shrapnel and pieces of water hose, all of which whined overhead like a mortar attack, they could see that The Devil's Cigarette Lighter, which had burned for half a year, was out. It was shortly before noon, Saturday, May 28, 1962.

Red stared at where the flame had been and smiled, but he didn't celebrate. The noise of the escaping gas was still deafening, and until that gas flow was stopped — until a new wellhead with blowout pre- venters was in place — GT-2 was a menace that could, in a fraction of a second, explode into another Devil's Cigarette Lighter. Red quickly put the rest of his crew to work. Using a water-cooled scoop on the end of a second boom-equipped bulldozer, he dug a trench around the wellhead, eighty feet in diameter and twenty feet deep. The well casing had to be cut off below the spot where it had been initially damaged, and the trench was necessary to provide working room to make that cut. It took eight hours to dig, and every shovelful was fraught with tension because of the heat generated by the bucket digging into the sand. Then, using 8,000 feet of cable moving at 300 feet per minute back and forth between two huge winches, the old well casing was cut off. Adair's technique worked perfectly; the cable sawed its way through the pipe without creating a single spark.

After the pipe was cut, Red and his crew worked frantically next to the flow of gas, installing the new pipe, the valves on top of it, and the two six-inch flow lines that ran from the wellhead into the desert. The gas could be bled off through these lines and flared safely until drilling mud was pumped down the well. So powerful was the escaping gas next to where the men worked that anyone stepping into it would be instantly cut in two. Red told Charlie Tolar that before they began this final phase of the job. "Whatever you do, Charlie, keep your damn head below that flow. Believe me, it is one powerful son of a bitch, so you have to concentrate on keeping low, even when the noise of it starts making you a little nuts."

Tolar took heed for a while, but eventually he became so caught up in the work and so frazzled by the sound of the gas, which by this time was making his feet buzz wildly inside his boots, that he raised up a bit too far and had his hard hat ripped from his head and thrown several hundred feet up into the air. Red just looked at him. Neither of them could say a thing because of the noise. That night, however, when they were celebrating the capping of the well, Red smiled at Charlie and leaned over close to him. "I hope you realize that could have been your head going up in the air instead of your hat if you'd have raised up a few inches higher," he said.

Tolar did indeed realize how close a brush with death he'd had, but it wasn't bothering him a whole lot at that moment because he'd been drinking wine steadily for almost two hours at the banquet. "Red, I been meaning to ask you for several days now, where'd all these blond German guys come from?"

Red scanned the room to see whether any of the several dozen German workers had heard Tolar's question. "See, when the Second World War ended," he said quietly to Tolar, "there were all these very young members of Hitler's Youth fighting with Rommel, and they just took off into the desert rather than be captured. Most of them live in Algiers now, but some of 'em still live out in the boon-docks."

"Hitler's Youth, huh?" said Tolar, and went back to drinking wine.

The banquet continued, and soon it was time for every member of Red's American crew to make a speech. Red talked about how glad he was that all the various factions working at GT-2 had coop-erated so well. Boots and Coots seconded Red's thoughts and added compliments for the excellent food provided by the kitchen staff. Now it was Tolar's turn. He stood, somewhat unsteadily, raised his wine glass and shouted at the top of his lungs, "Heil Hitler!"

Red's jaw dropped six inches and his eyes nearly bugged out of his head. A third of the men in the room had jumped to attention. The mess hall was absolutely still. Red grabbed Tolar by the collar and yanked him back down to his seat, noticing as he did that the colonel, sitting across the table from him, had turned an interesting shade of purple. "Goddamn, Charlie," Red hissed, "you trying to start World War Two all over again?" Out of the corner of his eye he could see Boots and Coots doubled over hysterically, though neither of them were making any noise. Tolar had his head on the table and was mumbling incoherently, while the Frenchmen and Algerians cast sidelong glances at the Germans, who stared glumly at the floor. "Christ almighty," Red thought. "It isn't any damn well that's gonna get my ass blown away, it's the human beings I keep having to contend with."

He got to his feet and in his most congenial Texas drawl said, "Gentlemen, I propose a toast to all the beautiful women of the world, American ones, French ones, German ones, who may not be here with us tonight but . . . well, we wish that they were."

"Well said," shouted the colonel. Everyone else applauded and the banquet concluded without further incident.

Defeating The Devil's Cigarette Lighter brought Red Adair immediate international acclaim. Geologists, praising his work, said that if he hadn't killed the fire when he did it would have burned for another hundred years — until the world's greatest natural gas field was depleted. *Life* magazine did a story about Red and the fire at GT-2 in their May 11, 1962, edition and included one picture; smaller than the rest and in black and white, reminding readers how potentially lethal the well had been. In the background of the photograph, looking tiny and insignificant against the wall of flame, stands Red Adair, in silhouette, partially hidden by smoke. In the foreground are three canvas stretchers, set out in a row, empty, ready.

As usual, Adair himself had little time to sit back and bask in fame and glory. By 9:00 P.M. on the day following his capping of the well, Red was back in Houston. He had a late-night dinner with Kemmie, told her the story about Charlie Tolar and the banquet, and promptly fell asleep.

Three hours later, he was awakened by a call from his answering service. "Mr. Adair," said the woman on call, "Texaco's got a blowout down in El Campo. I'm real sorry to bother you. I told 'em I'd call one of the boys, but they said to please call you . . ."

"It's OK, honey, " Adair said. "I'm on my way." It was 5:30 Sunday morning. There wouldn't be anybody on the road. He could make El Campo before breakfast.

THE NORTH ATLANTIC — 1988

He woke to a vision of thick, dark smoke rising from a stormy sea. A tongue of flame appeared where the smoke and water met, then the flame disappeared, then appeared again and began to grow. The vision tilted and he could see stumps in the water, or were they pipes? He couldn't be sure. His head cleared and the vision became more distinct. They were pipes, all right, twisted extrusions coming out of the sea where once an offshore platform had stood. He sighed and shook his head. Across the aisle, his men, Raymond Henry and Brian Krause, were asleep, as were the other passengers in the darkened first-class cabin. The flight attendant stood beside him, a steaming cup of coffee in her hand.

"It came on again," she said, gesturing with her head toward the movie screen. "You asked me to wake you."

"Thanks," he replied, but refused the coffee with an upturned hand. He put on the headset and listened to the BBC reporter.

Armand Hammer had issued a statement expressing his deepest sympathy for the families of the men lost in the Piper Alpha tragedy, the reporter said. Hammer was flying from California to Scotland that day. There was no way to tell as yet how extensive the damage was, but it was certain to run into hundreds of millions of dollars. Red Adair, famed Texas oil-well fire fighter, had been called in to deal with the fire, the reporter went on, and even now, as Adair travels to Aberdeen and then to the fire-fighting vessel *Tharos* he designed, and grief-stricken families wait for word about the missing men, the platform continues to burn, lighting the sky for miles around with an eerie amber glow.

The screen went blank. He took off the headset and closed his eyes again. How many times had he seen that eerie glow in the sky? Three hundred? Five hundred? A thousand? When had it begun? When had he seen the glowing sky for the first time? It seemed that his life had been entwined with it forever. Slowly, he drifted back, before all the foreign travel, before the newspaper stories and magazine pieces, before the TV cameras and the urgent late night calls from men he'd been bred to call "sir." He remembered seeing the glowing sky then, before anyone had known who he was, or anyone except himself had known what he could do. Young as he was he had known even then he would do something — something big — something more than what he saw around him in the tiny houses, on the dirt streets, on the edge of Houston.

CHAPTER FIVE

These young fire fighters come up to me and they say, "I want to be just like Red." They're wearing four-hundred-dollar boots and gold Rolex watches. They have expense accounts. They're driving big company cars, but they see Red's million-dollar town house and his million-dollar boat and his Mercedes and my Rolls-Royce, and they see how people flock around Red in restaurants, in airports, at football games, wherever he goes, and they say, "Tell me how I can be just like Red Adair." I tell them they'll never be like him. There just isn't any way. To be like him they would have to have been a little boy with no shoes.

Kemmie Adair

HOUSTON — 1921

Red Adair was born in Houston on June 18, 1915, when the city was emerging as the hub of the oil industry in South Texas. He was six years old the first time he heard about an oil-well fire. It was on a stifling summer night and he was standing in a weed-choked vacant lot on 6½ Street next to Ashmore's Filling Station, two blocks from the corner of Seventh and Oxford streets, where he lived, in the northwest part of Houston known as Houston Heights. He was with a dozen other boys, all older, all bigger, whom he had followed when they raced past his house, shouting and pointing at the sky east of town, which pulsed deep orange and crimson through the trees.

It was very late and Red's twin sisters, Faye and May, who were sitting outside with him, told him not to go. They were eight and felt it was their job to watch out for him, although mostly what they did was their best to keep up with him. Faye said, "Booger Red, carrot head, Daddy's gonna whip you if you ain't in bed." She always called him Booger Red, just as their father did, and Red didn't mind. In the whole family, Faye was the only one at all like him, restless, adventurous, full of mischief. She even looked like him, only she didn't have red hair.

"You'd come, too, if you were a boy," he yelled to her. And it was true.

May was more sedate, more passive, like their older sister, Dorothy, sixteen, and their brothers, Charlie, twelve, and George, eighteen. (Two more boys, Bob and David, would be born years later and neither would have Red's aggressive, competitive nature.) May called Red by his real name, Paul. Sometimes she even called him by his whole name, Paul Neal. "It sounds more grown up," she said. Red didn't mind that either. He loved both twins dearly and the three of them went everywhere together. The only time he got angry was when they crossed the big field with the bull in it on their way to the free movies in the park.

"I'll go with you," Red would say, "but you ain't gonna put that big ol' rag over my head."

"Booger Red, we have to," Faye would tell him, "or else the bull will see your red hair and come get us. And it ain't a rag, it's a shawl."

"I hate red hair," Red would say, "and I ain't scared of no bull." But he let them cover his head anyway, because they were his sisters and he wanted them to be happy.

In the vacant lot, the boys had a clearer view of the sky and fell silent for a time watching it glow, waiting for the occasional flares of white hot sparks. "What is it?" Red asked. "What's makin' the sky light up like that?" Even at six years old, as he rocked back and forth on the balls of his feet with his hands balled up in his overall pockets, and his jaw thrust out, you could see he was dauntless, ready for action.

"That's an oil-well fire," an older boy said. "My dad says there ain't nothin' on this earth hotter or more dangerous than an oil-well fire."

The boys were quiet again. They'd all heard stories about the black gold coming out of the ground at the vast East Texas oil field outside the city, and about the men who'd become rich overnight because of it, but this was the first time any of them but the one older boy had seen a well burn, even from a great distance.

"What will they do about it?" Red asked the older boy.

"My dad says sometimes they just let 'em burn," the boy told him. "Other times they try to put 'em out. Old Man Ashmore, he's tried it, but he don't get too far. That's what all his contraptions are for, but he ain't got nothin' there for this one. This fire's way too big."

The boy pointed across the field to Ashmore's station. Through the darkness they could make out the strange hulking carts with large iron wheels and coiled hoses on them, and the Model T truck with what looked like a huge cage mounted on its bed. Red had always wondered what the machinery at Ashmore's was for and once asked his brother George about it when they rode by in the truck George drove for a freight company. "Just a pile of junk," George said, though to Red it looked wonderful, like the abandoned engines of a defeated army.

"My dad had a friend who tried to put one out," another boy said.

"What did he use?" Red asked him. "How'd he do it?" He was excited now, jumping around from one kid who spoke to the next, intrigued by the notion that Ashmore's junk might truly have a mysterious, death-defying purpose.

"He didn't do it," the boy said. "He got burned up. My dad says you can make lots of money fighting oil-well fires, but ain't a man who's done it ever died a natural death."

Red stared at the eastern sky and tried to imagine the kind of men who would battle a fire that could make the sky shimmer and glow at night. They would have to be extremely brave, he thought, like the ancient warriors Faye and May told him stories about. They would have to invent great machines to help them do it. "I bet I could get it out, someday," he said. "I'd build this huge truck as big as a house with a ton of water in it you could drive right on up and dump on the fire. I could do that."

"Sure you could," said the boy who'd seen a well fire once before. "If a pig had wings it could fly."

"Where you been, Booger Red?" said Dorothy, when he got home. She was sitting in the parlor, in the rocking chair, sewing by the light of a small table lamp.

"I was over to Ashmore's field watching the oil-well fire in the sky," he said. He looked around nervously, though the house was quiet. This was the fourth house they'd lived in in various parts of the Heights in the last six months — shotgun houses, they were called, because you could stand at the front door and shoot a shotgun straight through the house and out the back without touching a wall. All of them were tiny, wood-frame structures, so similar Red could find his way around in the dark the day after the family moved in.

Red's father, Charlie, and his mother, Mary, had come to Texas from Missouri not long after the turn of the century, when the boom was on and Houston was changing from a small country town to an industrial city. Oil had been discovered nearby and the industry was growing. Factories were being built. Seventeen railroads joined in Houston, and the ship channel was under construction that would make the city a port. Charlie opened a blacksmith shop where he made springs for railroad cars and, later, for automobiles that raced on the tracks around Houston. Charlie Adair was a good blacksmith, diligent and honest, who kept a meticulous set of books in beautiful, flowing handwriting, but he was a lousy businessman and his ledger overflowed with receivable accounts. Hard as he worked, he never had enough money to feed and clothe and house his large family, so he'd pay a month's rent, stay until the landlord came knocking, and move to another house. Deep down, he was a good-hearted man, but his situation made him gruff and stern. He cussed a lot and wouldn't be crossed at home. The Adair kids did what Charlie said or they felt the sting of his wide Sam Browne belt. Red was waiting now for him to appear and give him the whipping his sisters had assured him he'd receive.

"Where's Daddy?" he asked Dorothy.

"He's not here," she said. "He had to go. He had to take Mamma to the hospital."

Red looked at her, his mouth tightening into a thin line. He had no shirt on underneath his overalls, and his freckled arms and shoulders were streaked with dirt. A fine coating of dust covered his dark red curls.

"What's Mamma got?" he asked. "What's gonna happen?" He had forgotten about the whipping and had moved across the room to a spot directly in front of the rocker so that when his sister leaned forward in the chair their knees touched.

"She has TB, Booger Red," Dorothy said. "That's what the doctor told her. She has to go to a special kind of place to get better. I don't know what's gonna happen yet. Daddy will know that. Why don't you go on to bed?" Their knees were still touching and she had taken both his arms in her hands. "Boy," she said, "you're gettin' to be a strong little booger."

"Will you take care of us like before?" he asked her. He was used to his mother being sick. It seemed that she was ill with one thing or another almost all the time, and that Dorothy was the one who took care of the house. In fact, he and the twins called their older sister Mamma Dot, and both May and Faye thought of Mary Adair not as their mother but as "that pretty woman in bed."

Dorothy sighed. She was a small girl with bright eyes and a beautiful smile who had been doing the work of a woman since she was nine. But then, all the Adair children worked hard. Even Red had been rising before dawn for a year to walk ten blocks to his father's blacksmith shop. There he built the fire in the stove his father used to heat the steel he beat and shaped into springs. If the fire went out, Red received a whipping.

"Daddy says I can't take care of everybody," Dorothy told him. "I can't take care of you *and* May *and* Faye."

"What will we do?" Red asked her.

"You and the twins are gonna go live in this real nice place for a while 'til Mamma gets better. It's called the Faith Home. It's downtown near all the big buildings and there's lots of kids there. It's run by the church."

He pulled his arms away from her and took a step back. Beneath the grime, she could see the skin at the corners of his mouth turn white as flour. "I'm goin' to bed," he said.

"Don't forget to wash your face," she told him.

In the morning it rained and rained, and all he could see of the well fire was dark smoke rising into the clouds. They rode in George's truck, each holding a small bundle of belongings, across 11th Avenue and down North Main, to the orphanage called the Faith Home.

"Look," Red said, when they crossed Congress, "the street's floating, the street's floating!"

He had his face pressed against the truck's side window, and began bouncing up and down on the seat. What he saw was a whole section of the cypress blocks used to pave Main and a number of the other downtown streets rising up in the torrential downpour.

"Look at it, George," Red said.

"I am looking at it," George said. "It's dangerous as hell."

"I could fix it so they wouldn't float, I know I could," Red said.

"Paul Neal, you could not," said May.

"I could, too," he said.

"How you gonna fix it?" May asked him. "Don't you think the men would do it if there was a way?"

"Maybe I got a way in mind and they don't," Red said. "I'd chain the street down."

"Paul Neal, there's no way you can chain down a street," said May.

"Don't ever say no way to him," said Faye. "He'll be runnin' all over Houston stealing chains."

"This is it," said George. They had pulled up in front of a large, three-story brick building. "This here's the Faith Home, where you're gonna stay. Y'all be good and mind your manners."

He wasn't scared there — even as a little boy, fear was an emotion he refused to acknowledge — but at first he was confused, and he was lonely, too, because the girls and boys slept in different dormitories and he was separated from his sisters.

"Where are they?" he kept asking Miss Holt and Miss Little, the two kindly, middle-aged women who ran the home. "Where'd May and Faye go?"

"They're OK," Miss Holt said to him.

"Don't worry. Just settle down and everything's going to work out fine. You'll make lots of friends here," said Miss Little.

"My sisters need me," he said, thinking, "my mamma needs me, too, and I don't know where she is either." For the rest of his life, no matter where he was in the world, Red Adair would insist that all of those close to him, from his wife, to his children, to each of his firefighters, let him know where they were at all times, because he cared about them, because he didn't want any of them ever to leave him.

The first night he climbed from his bed when the dormitory lights were out and went looking for the twins, wandering through the building until he saw a light. He walked through a swinging wooden door with a small circular window in it and found himself in the kitchen, where a black man with the biggest arms he'd ever seen sat at a table reading a newspaper and sipping a steaming mug of coffee.

"I'm Malone," the man said. "I'm the cook. Who are you?"

"My real name's Paul, but most everybody calls me Red," he told the man. "I'm looking for my sisters."

"They ain't in here," said Malone. "You hungry?"

Red nodded. He was always hungry, mainly because he rarely had enough to eat, but he had never said so before. He was too proud. Time and again, in the months before he entered the orphanage, he would stand in the driveway of the home of his friend, Bill Schultz, waiting for Bill to come out to play.

"Hey, Red," Bill's father would holler. "C'mon in and have some breakfast with us."

"Nah," Red would reply. "I ain't hungry. I just ate."

The truth was that more often than not Red hadn't had a bite in two days. Now, though, things were different. Now he wasn't at home and nobody would know there wasn't anything in the cupboard.

"I'll make you a sandwich," said Malone, "and you can have a glass of milk. That all right?"

Red nodded again.

"You the first kid ever come down here at night, you know that?" said Malone. "C'mere and sit down. I like you. You a tough little fella, lookin' for your sisters. You protect 'em, uh?"

Red nodded a third time.

"Well, Red, I can tell we gonna be friends. You ever get in a bad way, or you ever get real hungry, you come see ol' Malone. How's that?"

"That's fine," Red said. "I like you too."

The little redheaded kid looked like easy pickings. He was alone in the basement corridor of the school clutching the paper bag that held his lunch. He seemed lost, as though he didn't quite know where he was going nor anybody to ask who might be able to tell him the way. The two other boys in the corridor, older and considerably bigger than the redhead, blocked his path. They were tough kids from downtown Houston, and they wanted the paper bag. At eight years old they were already veteran street fighters. They knew the redheaded kid came from the Faith Home because he had on the shorts and blouselike shirt all the Faith Home kids wore. They knew, too, that this was his first day at the Fannin School because they'd never seen him before. What the two older boys didn't know was that Red Adair, the kid in front of them, had been given something special for lunch on his first day of school by his good friend, Malone, the cook, and that there was no way in the world he was about to give the bag up. Neither did the two boys know that the kid, who was quivering before them, was not shaking out of fright but in rage.

"Give us the bag," one of the boys said for the second time. "Give us the bag and you won't get hurt."

"If you'd 'a asked me, I'd 'a shared it with ya," Red finally said. "But now you're gonna have to kill me to get it."

For a moment the older boys hung back, surprised by the little kid's answer and just a touch uneasy about something they saw in his eyes. Small as he was, this new kid suddenly didn't look like a pushover. But the older boys had their reputations to think about, so they advanced, swinging at Adair with pudgy fists. Adair fought back the best he could, kicking, biting, striking at the boys who were after his food. The hallway became a blur of snarls and curses and bodies crashing into the metal lockers lining both sides until finally a teacher, hearing the noise, rushed to the corridor and intervened. When it was over, Red Adair was bloodied and his new clothes were torn, but the other boys were not much better off, and Red still had his lunch.

It would have been nice if Red's problems at the Fannin School had ended with that first fight, but unfortunately real life is often not like that, and the hallway battle proved to be just the beginning. The two boys had friends, a whole gang of young brawlers who taunted the Faith Home kids and lay in wait for them along the route between the orphanage and the school. Red's trip became a daily gauntlet run with older, stronger boys lurking behind trees and fences to pounce on him and beat him up, and in spite of Red's fearless nature, the fact was he didn't really know how to fight. So day after day he returned to the Faith Home with his clothes torn and his face cut and bruised.

One day, as he was walking into the home with blood still running from his nose, Miss Holt called him into her office. Miss Little was there too, and Red was certain he was going to be severely punished for ruining another Faith Home uniform. Instead, Miss Holt put her arm around him. "Paul, this has gone far enough," she said. "It's time Miss Little and I taught you how to defend yourself properly."

Red was dumbfounded. How were these nice ladies in their long skirts and clumpy shoes going to teach him to fight? "Let's go," said Miss Holt, and she and Miss Little took him to a small room off the kitchen where the two of them kicked off their shoes. They had two pair of boxing gloves, one for him and one for Miss Holt. "Miss Little will referee," said Miss Holt, "and help me give you pointers. We'll begin by teaching you how to throw a jab."

Red Adair was a perfect pupil, because in addition to great natural athletic ability he was a fanatic in his desire to be the best at everything he did. He learned to jab, to throw a cross and an uppercut, and how to block a punch. Within a month, he was whipping all the kids who'd been using him for a punching bag, no matter how big or how old they were.

"I'm gonna tell you why those two women taught you how to box," Malone said to him one night as they sat together in the kitchen. Years before, the cook had been a club fighter in Kansas City, but at first had refrained from instructing Adair, believing that was not his place. As time passed, however, he had begun to add fine points to Miss Holt and Miss Little's rudimentary instruction, including tales of backroom brawls that held Adair spellbound. Red had been in the Faith Home for nearly two years and was almost eight by this time. His mother was coming home from the sanitarium in San Angelo in a week and he and the twins would be returning to the Heights. "See, they was sick of you tearing up them little suits y'all wear, and they was scared, too, that you'd get hurt real bad. But there was another thing. They're very smart ladies, Miss Holt and Miss Little, and they knew you weren't going to run from those other boys. They could tell that wasn't your way, no matter what they said or did to you, so they had no choice. You get much better you be good enough to whip me."

"I bet I could whip you now," Red said.

Malone smiled, showing two gold teeth, one with a minute diamond in the center. "That's why I like you, Red," he said. "There ain't nobody or no thing in the world you don't believe you can't whip. You gonna be somethin' big someday, and when that day comes just don't forget who made you sandwiches at night."

"I won't forget," Red said.

FAYE

Red was fun. A little crazy, plenty different, but fun. I know there were things that happened to us that bothered him, but he never showed it. And no matter how bad things got he always managed to figure out some way to have a good time. I remember once he came home with a jackass. He couldn't've been more than nine or ten years old. I think he paid a quarter for it. Daddy was furious with him. He said, "We ain't got enough food on the table for all of us, how the hell are we gonna feed a jackass? Get rid of the damn thing."

You could see Red thinking. He really wanted to keep it. He said, "Daddy, the reason he was so cheap was 'cause nobody could ride him. What I'm gonna do is charge people money to see if they can stay on him." And that's what he did. And he made a bunch of money doing it, too. People came from all around to see if they could stay on it. And when he got tired of doing it, he sold that jackass to another boy for I think three dollars.

He gave most of the money to Mamma, but he took me and May to the movies and bought us ice cream sodas and Mrs. Bender's hamburgers. They only cost a nickel, unless you wanted a big one, which was a dime. I remember on our way home he got in a fight. (He was never mean, but he was always gettin' into a fight.) Some guy said something rude to me or May and next thing you know Red was on the ground with four of 'em. They got him at the bottom of the pile, so May and I started kicking and pulling 'em off and finally they ran away.

Red was angry with us. He said, "What'd you do that for?"

I said, "Booger Red, they were killin' you."

He said, "What do you mean? I'd 'a got 'em. You should have given me a little more time."

HOUSTON — 1925

Red met Stewart and Jimmy Wade for the first time a week after blowing up the coke-fired furnace in his father's blacksmith shop shortly after dawn on a Saturday morning in October. You could hear the furnace cut loose from three blocks away, and the mess it made was beyond description, but at least no one got hurt. "It was an experiment, Daddy," Red said. "I was just tryin' to get you a bigger, hotter fire. I was just bein' helpful, is all." Red had gone back to his old chores the day after returning from the Faith Home, and after two more years of rising before the sun to build the morning fire, he was getting bored. In truth, he had been increasing the pressure in the furnace steadily for days to find out how much it could take. Charlie Adair, who suspected as much, and who was experiencing a run of even worse financial distress than usual, yanked off his belt, but Red was quicker than his father and took off down the street. He ran all the way to Harvard and 7th streets, where the freights slowed down at a sharp curve, hopped into an open boxcar, and rode it to the railroad yard downtown.

There were about 140,000 people in Houston in 1925, along with 35,000 automobiles, seven oil refineries, and a number of oil field equipment manufacturers, including the Hughes Tool Company, which had just been taken over by Howard R. Hughes, Jr. Still, Houston had the feel of a small town. Despite the dredging of Buffalo Bayou from downtown Houston to Galveston Bay to create the Houston Shipping Channel, the Bayou's upper reaches, and all of White Oak Bayou, where Red and his friends swam, were still overhung with vegetation and crystal clear. Many of the streets in the city weren't yet paved, and the traffic signals along Main Street were controlled manually by men who sat in a tower in the center of the Capitol and Main Street intersection. Red would travel into town as often as possible with his twin sisters or his friends. Sometimes they would hop a freight, sometimes they'd jog three miles down the railroad tracks, and if it was a special occasion and they were lucky enough to have a nickel, they'd take a streetcar.

On the Saturday Red blew up his father's furnace, he watched the traffic controller, watched the cars and trucks, and watched the people all dressed up in fancy clothes walking in and out of the stores on Main Street, wondering whether any of the men he saw were wildcat oil men who drank bourbon and had gold pieces jingling in their pockets. He had a dime he'd earned for chopping wood in his pocket.

In the afternoon he walked up White Oak Drive, back to the Heights. He spent a nickel on a Mrs. Bender's hamburger and washed it down with water, saving his other nickel for the movie theater, where a man accompanied the silent films on piano. After the movie he went home, but waited in some woods nearby until after ten o'clock, when he knew (or thought he knew) his father would be in bed. Quietly, he climbed through the window of the bedroom he shared with his brother Charlie and the twins and crawled under the covers.

He'd been asleep an hour when the cold water hit him, a whole bucketful, drenching him from head to toe. He tried to jump up but was unable to move, because his father had wound the sheet carefully around him before dumping the water. Now, as he lay shivering, only half awake, the Sam Browne belt descended again and again, cracking like a bullwhip on the wet sheet, raising thick red welts on the skin underneath. "Don't ever run away from me again," his father said when he was through, and left the room.

The welts were still there a week later as he rode with his brother Charlie down Cortland Street in the Adairs' old Maxwell their father had assembled from several wrecks. As the Maxwell slowed at a corner, two boys named Stewart and Jimmy Wade watched from high up in a tree that overhung the street. They had a good supply of the heavy, thorny, spherical plants the boys in the Heights called sticker weeds and awaited the topless Maxwell eagerly. The first sticker weed missed the Adairs' car entirely, the second landed on the hood, but the third caught Red squarely between the shoulder blades, directly on one of the welts. He yowled in pain as the fourth hit him in the ear and was out of the Maxwell and next to the tree before Charlie got his foot on the brake.

"You sons o' bitches," he screamed. "Get down outa that tree so's I can kick your ass."

"You want us both together or one at a time?" Jimmy Wade yelled back. "Make it both together," hollered Red. "That way it won't take me as much time."

Jimmy Wade came first, but halfway to the ground he got a good look at Red and stopped. Below him was this short, skinny kid with red hair, lots of freckles, and the wildest look in his eye Wade had ever seen in a human being. Wade also thought he could hear the kid's teeth grinding together. "Wait a minute," he said. "I heard about you. Ain't you that redheaded kid that whipped Henry Marchese and Jim Cossasa?"

"That's me," Red told him. "And I'm gonna do the same thing to both of you."

Marchese and Cossasa were the leaders of an Italian gang in the Heights that had terrorized Red's neighborhood during the time he'd lived in the Faith Home. The Italian gang had waited daily at a feed store not far from the Harvard Elementary School, which most of the Heights kids attended, and had routinely beaten the daylights out of the rest of the boys on their way to and from school. Red Adair had personally changed the routine and brought about a truce between the rival gangs. Eventually, in fact, he and the Marcheses developed a strong friendship that lasted for many years.

"I don't want to fight you," Jimmy Wade said. "I'm sorry I threw the sticker weeds at you. Let's be friends."

Charlie Adair had by this time pulled the Maxwell over to the side of the road. "You gonna whip 'em, Red?" he yelled. Charlie wasn't in the least combative, but he was more than happy to egg Red on and would often pick fights for his younger brother.

Red glanced over at Charlie. He looked up into the tree. "I already got plenty of friends," he said to Jimmy Wade, but his fury had ebbed. There was something about the two boys squatting in the branches above him that he liked. They were both wearing old jeans and Western-style shirts, and Stewart, the older one, had on a wide-brimmed hat with a feather stuck in the band.

"You cowboys or somethin'?" Red asked.

"We're gonna be," said Jimmy. "We're gonna rodeo. If you want we can show you where there's wild horses to ride."

"What the hell's goin' on?" yelled Charlie. "You gonna fight 'em or not, Red?"

"They know where there's wild horses," said Red.

"Where's that?" asked Charlie.

"It's out past the Eureka Yards," said Stewart. "Out past Mangum and 18th."

"I ain't goin' all the way out there," said Charlie. "I gotta get this car back. Booger Red, you want to go chasin' critters, you go on. I'm goin' home."

Red and the Wades walked to Harvard and Seventh streets, where the freights slowed, and waited for a train. Red had a moment of hesitation, remembering his ride the previous Saturday and what had followed. He reached over his shoulder and scratched at the scab over one of the welts.

"Somethin' wrong?" Jimmy asked him. "Hell, I didn't hit you that hard with the sticker weed."

"It ain't nothin'," Red said, thinking, "This is different from last week. This time I've done all the chores and I ain't runnin' away from him."

They rode the train northwest out of town to the Eureka Yards, where the open country began. The day was cool and clear, and two hundred yards from the tracks, as they stood in a prairie rimmed by bands of oak and pine, the only sound they could hear was the wind. A hawk rose from a clump of pines to their right, caught a thermal and soared almost out of sight.

"That's good luck," Stewart said. "That's what the Indians believe. This feather in my hat's from a hawk."

"Maybe that's what saved you from having me whip you," Red said.

He had never been out here before and was experiencing a sense of exhilaration that made his heart beat in his ears and his legs feel like mush. The cramped houses and blacksmith shop and Harvard School seemed as far away as the moon. Not that he didn't like school. He was an excellent student, especially in math and science (although public speaking rendered him numb) and had already begun to distinguish himself in every sport that was offered. But out here there were no constraints. Out here there was room to do whatever you might imagine.

"C'mon," said Red to his new friends, "I'll race you to the woods on the other side of that hill."

"That's a long way," said Jimmy Wade. "I bet it's more'n a mile."

"So what," said Red.

They saw horses that day — small mustangs, of the kind that roamed the plains of East Texas back then — and managed to catch two, though Red was unable to ride either one. He kept sliding off and finally wound up taking off his shirt, which he tried to use as reins by slinging it around the animal's neck while holding either end.

"Jesus Christ, Red," said Jimmy, "you trying to ride the bastard or strangle him to death? What the hell kind of cowboy you gonna be?"

"I'm gonna be the kind that has a saddle and a horse with a bit in his mouth," Red said.

"Yeah, but Red, you gotta start with these fellas, and they don't come with saddles," Jimmy said. "You gotta work up to all that other stuff."

"I thought it was the other way around," Red said.

RED

Jimmy and Stewart Wade and I got to be real close. Along with Bill Schultz, they were my best friends. When we got a little older we went out and caught those mustangs and sold 'em for a buck apiece. Made us some good money. We'd break 'em and ride 'em ourselves too. We kept 'em tied up over at Bill Schultz's house 'cause he had more space than the rest of us. We used to ride 'em to school — to Hogg Junior High School — and keep 'em tied up outside. One day, those horses got loose and tore up the brand new flower beds they'd planted at the school. Boy, we caught hell! So much for riding horses to school.

The Wades really did become cowboys, too. Got to be real good rodeo hands. They were after me all the time to get into it with 'em, but I just wasn't interested. I loved goin' out onto the prairie with 'em, but I never cared to rodeo. What I liked was football, baseball, and swimming. I remember one rodeo where a 2,000-pound bull fell on Stewart Wade's leg and broke it. They had to cut his brand new cowboy boot off him to get his leg free. He didn't mind the broken leg as much as he minded losing that boot. Man, he was some kind of mad. It was right after that that we got into the bubbling grease with his daddy. I remember it, 'cause Stewart's leg hadn't healed all the way at the time.

HOUSTON — 1928

Old Man Wade was a bootlegger. He made white lightning in a still in the woods down at the river bottom, and they said it was the best stuff from San Antonio to the Louisiana state line. He'd have been a wealthy man if he wasn't a drunk himself, but try as he might he couldn't keep his hands off his product. Half the time he was too hung over to make deliveries.

"Boys," he said to Red and Stewart one day. "I got a job for you. I want you to take my car and deliver these here packages to the addresses I got written on each one. Now when you make a delivery, the person there's gonna give you a sealed envelope. You bring those envelopes on back here and don't you go openin' any of 'em, you understand? And don't open none of the packages either."

Old Man Wade was six-foot-two and had a voice like a phonograph record of a thunderstorm played at half speed. Red and Stewart understood, they said. "You do a good job and I'll give you each a quarter," he told them. A quarter sounded fine to Red, who was still hungry three days out of four. The fact that he and Stewart Wade were only thirteen made no difference to either of them. Both boys had been driving cars for a year already and out in the country where they were going nobody cared much about driver's licenses anyway.

The packages were often heavy, but Red didn't mind. The extra quarter a week, added to the money he earned making deliveries for a drugstore, put just a little more food on his family's table and made Red feel substantial and grown-up. Then one day, two months into their new job, after he and Stewart had made their final delivery, one of the envelopes between them on the seat of the Model B Ford came unsealed. It was stuffed full of money.

"Holy shit," said Stewart, "will you look at all those bills. Ain't no way in hell the old man's gonna miss a couple of 'em."

"Well," said Red, "maybe if we only take a few."

"What should we do with it?" asked Stewart. "What should we buy?"

"Food," said Red. "Lots of food."

They passed up Mrs. Bender's and went instead to a much fancier hamburger place on 19th Street, where they ate until they couldn't breathe. They drove around for an hour, stopped at a drugstore that made particularly rich milkshakes and drank three apiece. They re-sealed the envelope and brought Old Man Wade's car and what was left of his money back to Cortland Street, where Red left Stewart, went home, and passed out.

Red was sitting, the next morning, in his social studies class, on the second floor of Hogg Junior High School, in the very front of the room (since his name began with the letter *A*), when Old Man

Wade came through the door, three days' growth of beard on his face and blood in his eye. Stewart Wade was sitting at the back of the room (since his name began with the letter *W*), so Old Man Wade spied Red first. "Paul," he roared in his thunderstorm voice, and that was all Red heard. He leaped from his seat screaming, "Stewart, we better beat it," dove headfirst out the window, did a perfect half flip in the air, and landed on his feet and running, with Stewart Wade right behind him in the very flower bed their mustangs had torn up the previous spring.

The daring escape was to no avail, as Old Man Wade caught up with the two boys that night and, this being prior to the modern era of litigation, throttled both of them soundly. Red and Stewart got revenge, however. The following Saturday night they stole Old Man Wade's car.

"Where you want to go, Red?" Stewart asked, once they had quietly pushed the Model B down Cortland Street and gotten it started.

"To Woodland Heights," Red replied. He knew two very pretty, very willing young women there, whom he was certain would jump at the chance to go joyriding through the countryside. Ordinarily, a trip to the far more affluent Woodland Heights — made on foot — was quite treacherous for boys from Houston Heights, as the Woodland Heights boys didn't want outsiders dating their girls and would fight anyone who tried, but on this Saturday night Red and Stewart had a car and traveled with impunity.

The Woodland Heights girls loved Old Man Wade's Model B. They loved the flask of his home brew that was stowed under the front seat, too, and the evening went even better than Red and Stewart had planned. At least it did until they dropped the girls off, because on their return trip to Cortland Street, Stewart made a last-minute error in judgment and drove the car clean through the back wall of the Wades' garage.

"Don't worry, Stewart," Red said. "It's Saturday night. Your old man'll be so drunk we can tell your mother he did it and he'll never know the difference. Just go to bed, and I'll come over in the morning and help you convince her."

"Hell, I can't remember doin' it," Old Man Wade said to his wife, as he shook his head and looked forlornly at the splintered remains of the back wall of the garage, and at the Model B that rested in the mud in the alley behind it. "But I guess I got so drunk I did."

"We heard it, Mrs. Wade," Red said. "We were sittin' on the porch and it sounded like a bomb went off. We thought maybe a comet had struck or somethin'. It was scary, let me tell you. We came runnin', but it was too dark to see a thing."

"You boys help Mr. Wade winch that car out of the alley," Mrs. Wade said, and stormed into the house. And that was the end of it, so Red's plan worked out. But then Red's plans usually did if he was orchestrating, if he was in control. There were some things, back then, he could not control, though, some things that would shape his life in ways different than he had wanted.

HOUSTON — 1929

Red was flying high. He had graduated in June from junior high school with excellent grades and all-city honors in baseball, football, and swimming. The junior-high football team, on which he'd been the star halfback, was so good, in fact, they'd beaten the varsity of John H. Reagan High School, and Pop Adams, the Reagan coach, could hardly wait for Red to join his team. Adams was also the swimming coach and spent time with Red over the summer working on Adair's strokes. "You keep it up and you'll be in the Olympics, Red," Adams said to him on more than one occasion. "And I mean that seriously."

Red listened carefully to Pop Adams, who had become a role model for him. In addition to his full-time job delivering prescriptions for a drugstore, he cleaned the pool at the Heights Natatorium, which allowed him free pool time. Red trained there daily, swimming two to three miles each session. He also had begun boxing with a group of older boys at a club where Pop Adams instructed. Not that Red didn't take time out for fun. Dressed in a gaudy, candy-striped bathing suit, he put on exhibitions of trick diving at the Natatorium for the local girls, at least three of whom considered him their boyfriend. One, Rosemary Cole, was thought to be the most beautiful girl in the Heights.

In the fall he enrolled at Reagan High and immediately made an impact on the school's football team as a starting halfback. At fourteen, he had reached his full height of five feet, six inches, and weighed only 135 pounds. He wasn't the fastest man on the team, but he was quick, and had the kind of incredible balance that allowed him to bounce off would-be tacklers, remain on his feet, and slash for extra yardage.

One night, after a game in which Red had scored three

touchdowns, Pop Adams took him aside. "I know you're only a freshman, Red," Adams said, "but have you thought at all about what you want to do after high school?"

"I want to go to college and play football," Red said without hesitation, "and then I want to become a coach like you. That's what I'm going to do."

"Well, Red," Adams said, "you keep doing just what you're doing and you keep on getting good grades and I can guarantee you you'll get a scholarship. I will personally see to that."

When the football season was over, Red went back to his job at the drugstore, working forty hours a week in addition to going to school. He still managed to swim on Pop Adams's team, but things at home were worse than ever, and he didn't know how long he could keep up the swimming. The Great Depression, which hadn't yet hit the whole nation full force, was already having its impact on the Adair household as Red's father fought desperately to hold onto his blacksmith shop.

There was a swimming meet one cold night in December. Red's feet had grown a size in the month before, but there was no money to buy him shoes, so he had been wearing an old pair of his father's. He wore them now to the meet. Red had been practicing very hard for weeks, and on this night his arms and legs moved through the water with power and rhythm he had never before felt. He won the two backstrokes, two breaststrokes, one butterfly, and an individual medley before his favorite, the hundred-yard freestyle, was announced.

From the starter's gun he knew it felt right and at the fifty-yard turnaround could hear Pop Adams screaming, though the words were indistinct. "You're ahead of Weismuller's world record," was what Pop Adams hollered, "don't let up, don't quit." Red was still at a world-record pace with ten yards to go when his strength gave out. He won the race, but missed Weismuller's record by a half second.

"It's my fault," Pop Adams told him. "I never should have put you in all those events. I wore you out. I'm sorry, Red, you would have been famous."

"It wasn't you, coach," Red told him. "It was me. I should'a had somethin' more to eat than I did before the meet." He wouldn't tell Pop Adams that the only thing he'd eaten all day was a bowl of oatmeal and a single slice of toast.

After the meet, Red waited around the pool until everyone else had left. His father's feet were very skinny, and the shoes he'd worn before swimming were too tight to fit him after so much time in the pool. In the early evening, when it was too dark for anyone to notice, he walked home barefoot, clutching the seven blue ribbons he had won.

It was a week later that Faye Adair saw her brother crying for the first time. He was sitting on the ground behind their house, on the slender strip of grass that ran like an alley of vegetation behind all the houses on their street. She saw him through the window. He had his head in his hands, and that was so unlike him she thought that he was hurt. She came up behind him, calling his name, but he didn't answer. Then she saw the tears running down his face.

"What's wrong, Booger Red?" she said. She still called him that, and now she was the only one who did. "What is it?"

He looked up at her and moved his mouth, but no words came out. She put her arm around his shoulders, thinking, he's so skinny, how can he be so strong?

Finally he spoke. "I gotta quit school," he said. "Daddy's lost the shop and I gotta go to work. I won't get the scholarship now. I won't go to college."

"You'll go," Faye said. "Things'll get better, you'll see."

"I don't mind workin', Faye, you know that. I've always worked," Red said, "but if I can't go to school, how am I gonna be something? How am I ever gonna do what I really want to do?"

"Booger Red," said Faye, "school or no school, ain't nothin' gonna ever keep someone like you from doin' what he really wants to do. Nothin' in the world."

CHAPTER SIX

*See, once I finally got into the oil field, I never sat and waited
for jobs or people to come to me. I went out and got 'em, because
I waited in the railroad shop too damn long. That's what cured
me of that. And in the oil patch, I never, ever, took anything for
granted either, because before the railroad shop, when I worked in
the drugstore, I thought I had it made, and along comes this other
guy with a better bicycle than mine and he took my job. I said,
"That ain't never going to happen to me again."*

Red Adair

HOUSTON — 1932

Red followed closely as Bill Williamson chased the pig along the
pipeline, up and down the little creeks, through the stands of scrub
oak and cypress, south of Baytown, near where Cedar Bayou ran
into Galveston Bay. The pig, or "go-devil," was a mechanical device
with whirling blades or brushes that ran under pressure through the
pipeline to scrape and clean the pipe. It also searched for blockage
in the line, and when it found any, it stopped. Williamson, the
chaser, could hear the pig where it found obstruction, gurgling and
thumping in the pipe. With his two-way radio he notified another
man at the pumping end of the pipeline, who increased the pressure
until the pig was free once more and the chase continued. To Adair,
it seemed that Bill Williamson had the most wonderful job in the
world, for he was out in the oil field, where Red could feel the excitement and romance.

Around them, as they ran, were drilling rigs, some with old-style
wooden derricks, others with newer steel ones. The rigs were everywhere they went, in among the trees, or in the marsh grass and sand,
or set out in the shallow inlet waters, connected to land by a network
of wood-plank roadways. There were pump jacks too, droning stead-

ily as they brought oil to the surface, their long, thick, steel necks rising and falling, like a grazing herd of prehistoric beasts. Here and there, work crews on barges in the water, or surrounded by equipment-laden flatbed trucks on land, attended to the rigs, cleaning, repairing, or forcing pipes deeper and deeper beneath the ground. Inland, in the distance, loomed the buildings and tanks and maze of giant overhead pipes of the Standard Oil refinery.

It was at the refinery that Red had met Williamson, two months before, in a number of violent collisions on the refinery football field. Red played halfback and defensive back on a semipro football team, earning five dollars a weekend in games around Houston, in Baytown and Galveston. Williamson played end for Baytown. He was eight inches taller than Red and outweighed him by sixty pounds. In a game for the tri-city championship, with a three-dollar bonus for every player on the winning team, he caught three passes in a row in front of Red, whose coach was livid.

"Dammit Red," he said, "you let that guy catch another one and I'm going to cut your pay. Even if we win, I'll keep your bonus."

At the time, Red was the only member of his family to have a steady job. He was working in a drugstore six days a week, eleven hours a day, for twelve dollars a week plus tips, which were few and far between. The coach might just as well have told him he was going to cut off a finger. The next time the ball was thrown to Williamson Red slammed into him at full speed, jamming the heels of both hands into Williamson's neck, causing him to fumble. The time after that, Red slapped the ball away with one hand and buried an elbow in Williamson's ribs. The third time, he hit Williamson so hard the big man's helmet flew off when he hit the ground and he left the game with a concussion.

Red's team won the championship, fourteen to seven, and after the game Red went over to Williamson and apologized for playing so roughly.

"No problem," said Williamson. "It's a rough game."

"I just wanted you to know it wasn't personal," Red said. "I need the money, is all."

"For a little guy, you sure hit like a ton of bricks," said Williamson. "What the hell you do for living, lift railroad cars?"

"I work in a drugstore," said Red. "How about you?"

"I chase a pig," said Williamson.

"You get paid to chase pigs?" said Red. "That don't sound like such a bad deal. They got any other animals over here need chasing?"

"It ain't an animal," Williamson told him, "it's a scraper that cleans the pipeline. You ever get over this way again I'll show you."

It was two months before Red managed to get a day off from the pharmacy. He had begun his drugstore career two days after he quit school, keeping the store clean, waiting on tables, and delivering prescriptions to customers' homes. The bicycle he used was a rusty wreck he bought for a dollar from the old one-eyed man who sat stony-faced on his porch over on 7½ Street scaring the hell out of the little kids in the neighborhood, who told each other the old man was the devil. When Red got the drugstore job, the owner said, "You'll need a bike," and Red said, "Yes sir, I'll have one tomorrow morning." He had seen the rusty wreck leaning against the one-eyed man's house for over a year and actually considered stealing it, but the old man was home, sitting on his porch, as always.

Red took a deep breath, walked up, and said, "I'll give you fifty cents for that bike you got."

No one he knew had ever heard the old one-eyed man speak. "Make it a buck," said the old man, in a voice that sounded surprisingly like the croak of a bullfrog. "But," he added, "you can pay me ten cents a week."

The headset of the bike was so rusted the handlebars barely turned. The rims were both bent, so the tires kept coming off, and no matter how many times Red adjusted it, the bike kept throwing its chain. Still, it did get him around the Heights faster than walking, and it seemed for a while that the job would work out fine. The owner didn't even mind if he took an occasional scoop of ice cream for himself, as long as the store was empty at the time. Then one day, when the bike threw its chain for the fifth time, and Red walked back into the store, covered with grease, a half hour later than he should have, there was a tall, black boy, a year older than he, leaning against the counter.

"I'll get cleaned up before I make more deliveries," Red told the owner.

"That won't be necessary, Red," the owner said. "Mitchel, here, is going to be making the deliveries from now on. He's got a brand new bike. Deliveries will be much faster for us that way."

"What will I do?" Red asked.

"I'm real sorry, Red," said the owner. "There isn't anything for you to do in this store anymore."

Red stared impassively at the owner. Inside he was furious, hurt, and embarrassed, but he would show no emotion. He turned and left the store, and if you had seen him, as he walked his bicycle down Yale Street, you would have thought he was a typical, happy-go-lucky, freckle-faced teenager, a little ragged, but content. That's what his friends all thought. That's what his family thought, too. Only rarely — almost never, in fact — did he reveal his inner feelings to any of them, but the abandonment he felt when he was put in the Faith Home, the pain from his father's Sam Browne belt, and the broken dream of a college scholarship left deep scars. From the time he was old enough to talk he'd been taught that a man's role in life was to work, work hard, work some more. That was the only hope, he was told, against a world with no mercy. To that he added his private code, his personal defense system, his shield against physical and emotional vulnerability: Take nothing for granted. Always leave yourself an escape route, a way out (a hind door, he called it). And never trust anyone but yourself.

He crossed White Oak Bayou, left his bike in a clump of fragrant magnolia trees, and walked east down the tracks of the Southern Pacific Railroad, past stands of cedar, oak, and ash intertwined with vines and dense underbrush. A thick layer of silt covered the low-growing bushes, a reminder of the Great Flood of 1929, during which two-thirds of Houston was underwater and Buffalo Bayou, the city's major waterway, overflowed so badly a four-foot-deep river ran through the downtown streets. Through the swath cut in the vegetation for the railroad right-of-way he could see all the way from the Heights to downtown Houston, where the tall buildings sparkled in the late morning sun.

Jesse H. Jones, a flamboyant lumber tycoon and major developer in Houston during the early part of the twentieth century, had originally tried to keep the city's skyline at one level, with buildings no more than ten stories high, modeling it after his impression of Paris, but one of his competitors went to fifteen stories. Jones, who by the mid-1920s owned more than thirty commercial buildings, was not about to have someone else build Houston's tallest structure. He abandoned his Parisian fantasy and began, so to speak, raising the ante, first to sixteen stories, then twenty-two. By 1929 he had built the thirty-seven-story Gulf Building.

It was Jones, an emerging political force in Texas, who was instrumental in luring the Democratic National Convention to Houston in June 1928, but that proved to be a fiasco of major proportions. For one thing, the Democrats nominated Alfred E. Smith of New York, a northern, big-city, Catholic antiprohibitionist, to run against

Herbert Hoover. Throughout Texas, throughout the nation, for that matter, fundamentalist Protestants decried "the Pope's candidate," who, they claimed, was bent on putting a saloon alongside every church. Furthermore, although air conditioning had come to Houston as early as 1923, when it was installed in the Second National Bank, it was not available in the convention hall, a large auditorium open at both ends. There, delegates swatted mosquitoes and broiled while being serenaded by a raucous, around-the-clock, anti-Smith, pro-prohibition prayer meeting conducted two blocks away by Houston's First Baptist Church.

The polarity between the wild-eyed prohibitionists and progressive delegates at the convention mirrored life in those days in the state. Hooded Klansmen rode through the countryside at night, but in 1924 voters in Texas elected anti-Klan Miriam "Ma" Ferguson as their first and only woman governor, returning her to office when she ran again in 1932. Atheist schoolteachers taught with impunity in small, rural communities, yet freethinkers who spoke out on Houston street corners were arrested. Prohibitionists preached at camp meetings and on street corners to huge, wildly enthusiastic crowds, yet the flow of moonshine in Texas was second only to the flow of oil. Hoover carried Texas by 26,000 votes in 1928, a victory to the P's — Prosperity, Prohibition, and Prejudice, the liberal members of the press called it — but incumbent U.S. senator Earl B. Mayfield, an ardent Klansman, was defeated by anti-Klan Tom Connally. But then, Texans weren't any different from the rest of Americans who elected Hoover president, choosing to believe in his vision of economic bliss while the world around them shuddered toward financial collapse.

Red Adair, apolitical, and thoroughly pragmatic even as a very young man, took no sides in any of the controversy. He was far more interested in the standings of the Texas League — the Class AA professional baseball league that reached its pinnacle during the late 1920s and 1930s — and the progress of its stars, Dizzy Dean, Carl Hubbell, Joe Medwick, and Hank Greenberg, all of whom went on to major-league fame, than he was in political races. And while he possessed considerably more propinquity for rumrunners like Old Man Wade than he did for any moralizing preacher, he kept his feelings to himself. He played on two baseball teams, one sponsored by the All Saints Catholic Church, where his mother belonged, the other sponsored by the Heights First Baptist Church. He attended both churches (although very sporadically) to maintain his eligibility and got along just fine with members of both denominations.

As he walked along the Southern Pacific tracks, however, he wasn't thinking about baseball. He was thinking about his next meal and how hard it would be to go home before finding another job. He thought about his mother, who was sick again. He would never say this to anyone, but there were times he wondered whether she exaggerated the severity of her illnesses, or whether they were not excuses for her to avoid the reality of the pain and poverty in her family's life. She always seemed to get sick on someone's birthday, if a relative was getting married, or if someone else in the family was sick. It bothered him to think these things, but they were the truth.

He had walked almost into downtown Houston, where buses, trolleys, cars, and trucks clogged the streets. There were almost 300,000 people in Houston now; it was the most populous city in Texas, and ranked twenty-sixth nationwide. It had become a major distribution center for cotton and lumber as well as oil, and throbbed with activity day and night, but at the moment its glitter and bustle seemed as far away to Red as the moon.

He turned and retraced his steps, jogging now instead of walking. He *would* get another job, he told himself, that very day, if he had to knock on the door of every drugstore in the Heights. Somehow he'd fix the bicycle, he told himself, but more important, he would never again get caught by his own complacency. "I should'a seen it coming," he said aloud. "My eyes were open, but I was staring at the wall."

Red walked through the Heights for hours, but didn't find a job that day. When he returned home, well after dark, his father was standing outside their house sorting through some scrap metal he had managed to salvage from his failed blacksmith shop. Since he lost the shop, he'd been unable to find steady employment and the supply of saleable equipment and parts had dwindled to a pile of junk.

"Where you been?" he asked.

"Looking for work," Red said. He was as strong as his father now and no longer feared him physically, but still dreaded Charlie Adair's scorn. "I lost my job at the drugstore."

"What do you mean you lost your job?" his father said. "What the hell did you do wrong?"

"It wasn't me," said Red. "It wasn't my fault. This black kid had a better bike."

"You lost your job to a damn nigger," his father said, spitting in the dirt.

"It wasn't his fault either," Red said. "He just had a better bike. That's all it was."

"You sure?" said his father, turning and walking into the house.

It was more than a week until another drugstore hired him, but during that time Red scrounged enough parts to fix his bicycle. He also made ten dollars at a traveling tent show out of New Orleans that was holding forth over on White Oak Drive. Traveling tent shows were common throughout rural America in those days, and this one had the typical array of entertainment. There was a small midway with a couple of rides and several games of chance — a ring-toss, wooden bottles to knock down with baseballs, an impossibly difficult dart board — with stuffed animals as prizes. There was a sideshow where an assortment of sad-eyed freaks paraded their deformities and a weasely little man with a mouth like a lizard presided over an exhibit of snakes. But the attraction that magnetized most of the local young men was a boxing ring set up in the far corner of the show. There, a prize of ten dollars was offered by a defiant, bare-chested carny with a sailing ship tattooed on his back to anyone in attendance who could knock him down in a two-minute round. If the carny knocked the challenger down in less than two minutes, the fight was over.

The carny strode around the ring, flexing his muscles and challenging the men in the crowd. "One of your dollars against ten of mine says there ain't a man out there who can put this sailor on the deck," he shouted. He had two parrots tattooed on his chest and a half-clad woman on the bicep of one arm. "You're a bunch of weaklings," he roared. "You got no guts."

One by one, challengers succumbed in less than a minute to the carny, who snarled at the crowd derisively, spraying them with sweat as he leaped around the ring after each victory. Red, who was watching with his friends, Stewart and Jimmy Wade, noticed there was a pattern to each fight. The carny would quickly maneuver his opponent to the side of the ring that was flush against one canvas wall of the tent. There he would push and butt the man while hitting him with a flurry of punches, the man would stumble, and the carny would club the man to the ring's dirt floor.

"They're falling forward," Red said to the Wades.

"What do you mean?" said Stewart.

"C'mon," said Red, and he crept quietly, with his two friends close behind, around the outside of the tent to the side positioned against the ring, which was in an area of thick bushes. Red got down on his hands and knees and crawled through the bushes until he reached the bottom corner of the tent, where he saw a tiny canvas flap, no more than two feet square. He signaled to the Wades to be still and lifted the flap, exposing a narrow passage between the actual outside wall of the tent and the wall next to the boxing ring. Halfway down the passage, directly behind the ring, stood a man with a large wooden mallet. "See what that sailor does?" he said to the Wades. "He gets 'em backed up to this wall and makes a big commotion while this other guy whacks 'em in the head with the mallet. Next thing they know they're on the ground and they got no idea who hit 'em with what. Loan me a dollar. I'm gonna knock that sailor on his ass."

"Well, well, well," the carny hollered. "We got done with the men and now we're down to the boys. Don't matter to me. A buck's a buck, although this kid's kinda skinny." He closed with Red, immediately cutting off the ring and herding him toward the canvas wall, but the carny had grown accustomed to large, ponderous contestants and hadn't counted on Red's speed. Adair ducked under the carny's arms, jabbing him twice in the kidneys on his way, whirled, lowered his head, and rammed the man as hard as he could toward the canvas wall. The surprised carny took two steps backward, cocked his fist as Red charged again, and was about to deliver his Sunday punch when suddenly there was a sound like a ripe tomato hitting cement. The carny stumbled, he groaned loudly, his eyes bugged out, and as he lurched forward Red hit him as hard as he could square on the chin. The crowd roared as the carny's knees buckled and he fell to the ground.

"It seemed funny to me 'cause all the guys kept fallin' forward *toward* the sailor instead of away from him like they should've when he hit 'em," Red said to the Wades, his mouth filled with a Mrs. Bender's hamburger. In the week since he had been fired from the drugstore he had been so ashamed he had barely eaten, believing he didn't deserve to dip into the family's meager supply of food. This was the sixth hamburger he'd wolfed down in the hour since the fight.

"You got a new job yet?" Jimmy Wade asked him. Most families in the Heights were poor, but it was common knowledge that the Adairs' circumstances were dire. Jimmy was still in school, his clothes were patchless, and he had plenty to eat. He was well aware of Red's pride and, not wanting to make his friend feel bad, hadn't mentioned the drugstore to him until that moment. Now, after the triumph at the tent show, it seemed all right.

"I ain't got one yet," Red told him. "But I will. I'm gonna get one today, in fact. I can feel it."

Red did get a job that day, but he kept it only a month, moving to a third drugstore when a position opened up there for fifty cents more a week. By the time he went to visit Bill Williamson, he had worked at six different pharmacies. By the time he switched to a different line of work he'd been employed by every one in the north-west end of Houston. After the third store, he no longer had to look for better jobs. His reputation for working hard had drugstore owners looking for him.

Late one August night, in the week before Red traveled to Baytown to watch Bill Williamson chase the pig, he walked from gas station to gas station with a five-gallon can, collecting the gas that was left in the hose of each pump. His friends Bill Schultz and Stewart Wade did the same, and by the weekend they had enough gas to make the trip, in the Wades' old Model T, over the rutted, backcountry roads between Houston and Baytown. Often, they wheezed axle-deep through the brick red, Southeast Texas gumbo, mud so thick it could stop a train, and it took three hours to cover forty-five miles. When they finally arrived, Schultz and Wade were exhausted and wanted to get something to eat. Not Red. "You guys go on ahead," he said. He was too excited, anyway, to have an appetite.

"What do you think?" Bill Williamson asked. He and Red were ankle deep in swamp water, covered with mud, fifty feet from a chugging pump jack. Mosquitoes swirled around them, brambles had scratched their arms and necks, and there were probably snakes in the water.

"This is great," said Red. "How do I get into the oil field?"

"It ain't easy," said Williamson. "In fact, unless you know somebody, it's impossible."

"I know you," Red said.

"I wish I could help you, Red," Williamson said. "If I could I would, 'cause anybody who plays football the way you do could make it in the oil patch, and I know you'd work your ass off, but I ain't in that kind of position. I'm twenty-two years old, and I've been waiting since I was nineteen to get this job. I'd about given up hope, and my uncle works for Deep Water Refineries, too. If I ever do hear about somethin', I promise I'll put in a word for you, but don't go gettin' your hopes up."

What Williamson said was absolutely true. Two years earlier, on the Daisy Bradford Farm in Overton, a little town just east of Tyler, Texas, Columbus Marion "Dad" Joiner had discovered the great East Texas Field, the most abundant of any oil field in North America. So prolific were the drilling rigs in this field at one point that a man could walk all day from the drilling floor of one rig to the drilling floor of the next and never touch the ground. Farmers and ranchers under whose land the oil lay became instant millionaires, and people from every walk of life bet their life savings on wildcatters, some of whom struck it rich, many of whom went broke. Hamlets in the East Texas field no one had ever heard of before became world-famous boomtowns overnight: Petrolia, Electra, Ranger, Desdemona, and Burkburnett. Speculators and dreamers of every persuasion flocked to East Texas, where gamblers, prostitutes, murderers, and thieves mingled with drillers, tool pushers, derrickmen, and geologists. So frantic was the pace, so lawless and unrestrained, that one night, when a man murdered his partner in Ranger, he was tried, convicted, fined $100 and told to get out of town, all before the sun came up the next day.

Then the pace slowed to a crawl, because the market was suddenly flooded with foreign oil, brought to America by oil companies with vast overseas holdings. The price of Texas crude fell to fifty cents a barrel, then twenty-five. By the time stringent regulations were enforced by the Texas Railroad Commission, which controlled petroleum production in the state, the price had dropped to ten cents a barrel. By then, in the depths of the Depression, producers were allowed to pump oil from their wells only eight days a month. Work continued, but for a new man, finding a job in the oil patch was like finding apple seeds in a pear.

Red listened to Williamson, but said nothing. A hundred yards away he could see a work crew next to a derrick, pulling sucker rods. The steel sucker rods, thirty feet long, an inch in diameter, and threaded at either end, were the mechanical link between the pumping arm of the rig on the surface and the "sucker pump" at the bottom of the well. As a well went deeper and deeper, more and more rods would be strung together. Every so often, they would have to be removed and cleaned of sand and other debris so that they wouldn't bind or overheat while the well was pumping.

Red watched as the crew removed the rods and hung them in the derrick, where they swung slightly in the breeze like a gigantic set of wind chimes. As the men hopped confidently from beam to beam, Red had the urge to join them. He felt the same as he had on the day Stewart and Jimmy Wade had first taken him to ride wild mustangs on the prairie. There, it was a wide-open, unpopulated, empty space. Here, there were men, machinery, noise, and activity, but both places spoke to him of limitless, unfettered possibility. He wanted to leap into the air, to run, but he stayed in the water where he was, wondering if things would ever change, or if he would go from drugstore to drugstore for the rest of his life. Little did he know that thirty-five years later, in the sand ten feet from where he now stood in the Goose Creek Oilfield, John Wayne would act out a scene in a movie about fighting well fires based on his work in the oil patch.

A month passed and it was late September, when Old Man Orton came to see Red one Sunday afternoon. Some of Red's friends had left the Heights to attend college. The Wades were off rodeoing every weekend. Red was still working day after day in the drugstore. Old Man Orton worked for the Southern Pacific Railroad and he knew Red's father from the days when Charlie Adair made springs for railroad cars. "Red," he said, "how'd you like a job laying track for the railroad?"

The night before, Red boxed against a man he had previously beaten twice by knockouts, and though he won again, it was a dispiriting, split-decision victory. After the bout, he told Pop Adams he had definitely made up his mind not to turn pro.

"Coach, my heart just isn't in it anymore," he said.

"You ever reconsider, come see me," Pop Adams said. "I'll make you a champ."

Now Red rubbed his chin and studied the ground between him and Old Man Orton. "What's the job pay?" he finally asked.

"Thirty cents an hour, sixty hours a week," Old Man Orton said. It was three dollars more per week than he was earning in the drugstore.

"When do I start?" he asked.

For three months, Red worked with a road gang laying track west of Houston. Then he was transferred to the Southern Pacific Maintenance of Way Repair Shop just off Center Street, halfway between his house and the middle of downtown Houston. He unloaded boxcars, unloaded gondolas of coal, cleaned locomotive engines and other machinery, and went out with crews to lay more track.

In the beginning, he made mistakes. When Mr. Miller, the shop foreman, told the men the first one to get his engine clean would earn an extra half hour of pay, Red decided scrubbing by hand with a brush was the wrong way to go. He hooked the engine he was assigned to a block and tackle, lowered it into a vat of sodium hydroxide, or caustic soda, and went on to another job while his coworkers sweated and strained.

"Where's your engine?" Mr. Miller asked, when he saw Red sweeping out a coal bin.

"Oh, it's already clean, Mr. Miller," Red answered.

"Where is it?" Mr. Miller asked.

"It's right over there in that vat," said Red.

"Let's have a look at it," said Mr. Miller.

Red began hauling on the chain of the block and tackle and noticed it was kind of light. He peered over the edge of the vat with Mr. Miller looking over his shoulder.

"It's gone, Mr. Miller," Red said. "My engine's not here! Someone must've taken it when I wasn't looking or I'd've won the extra half hour of pay for sure."

"The vat of caustic soda's what took your engine, son," said Mr. Miller. "It dissolved every last little piece of it. Good thing you didn't think to get in there with it or it would have taken you too. I know you're eager, but from now on, you do your engine cleaning with a brush like everyone else."

Shortly after the caustic soda blunder, Red was paired with a man named Bill Ludke — a giant Pole who stood six-four and weighed 225 pounds — to move and unload boxcars and gondolas. At first, Red nearly tore himself in half trying vainly to pit his strength against Ludke's. Red's back ached every night, his legs and shoulders felt like they were permanently on fire, but there was no way he could outmuscle his partner. Then one day, as he jogged to work down the railroad tracks from the Heights to the yard, Red had an idea. That day he stayed late, after everyone else in the shop had gone home, and fashioned an eighteen-inch extension out of heavy-gauge steel pipe that fit over every handle on the boxcars, gondolas, and pushcars in the yard. From then on, with this mechanical advantage, he could actually raise more than the much taller and heavier Ludke.

When he saw how well the handle worked, Red made up his mind to find himself an edge, an upper hand, for everything he had to do in the yard. He stayed late and drilled holes in all the wooden blocks he used to hold the boxcar doors open so when he went to drive nails through the blocks they'd penetrate quicker. He also greased all the nails he used, and oiled his shovel every night so it would scoop coal faster when he unloaded a gondola. By this time, Red had been given the job of coming into the shop a half hour early each day to load the coal bins and was also putting in a half day on Saturday cleaning the shop. Monday through Friday he worked from six-thirty in the morning until six at night. Saturdays, he worked seven in the morning until one in the afternoon — sixty-three and a half hours a week, $38.10 every two weeks.

It was winter now, and the cold northwest wind, whipping down off the high plains above Amarillo, pushed Red along as he jogged down the tracks to work, hunched in an old woolen jacket, his lunch in a small paper sack hooked to his belt. His face had weathered, his shoulders broadened, his hands grown thick with calluses since he'd left the drugstore, and his eyes gleamed like a cat's. If anything he was even leaner than before. At noon, he would join the other men gathered round a small potbellied stove in the railroad shop, warming their hands and toasting their sandwiches. Red would toast the two pieces of bread he took from his sack, pretending he had a sandwich as well, although there was rarely anything between the slices he brought. He would wash the toast down with water, joking with the others, who sometimes offered him an apple or a slice of lunch meat he was too hungry to refuse. In time, he took to bringing dry oatmeal in his sack, mixing it with water that he boiled on the stove. The oatmeal, he found, gave him energy that lasted through the afternoon and evening, helping him to work without thinking constantly of food.

As the men ate in the corrugated sheet metal building at one end of the yard, they could hear the grinding gears and groaning metal plates of the roundhouse next door. They could hear the chuffing sound of vented steam, the screech of steel on steel, and shouts of brakemen and engineers as locomotives shuddered to a halt, were turned around, and labored off again in the direction from which they'd come. This was an era of great railroad activity in southeast Texas, with six major systems — Southern Pacific; Missouri Pacific; Missouri, Kansas & Texas; Santa Fe; Burlington; and Rock Island — all meeting in the Houston area. The Southern Pacific had just constructed a $3 million, four-story depot not far from its main repair shop where Red worked; other lines had switching yards and repair shops nearby, and it is likely that the locomotives and railroad cars coming and going in all of them rolled on wheels manufactured by

Houston's Dickson Car Wheel Company. Looking around him, there was no reason for Red Adair to believe he couldn't spend the rest of his life working for the railroad.

Directly across Center Street from the railroad shop was a large two-story wood-frame building owned by a woman named Mrs. Small who rented out rooms to a dozen or so single men working for the Southern Pacific. One of these boarders was a man named Spot Gaines, so called because of a snow white streak in his otherwise coal black hair. Spot shared a room in the far corner of the second floor with a man who had to move back to Oklahoma.

"Red, my roommate's gone," said Spot one day at lunch. "Why don't you move in with me?"

Spot Gaines was a few years older than Red. He was a foreman's helper, a respected man at the railroad shop, who earned forty-nine cents an hour, and Red, who had been at the shop for almost a year, was flattered by the offer. He was also tired of living at home.

"What's it cost?" he asked.

"The room's three-fifty a week," said Spot. "A buck seventy-five apiece. You can eat across the street at Howard's Café. Fifteen cents a meal and they give credit. You can settle up with 'em every payday. Good food, too, Red, and lots of it. They give you so much for breakfast you can stick some in a sack and bring it for lunch. Put some meat on your bones."

Red did some quick calculating in his head. He could room with Spot Gaines, eat at Howard's Café, and still send several dollars a week home to his parents.

"I'll do it," he said. "I'll move in with you tomorrow."

There is a picture, taken on July 13, 1936, of the forty-nine men who worked then at the Southern Pacific repair shop, and there isn't an overweight man in the group. Many of them wear overalls, some have on jeans or dark cotton work pants, some khaki trousers. All but two wear light-colored summer work shirts, the sleeves rolled or cut off; the other two, the foreman and clerk, wear white dress shirts with ties. Whether they are clean or grimy, smiling or somber, there is a uniformity to all these men, or almost all of them. In the angle of their shoulders, in the way they hold their heads and their arms, in the expressions on their faces, almost all appear resigned, settled, rooted to this place forever.

Then there's Red Adair. He is sitting, in this picture, in the middle of the front row, though crouching there might be a better way to phrase it, as though at any moment he might spring. His shirt is unbuttoned to his navel, his biceps bulge, and with his jaw out-thrust and shoulders rounded forward, his fist clenched and right arm resting on his knee, he looks like a football lineman getting set to charge. He seems to be grinning slightly, but it's an aggressive, self-reliant, almost predatory smile. "Look out, I'm coming to get you," is what it says. "Nothing can stand in my way."

That's the image Red presented to the world; that's what he wanted everyone to think, and in many ways it was true that his life had never been better. His father had a job driving a bus, only his two younger brothers, Bob and David, were still at home, and the improved financial situation meant that Red could spend more on himself. He had a car, a 1927 Chevrolet he bought for eleven dollars, and on the weekends he would drive it, or ride with friends, down to Galveston to swim, drink beer, and party. He'd given up football, but played on two softball teams, Heights First Baptist Church and I. Smith Compactors, and in the winter played some basketball and even boxed. But there was nothing new about his job, and as the years went by, the sameness of the days began to gnaw at him.

RED

There was this high chain-link fence around the railroad yard. Some-times I used to stand and look through it and think, "There's a whole world out there, there's all these places to see and things to do. Will I ever see 'em? Will I ever do 'em?" Then I'd look arond the railroad shop. I knew exactly what I was going to do every day. There were no surprises, no challenges. That really began to get to me. I'd think, "The only way I'm gonna advance in this place is if someone quits or someone dies. None of these guys are quitting, not in times like these. They're happy. They're here for life. And they all look too healthy to die. And even if one of 'em does quit or die, what's next for me? Forty-nine cents an hour instead of thirty?" Every morning the gate on that chain link fence would clang shut behind me. It got so I'd hear that gate clanging in my dreams.

He never let on. He came to work smiling, whooped and hollered with the guys as he sweated all day, then played ball or drank beer and chased women with his friends at night. Then one day, when he'd been working for the Southern Pacific Railroad for five years, he met a young woman who was different than the others, different from anyone else he'd ever met in his life. Her name was Kemmie Lou Wheeler, and the first time Red saw her he fell in love.

CHAPTER SEVEN

I'd heard all about him from my friend Alice Rogers. She went on and on about this guy she knew named Red Adair and how terrific he was. When I first saw him I thought, "What's the big deal? What's so great about him? He's real short." But right away I could sense something unusual, something electric, as though all the energy in the world was concentrated in this one person. He told me he was going to be something big someday, and when he told me, I believed it too. That's the kind of person he was.

Kemmie Adair

HOUSTON — 1939

The first time they met, Red knocked Kemmie out. Literally, he knocked her out cold as a fish in a freezer. Red was with Alice Rogers and Kemmie was with one of Red's friends, whose name she'd forgotten within a week. Red had taken Alice to a couple of softball games and invited her to go swimming one Sunday down in Galveston. Alice said fine, but wanted to bring along her friend Kemmie Lou Wheeler and asked Red to bring a date for Kemmie Lou. They took Red's car and Alice sat in front, talking up a storm, but Red didn't hear a word she said. All he could think about was the girl in back with large, sparkling eyes and long blond hair billowing around her head like windblown wheat. She sang as they rode, too softly for him to make out the words, but he was certain it was the most beautiful sound he'd ever heard.

They drove south, crossing from the Texas mainland to Galveston Island on the new causeway. Despite the Depression, the influx of tourists in automobiles to Galveston during the mid-1930s had become too heavy for the original causeway to handle, and a second road, parallel to the first, had just been opened. The old Chevy's tires hummed on the new macadam surface, and brilliant sunlight bounced off its radiator's aluminum trim. Halfway across the causeway, the salty gulf breeze hit them, cutting through the mid-June heat, and Red's heart soared as it always did when he neared the sea.

In those days Galveston beckoned to Red, enticing him with its promise of freedom and adventure. It was a wild, exotic place, a place where he could escape the confines of the fenced railroad yard, the squalid Heights, his sidetracked dreams. As often as he could, he would drive there with his friends, or by himself, and wander along wharves piled high with cotton, sulfur, and grain, mingling with sailors from Europe, Africa, and the Orient, or with the Cajun and West Indian longshoremen who wore earrings and spoke in the musical rhythms of the wind and the waves.

There was a stretch of beach he particularly liked where the sand was always clean and smooth. From there he would swim, with a powerful, steady stroke, through the gently rolling surf, to a point of land just over a mile away. Sitting on the point, he could look back at Galveston Harbor and see the smokestacks of the grimy tramp steamers, rusty oil tankers, and trim passenger liners — ships from a hundred different ports — that crowded the berths of Galveston's docks. He could see the tall grain elevators that marked the city's skyline, and further off, across a narrow channel, the dry docks and ship repair yards stretched along a sand bar called Pelican Spit. He would swim back to the beach and lie exhausted in the sun, imagining what it would be like to sail away, on any one of the ships, to some foreign land, it didn't really matter where.

Red, Kemmie, Red's friend, and Alice Rogers swam for hours on that Sunday in June, and then played horse, waist deep in the water, shouldering each other into the surf. Kemmie was on Red's shoulders when she fell and struck her head on a rock. She was only out for about a minute, though it seemed a week to Red, who thought at first that she was dead, and knelt beside her cursing himself and looking skyward like a lonely wolf. When she came to, he was beside himself with joy and carried her across the sand, past the sea wall, to a small café, where he bought her a Coke and got an ice-filled dish towel for the walnut-sized lump on the back of her skull. He apologized the whole time while she laughed and told him not to worry, she was fine. When she touched his arm, smiled at him, and brushed her hair back from her face with her free hand, he felt as though his soul had suddenly been cut loose from his body and was whirling above him, perched on a blade of the café's paddle fan.

"C'mon," Red said, "let's all go dancing."

Alice Rogers and Kemmie's date looked at Kemmie. "It's OK with me," Kemmie said. "I feel great."

They changed clothes in the restrooms of the café and discovered that one of Kemmie's new white sandals was missing. "It's probably back on the beach," said Red, who went charging off to find it, but the sandal was gone, washed into the gulf on the incoming tide.

"It doesn't matter, I'll dance barefoot," Kemmie said, skipping ahead of the other three. The sea breeze blew her flowered sun-dress against her legs and tossed her hair high over her head. She was seventeen and had never met anyone like Red before. He seemed like such a happy person, so full of energy, so full of life. He was so sure of himself, too, but in a nice way, a comfortable way. She felt that no matter what might happen, if she were with him he could take care of it. He had just turned twenty-four.

At the pavilion, Red asked Kemmie to dance, and she accepted. The song they were playing was an instrumental version of Gershwin's "I've Got a Crush on You," and she sang along while they danced. He was amazed that she knew the words and said her voice was beautiful. She had totally forgotten he was short and marveled at the strength in his arms. He asked her for another dance and then a third, and suddenly she realized he was dancing only with her. She felt terrible because she was sure Alice Rogers was upset, so when Red asked her to dance a fourth time she said no, that she was tired and wanted to sit down. In fact, she had never felt less tired in her life.

Before they left the pavilion, Red asked Kemmie to go to a softball game with him the following night. She wanted to say yes, but told him instead she'd let him know later. She felt she had to ask Alice, and if Alice didn't want her to go she wouldn't, but by this time Alice was so angry at Red she told Kemmie she didn't care. "You go ahead," she said. "I'm not ever going out with him again."

So Kemmie went to the game with Red on Monday night, and then she went to another on Tuesday. On Wednesday night they went for a long walk and on Friday attended a free concert in the park, after which he took her to Howard's Café, across from the railroad yard, where they ate hamburgers and drank Cokes that he put on the bill he paid every payday. The brightly lit café was overflowing with boisterous railroad men wearing bibbed overalls who came in out of the darkness smelling of coal dust and lubricating oil. Smoke from the grill hung like a cloud bank just below the ceiling, and when a train went by the walls shook and the stacks of dishes clattered.

"What do you think?" Red asked her.

"I think it's exciting," Kemmie said. "And these hamburgers are the best I've ever eaten."

They were both broke; he'd spent his last thirty-seven cents on gas. When they left the café and he started up his car the throttle linkage snapped with a sound like a bullet ricocheting off a rock. "It's happened before," he said, smiling at her and reaching under the seat. He pulled out a thick rubber band, got out, and crawled under the car. In a few minutes he was back. "It's fixed, sort of," he said, "but this car'll never make it all the way out to the east end. We'll go on over to my house and borrow my daddy's panel truck."

Kemmie Wheeler had lived all her life in the east end of Houston, in a quiet, middle-class neighborhood of neat, wood-frame houses with well-kept lawns set along wide, clean streets lined with tall shade trees. Her parents were both well-educated teachers, and their home was always filled with books. Her father also sold real estate to make ends meet during the Depression. He loved music and encouraged Kemmie to develop her musical talent. She studied voice; she sang in her church choir and in a choral group at high school. She had never been to the Heights, and when they got to Red's house he went inside, leaving her sitting on the front steps. She felt suddenly as though she'd been deposited in a foreign country.

Behind her, inside the house, she could hear Red's father shouting at him and cursing. When Red came outside with the keys to the truck, she was rocking back and forth on the steps, hugging her knees.

"Let's go," he said, walking fast from the house to the panel truck parked in the side yard. "We better get you home." As they drove, he talked nonstop, about his car, about the truck, about the men from the railroad shop they'd seen in Howard's Café, about everything except what had just gone on in his house. She was too upset then to realize he was avoiding it, though years later it would occur to her when she thought back on that night.

"I was so scared," she said to him now. "Your father . . . he's so angry at you."

"Aw, the old man don't mean nothin' by all that racket," Red said. "It's just his way. The Heights isn't so bad either. Folks there are different than where you come from, but they're good people, you'll see. Don't be scared." There was a certainty in the way he spoke that calmed her, as though he saw the future as clearly as you could see down a brightly moonlit path cut through deep woods.

She leaned over and kissed him quickly. "I'll be all right," she said, and ran up the walk to her house.

It was the house where Kemmie had been born, where her parents had raised her, although her parents weren't there any more. Her mother had died the year before, when she was sixteen. Her father had stayed in the house for about six months after his wife's death, growing more miserable by the week, until finally he was emotionally unable to remain there any longer. One day, in the spring of 1939, he announced to Kemmie, her two brothers, and her sister that he was going back to Alabama, where he'd come from and where his kin still lived.

On the night he left, they gathered in the dining room to sort things out. Kemmie's oldest brother, Lionel, who was twenty-one, had a job with Tubescope, an oil-field equipment company. Her other brother, Bill, twenty, worked for an outfit that made duck decoys, and her sister, Jonilee, nineteen, was a bookkeeper for the electric company. Kemmie had just graduated from high school and as yet did not have a job. "Why don't you take care of the house and cook for us all?" Lionel said to her. "We'll chip in and pay you a salary."

The money wasn't much — only a dollar or two a week — because although all three of them were working, their income was quite meager, and they were faced with monthly payments on a $2,000 home improvement loan their father had taken shortly before her mother died. Still, Kemmie was content. She felt useful taking care of her brothers and sister, and secure, too, even though her mother and father were gone. But this arrangement lasted only a couple of months, because her brothers and sister were unable to keep up the loan payments, the bank foreclosed, and the Wheelers lost their house.

Kemmie took a job selling candy at a movie theater for twelve dollars a week and moved into the house of a woman named Merle Wellburn. Merle was an alcoholic, but treated Kemmie like a daughter, always leaving a plate of food on the stove at night so Kemmie would have something warm to eat when she got home from the theater.

Within two weeks of her first date, Red and Kemmie decided neither of them would go out with anyone else. In order to impress

Kemmie, Red traded in his old car for a 1936 Pontiac, a magnificent dark green sedan with a brown interior as comfortable as the plush couches in the movie theater's lobby. The only problem was Red couldn't make the payments on it and after two months the Pontiac was repossessed. Now, when they went riding together, Red and Kemmie had to depend on a friend's borrowed car or Charlie Adair's old panel truck.

One night, when they were out for a drive in the country, they stopped at a railroad crossing while a train passed. Red turned suddenly to Kemmie and said, "Well, I guess I'll be getting you some hardware pretty soon." She knew instantly what he meant, although she had never heard that term for a ring before and never heard it again. The next night, he gave her the ring — a gold band with a tiny diamond mounted on it — which he bought from Levitt's Jewelry Store for sixty-two dollars and fifty cents, five dollars down and two-fifty a week.

"Oh it's beautiful," she said, and meant it, although she was secretly concerned because of what had recently happened to the car. The following evening, Kemmie told Red she thought maybe they shouldn't be engaged, maybe they should go out with other people and just see each other on weekends. Red had worked all day at the railroad shop and walked clear across town to Merle Wellburn's house to see Kemmie, which, from her point of view, was part of the problem. He was doing that every night, ever since he lost his car. Then he would walk or hitchhike back to the rooming house and somehow get up and go to work again the next day. The pressure of it may not have been affecting him but it was sure beginning to gnaw at her. Furthermore, she wasn't all that certain she wanted to get married at all. "We can't go on like this, Red," she said. "It just isn't going to work."

This turn of events was not at all pleasing to Red, who viewed the loss of the Pontiac and his present transportation problems as momentary obstacles — a couple more of the hurdles placed in front of him — and was perfectly willing to go without sleep to spend time with the girl whom he'd already decided was going to be his wife. "Well, Kemmie, it's nothin' but a car," he said. "There'll be another one. There'll be lots of 'em. You just wait. Someday we'll both have our own cars, and our own house, too."

It was more than the car. Now that she'd known him for a while they seemed so different from one another. He was outgoing, effusive, a streetwise hell-raiser; she was naive and sheltered and would rather read a book than party. But she was only seventeen and she did love him, and as he talked on and on, enveloping Merle's living room in his luminous vision of the future, her fears were silenced.

"If how we're gonna get together all the time is the problem," he said at last, "the only thing for us to do is go and get married."

"When?" she asked.

"Hell," he said, "let's do it right now."

KEMMIE

On Sunday, December 3, 1939, Red got his daddy's panel truck and picked me up along with my friend Olive Evans and her boyfriend and we went down to Richmond-Rosenberg and got married, but first we went and rented a little apartment over on Columbia Street in the Heights, right near Reagan High School. I borrowed a yellow night-gown from Olive for my wedding night, and I wore one of her dresses, a black print. Red wore slacks and a sport shirt. After we got married we went back to the railroad café and ate hamburgers for our wedding dinner, because by the time we paid for the blood tests and the marriage license we only had two dollars left to our name, and Red could charge our food there. After we ate the hamburgers, he gave me a quarter to play the punchboard. Those were boards filled with numbers that you could punch out, and they had them at all the cafés and bars around at that time. You paid a quarter and got to pick one number and punch it out. I was a whiz at playing them. It was like I could feel which number was a winner. So I played and I won a pound box of candy that was dessert for our wedding dinner.

CHAPTER EIGHT

HOUSTON — 1940

On a scorching day in late July, Red Adair quit his job at the railroad shop. He went around after work shaking hands with all the men, who slapped him on the back and wished him luck, shaking their heads in disbelief when he turned away. They all spoke about getting out of the yard, about looking for something better, but none of them ever did anything about it. As bad as the railroad shop was, leaving was far too frightening to them, and now they shrank back from Red when he wasn't looking, as though they feared some of his audacity might rub off.

As Adair was leaving, F. J. Miller, the shop foreman, took him aside. "Red, you're the best man I've got," he said. "I wish there was something I could do to keep you, but there isn't. Hell, I don't blame you for quitting, but if you ever want your old job back, just come ask me and you got it."

"I appreciate that, Mr. Miller," Red said, "but I'm gonna make it. When I come back it'll be to pay y'all a visit."

It was a risky decision, with his wife six months pregnant and he himself with no other work. Nevertheless, Red felt if he listened to the gate of the yard clang shut and stayed behind that metal fence much longer, among the men with sagging shoulders and lifeless eyes, where every day was exactly like the last and his chances for advancement were next to none, he'd truly go mad.

Kemmie saw it coming. For months, Red had talked to her at night about what a dead end the railroad shop was, and how it was driving him crazy. He was twenty-five years old now and had worked for the Southern Pacific for six years, yet his pay was the same $38, every two weeks, that it had been in 1934 when he'd started there.

"I had to get out of there, Kemmie," he said on the night he finally left. "There's no way in the world I could support a family on what they were payin' me, and it wasn't gonna get any better. If I stayed there, I'd have no time to even look for something better." They were living in the east end of Houston by then, already having moved twice to save money since they'd rented the apartment on Columbia Street the day they got married. In March they'd taken a room for six dollars a week at the edge of the Heights, on Sixth and Studewood, across the street from a noisy beer joint.

In April they had moved to an apartment on the second floor of a three-story house off Harrisburg Boulevard in the east end, for five dollars a week. They had a little bedroom, a tiny kitchen, and they shared a bathroom with several other people who lived on the same floor. Kemmie was sitting in the kitchen on the evening Red came home from the railroad shop and told her he'd quit. Even though she'd expected it, she was so terrified at first that she became dizzy and had to grab hold of the table to keep from falling over. "How will we pay for the baby?" she said. "How will we all eat? Oh Red, I know you had to do it, but I'm so scared."

He pulled her to her feet and put his arms around her, and she lay her head on his shoulder. "Don't you worry," he said. "Don't you worry at all. Everything's gonna turn out great. I know it. There's no doubt about it in my mind." Listening with her eyes closed to his deep, soothing voice, she felt safe, reassured, and she believed what he said was so.

She had felt the same way five months ealier when she told him nervously she was pregnant. She was frightened that Red would be angry, and for two weeks had said nothing to him about it, but instead, when she finally told him, he was thrilled. "Oh, that's great," he said. "That's wonderful news. Don't worry, there'll be plenty of money to pay all the doctor bills. Everything's gonna work out fine. I'll bet you anything we're gonna have a boy."

He was positive the baby would be a boy and talked about it all the time, to his friends, to the other men at the railroad shop, and to his family when he and Kemmie dropped over to his parents' house on Sunday for a visit. "My boy's not gonna have to quit school like I did," Red would announce to them. "My boy's goin' to college when he gets old enough. I'm gonna see to that, believe me."

So on that hot July night, when Red told her again not to worry, Kemmie smiled at him and nodded. She was sitting now, swollen-bellied, her forehead beaded with sweat, in their bedroom, in the chair her old boyfriend had made for her and insisted she keep. It was a beautifully crafted armchair, the only piece of furniture they owned, with scrolled wooden legs that reminded her of lion's paws, and feather-filled cushions so thick and soft that when she sat in the chair she felt as though she were swimming underwater.

"I'm gonna get into the oil patch, Kemmie," he said, "'cause they're gonna be needing more men, and they're gonna be needing them real soon. Last month Congress appropriated — what? — three billion extra dollars for defense? And the paper says they're about ready to appropriate a whole lot more than that. Never mind what all those America First people are saying, President Roosevelt's not about to let Hitler keep on chewin' up Europe forever without doin' somethin' about it. No sir, he's not."

He was pacing back and forth in the narrow space between the dresser and the chair, bobbing his shoulders up and down and waving his arms. Finally, he stopped and stood in front of her, his hands on his hips. "This country's gearin' up to defend itself, Kemmie, and we're gonna need more oil to do it. And see, we're not gonna be able to depend on foreign oil supplies as much, so we're gonna have to drill more here, and that means more work in the oil patch."

The need for domestically produced petroleum products would indeed take place, but not for at least six months. So while Red Adair's vision of a boom in the East Texas oil field was accurate, it was just slightly premature, and when, on the morning following his departure from the railroad shop, he began searching for work in the oil patch, he found nothing. He looked for weeks with no success, leaving the apartment at daybreak, walking or taking a streetcar (he still had no car of his own) from oil company to oil company, returning home well after dark, footsore and exhausted.

He left his name on lists as long as his arm at every oil-field service company in Houston — drilling riggers and mud suppliers, pipe and valve manufacturers, and wire-line outfits, whose business it was to place various sensing and testing devices deep inside the well bore — and while several were encouraging, none had an immediate opening. It would only be a couple of months, they told him, a half a year at the outside, before jobs would open up, but Red couldn't wait that long.

It was late August now, and he still had no job. He had walked eleven miles that day, been turned away from twenty-eight oil-field companies, and the soles of both his shoes were completely worn through. He knew there was only an apple, some plain biscuits, and a can of peas in the cupboard for him and his pregnant wife to eat, but he had only fifteen cents left to his name and could buy no other food. There was no way he could pay the rent on their five-dollar-a-week apartment, either, so earlier that day he called his parents and asked if he and Kemmie could come and live with them for a while. The call had been excruciating for him to make. In his mind, it was an admission that for the first time in his life he had failed. On top of that, he had been unable to deliver on his promise to Kemmie that everything would work out fine. His mother said yes, but he knew she was no happier about it than he was.

There was no hot water, so he took a cold bath. Afterward, in clean clothes, he sat silently at the kitchen table for an hour, staring straight ahead. Kemmie, too, sat at the table, watching his expression oscillate between anger and despair, an emotion she had never seen in him before. Finally, he got up and walked to the door. "I'll be back later," he said, without turning. He had made up his mind he wasn't coming home without a wallet full of money, no matter how he had to get it.

Hours later, Kemmie heard the door of the apartment open and close, and heard Red come into the bedroom. She waited for him to climb into bed beside her but when several minutes passed and he didn't, she switched on the night-light and saw him sitting in their chair, his face streaked with tears. Slowly, she pulled herself out of bed and knelt in front of him. "Red," she whispered, "what happened? Please tell me what's wrong."

He had walked west on Harrisburg Boulevard in the direction of downtown Houston, hands thrust deep into the pockets of his pants, until he came to a tavern he knew catered to a wealthy clientele. He went inside and sat alone at a small table in the far corner of the room where he could survey the entire place without attracting any attention. He bought a Jax beer with his last fifteen cents and studied the other men drinking there, until finally he found his mark. The man he picked looked at least fifty and was overweight, a hard drinker in an expensive suit with a roll of cash thicker than Red's fist, who had come in by himself. Red nursed his beer while the man drank steadily for an hour and a half, then rose and made his way across the bar to go to the bathroom, grabbing onto tables as he walked to keep from falling down. When Red saw this, he left the bar, crossed the street, and waited in the shadows beneath a large oak tree, leaning almost invisibly against the trunk until the fat drunk appeared, alone, on the sidewalk, his bulk outlined by the lights in the window of the tavern. As the fat man began stumbling up the street, away from the lights and into semidarkness, Red moved as well, silently closing the distance between them.

Kemmie's head was resting on his knees, so that when Red bent over his mouth was only inches from her ear, yet she had to strain to hear him. She reached a hand to his face and touched the wetness, then ran her fingers gently through his hair. "I couldn't do it, Kemmie," he whispered. "I was going to roll him and take his wallet. I could have hit him, knocked him out, and been gone in thirty seconds, but when I came up on him, I couldn't do it. How could I even think of hurting somebody for money? How could I do something like that?" That was all he said, and she said nothing in reply. For the rest of their lives, he would never speak to her about that night again.

The next afternoon they moved to Red's parents' house in the Heights, where they would stay for almost three months. Red resumed his search for work in the oil patch, leaving early in the mornings with his father, who by then was working for the University of Houston. Every night he'd come home empty-handed, telling Kemmie he felt as though he were getting closer to finding a job.

In fact, Red was much closer to entering the oil field than even he realized. In September 1940 Congress adopted the Selective Service Act requiring all men between the ages of twenty-one and thirty-five to register for a year of military training. The United States was expanding involvement with its embattled ally, Britain, and many young American men were beginning to accept war as an inevitability.

Bill Wheeler, Kemmie's brother, was one of these, and he decided that when war came he would much rather be an air-force pilot than an infantryman. Like Red, Bill had also been trying to find work in the oil field and had placed his name on many of the same lists as his brother-in-law. In the meantime, to save money, he was living with Jonilee and her husband.

One night in late August, Kemmie got a telephone call from Jonilee, who was speaking so fast her sister could barely understand her. "Well, Daddy finally signed the papers and sent 'em over from Alabama," Jonilee said, "so Bill's going in the Air Force, and he's leaving for basic training next week, and wouldn't you know it, the very same day the papers come from Alabama, Otis Pressure Control calls saying they got a job for Bill working on a rig way down in South Texas somewhere, and for him to show up first thing tomorrow morning at the Otis offices here in Houston. Right away I said to Bill, 'I'm callin' Kemmie this very minute, 'cause I think if Red goes instead he can take your place and get that job.'"

Otis Pressure Control was an oil-field service company owned by a man named Herbert Otis. Trained originally as an engineer, Otis was a very smart man who developed techniques for maintaining equipment used on drilling rigs and performing a number of tasks critical to effective rig operation while the rig was in production. Among other jobs, his company cleaned and adjusted the huge valves, or blowout preventers, at the wellhead. They also removed and cleaned drill tubing — the piping through which gas and oil is brought to the surface — and forced pipe and various sensing devices, or "tools," into wells that were in production, working against the well's high pressure, in a dangerous operation known as "snubbing." Otis and the men who worked for him were highly respected in the oil patch, for they did not take the words "pressure control" in the company's name lightly. Every one of them knew that if, in the course of their work, the well's pressure became uncontrolled, all hell would break loose in a hurry.

At daybreak on the morning after Jonilee's call, Red stood in the equipment yard of Otis Pressure Control, talking to the company foreman in charge of hiring. Behind him the long line of other unemployed men already wound its way down the block and around the corner. "You called for Bill Wheeler, my brother-in-law," Red said, "but he's goin' in the Air Force. My name's on your list, too, and I could sure use the work."

"It's only part-time work when you start here. You realize that," the foreman said. "You get paid by the job."

"That's fine with me," Red answered. "Whatever you got, I'll be glad to take it, and I'll do a good job for you, too."

"What we've got is two, maybe three days' work on a rig near Alice, Texas," said the foreman, "about fifty miles west of Corpus Christi. You'll stay out there 'til the job's done. Why don't you call your wife and tell her you won't be home for a couple of days."

"Yes, sir," said Red. "And thank you. You won't regret hiring me, I promise you that."

It is late in the afternoon, and the crew from Otis has knocked off for the day. Arms and faces streaked with dirt, the dozen or so men lean against cars parked near the drilling rig, or against the back of a large flatbed truck piled high with equipment. They are strong, confident-looking men, at ease with their bodies. Some are shirtless, several wear battered fedoras with brims turned down over their eyes. They are about to drive into town to wash away the dust in their throats with a few beers, eat some dinner, and rest from a day of backbreaking labor under the South Texas sun, which even in late September is brutally hot.

After the other men leave, Red unwraps a chicken sandwich he has saved from lunch and washes it down with a cup of tepid water from a cooler kept in a small enclosure on the rig floor, the size of a tool shed, known as the doghouse. Then he takes a small notebook and the stub of a pencil from his pants pocket and walks around the rig, noting in the book how the valves at the wellhead, below the rig floor, are positioned, and how the valves' adjustable openings, or chokes, are set. He sets the book down, takes a steel tape measure from his pocket, and calculates where he will set his block and tackle in the morning so that they will be directly over the well bore, or "hole." The crew from Otis will be using this block and tackle the following day when they force pipe into the hole, and his preparation will allow them to rig up faster, saving precious daylight hours. No one has asked him to do this, nor will anyone say anything to him when they see what he has done. Neither will he mention it to them, but everyone on the job, including the foreman, will be grateful.

Red is not oblivious to this, and in fact, as he climbs down a ladder to the ground, he sees, in his mind, the long line of men waiting outside the Otis Pressure Control offices for work on the day he was hired. "They all want my job," he says to himself, "but not one of 'em's ever gonna get it."

Now, he fills an empty coffee can with kerosene from a fifty-five-gallon drum, finds himself several clean rags, and begins to clean the equipment piled on the flatbed truck, though no one has told him to do this either. From time to time he pauses in his work, taking out the notebook to jot down a few words or make a sketch of the apparatus he is cleaning. This is the beginning of a long, deliberate, and thorough process of self-education. In several years, when it is complete, he will not only be familiar with every working part of a drilling rig, but will begin to improve on many of them.

The sun has not quite set when he puts the coffee can and the rags away, washes his hands in a pail of water, and quickly returns to the drilling rig. Using the steel supports that run diagonally between one cross-brace, or girt, of the derrick, and the girt above it, he climbs agilely to a small steel platform, called a monkey board, 150 feet above the rig floor. Leaning against the railing of the monkey board, he unbuttons his shirt and lets the west wind, blowing across the parched Rio Grande Valley from Mexico, cool his body. Here and there, in the distance, he can see other drilling rigs, rising above the rolling, mesquite-covered land. He sees some cattle, moving slowly toward a watering hole surrounded by a clump of trees, and a flock of birds silhouetted against the sinking magenta sun. Otherwise the endless landscape is empty, and its vastness exhilarates him, charging him with energy and boundless expectations.

He sits on the monkey board, letting his legs dangle over the side, and thinks about his wife, who is almost eight months pregnant. He sees the expression of joy on her face when he showed her the check for thirty-eight dollars he earned for two and a half days' work — his first job for Otis. "Look at it, Kemmie," he said. "It's as much as they paid me for half a month at the railroad shop." Though she protested, he went out and bought her a new pair of shoes with some of the money, saying, "Don't worry, this is just the beginning." He has been on this job, his second in the oil field near the town of Benavides, for four days. He will remain for another week and a half and earn $200, more than the Southern Pacific paid him in two and a half months.

Now it is dark. Red takes a thick blanket and a jacket from behind the seat of an old pickup truck belonging to the rig's night watchman. The watchman, who will spend the night in a tiny shack erected by the oil company, fifty yards from the rig, offers Red a cup of coffee, but he declines, saying he needs to sleep. He spreads the blanket in the truck's bed, lies down on his back on half of the blanket and covers himself with the other half, propping his head on the rolled up jacket that is his pillow. He turns his head slightly and can see the outline of the derrick against a black sky filled with more stars than he has ever seen in his life. He imagines he can feel the pressure of the oil pushing upward from a mile below the rig, pushing with incredible force against the valves the Otis crew adjusted earlier that day, but he is not nervous. In fact, he is calmer than he can ever remember. "This is my place," he thinks. "This is where I belong."

CHAPTER NINE

If you don't pay a guy enough to drill your well, it can cost you a helluva lot more in the long run, because that driller's insurance just says there have to be blowout preventers on the wellhead. It doesn't say whether they have to be working or not. You have to make damn sure you test it. That's the reason you have blowout drills. And you have to check the mud weight often, and check the temperature and what's in the mud. Is there any gas coming up with it? Old-time drillers used to check their cuttings all the time. They could tell what was in that mud by tasting it. Nowadays, drillers don't do that. They find someone to do it for them. They hire consultants with computers. Then they get in trouble.

Red Adair

SMACKOVER, ARKANSAS — 1940

There was no warning before the gas well blew out. The well was in the wilds of southern Arkansas, near where the Smackover River joins the Ouachita and the bass fishing is beyond compare. One moment there were only the normal sounds of work on a drilling rig, distinct in the clear, cold, December morning air. A section of chain clanged on a steel floor. Diesel engines powering the rig droned steadily. The transmission of a truck loaded with a spool of cable whined as the truck slogged its way through hubcap-deep mud up a recently bulldozed dirt road, turned around in a small clearing and backed toward the well. Men shouted to one another, communicating in short, staccato bursts of speech, and a dog barked somewhere in the underbrush a half mile away. The next moment these sounds were obliterated by a roar so deafening it seemed to reach into the core of every man's body like a white-hot iron hand trying to turn him inside out.

The oil patch is filled with tales of the strange things men have done when they were next to a well that let go, like the one about the man who jumped from the top of a derrick on a floating-barge rig that blew out in the Mississippi Delta. He broke his collarbone and both legs, but was so wired with adrenaline he managed to swim half a mile to shore and crawl another six miles through the swamp to his house. When he woke up two days later he had no idea where he was or how he got there. Another rig worker ran in terror a quarter of a mile into a bramble thicket so dense that when he finally stopped to catch his breath he was trapped. It took the rest of the crew two hours to reach him and cut him loose with chain saws.

The roar of a blowout has caused men to lose control of their bowels, tear their clothes off in sheer panic, and run screaming down a mountainside or into the desert. Wild wells have driven men totally mad. There is a story about a driller on a rig near Jal, New Mexico, who fled from the noise to his pickup truck. He couldn't find his keys and began pushing the truck down a dirt road by himself. When the other rig workers found him he was dead from dehydration, inside the truck's cab with the windows rolled up and the doors locked. He had somehow managed to push the truck three miles from the rig.

Owls near blowing wells have flown from their nests in broad daylight. Blowouts have brought bears out of hibernation and provoked fish to jump out of the water onto riverbanks. Once, at a blowout on a Shell Oil well in northern Sumatra, the sonic intensity so disoriented a tiger that the cat rushed from the jungle into the drilling camp, ripped through several tents, and leaped into a manmade reservoir where it swam, screaming, in circles for an entire night. The next morning a native hunting party killed it with spears, saying the beast was possessed by demons.

Nobody knows how he will behave when a well blows out, no more than anyone knows how he will behave during an earthquake or an artillery barrage, for the noise of a blowing well is so violent it drives a man beyond all hope of reason to the point of purely reflexive response. One reaction, however, has remained reasonably constant throughout the history of the oil patch. When a well comes loose, every man working on it, no matter how tough, no matter how strong, will almost always run as fast and far as he can to safety. It came as quite a shock, therefore, to the others on the well in southern Arkansas that cold December morning, when one of the men who had come up from Houston with the Otis Pressure Control crew to do a snubbing job stayed right where he was, beside the wellhead, two feet from a stream of gas loud enough to reprogram the beating of his heart; forceful enough, should he stumble or lean into its flow, to cut him into little pieces and hurl them halfway to the Louisiana border.

Afterward, some of the men who were there working for the drilling company claimed they'd noticed something different about this short, redheaded man whom none of them had seen before (this being only his third job with Otis). The crew employed by the drilling company was working up on the platform, or floor, of the rig. The redheaded guy, and the other men from Otis, had been carrying out their snubbing operation on the series of valves at the wellhead in the ten-foot-high space below the floor known as the cellar. Right away, they could see the redhead was light on his feet, and good with a wrench, too, but then that was true of all of them. One night, they remembered, he stayed on the job until three A.M. cleaning every piece of well bore–sensing equipment on the wire-line truck, and though that was a little unusual, inasmuch as no one was getting any overtime pay, he didn't brag about it and was right back on the job at seven in the morning, trading wisecracks and good-natured insults with the rest of them, so nobody thought he was a show-off or a brownnose, and they certainly didn't think of him as peculiar.

Later, when Red Adair was known in the oil patch, the confidence he inspired would cause men to stay with him at a blowing well or follow him up to one on fire, but on this day when the well blew out he stood there in the cellar all by himself, in a cloud of natural gas spiked with distillate, a petroleum vapor much like gasoline. A drilling rig, shuddering and clanking its way toward self-destruction while enveloped in an ever-thickening shroud of distillate, is about as explosive an environment as you can find on earth. This is precisely why the other rig hands, who instinctively broke and ran for their lives the instant the blowout began, continued sprinting in every direction through the woods and over the fields, like a herd of terrified deer, praying fervently that they could put enough distance between themselves and the well to keep from being burned to a crisp when it blew up.

It felt, to Red Adair, as though the earth itself had ruptured right next to him and was spewing its innards into the air, but *his* instinct, when confronted for the first time in his life by this unimaginably powerful natural force, was *not* to run, in spite of the fact that the vibration of the ground had forced his legs into a grotesque, spontaneous dance. Instead of fear, he was gripped by the need to find out what was wrong. Instead of being filled with terror, he was filled with an overwhelming desire to fix whatever the hell was screwing up the hard work he'd been doing for almost a week. He didn't have to will himself to stay by the wellhead; he took this blowout as an attack on him, personally, as if the well were shaking its fist in his face, so there was no way in the world he was going to turn his back on it before he could figure out why it was making all that noise and make an attempt to stop it. He looked around and, unbelievable as it may seem, was able to see, through the veil of gas, that a flange on the primary, or annular, blowout preventer had worked loose.

In an oil or gas well, there is a hole — the well bore — that goes from the surface down into the formation. Within that hole, sitting one inside the other, are lengths of pipe — conductor pipe, casing pipe, and drill pipe. Any one of these, under various conditions, may be an avenue through which the oil or gas can escape. Basically, the function of every blowout preventer is to cut off one or more of these avenues when gas or oil is making its way uncontrollably from a hydrocarbon formation to the atmosphere. If the preventer system on a well works (and these days they generally do), some of the well's pressure can then be bled off through pipes attached to the blowout preventers, while mud is pumped downhole to create a hydrostatic balance.

The annular preventer, a valve that looks like a plump fire hydrant and may be as large as the barrel of a cement mixer, is positioned at the top of one or more other blowout preventers on the well in an assemblage known as the preventer stack. The annular preventer is so named because the piston inside it seals off the annulus of the well — the space between the drill pipe and the side of the hole. An annular blowout preventer can also be used to seal off an open hole — one that has no pipe in it. Under normal conditions, when the gas or oil in the well begins grumbling and surging — or "kicking" — somewhere down in the well bore, but the well has not yet blown out, strong rubber fingers around this piston allow fluid such as drilling mud to be pumped down the hole to control the pressure, while the preventer keeps anything from coming out.

The blowout preventers below the annular preventer are called ram preventers because they use rams — large, rubber-faced blocks of steel that are rammed together, like the butting horns on a pair of angry rams, to seal off the well. They generally can withstand more pressure than the annular preventer and are the well's second line of defense. There are blind rams, which seal off an open hole, and pipe

113

rams, used to close the hole when drill pipe is in use. There is also a shear ram that simply cuts the pipe off. Using a shear ram is an admission that all else has failed, an emergency measure of last resort similar to cutting your fishing line when you realize you are about to haul a great white shark into your rowboat.

Imagine, for example, that you are working on a floating drilling rig in very bad weather. Suddenly, you get a violent kick — an enormous surge of well pressure — you can't handle, and the rig is about to capsize. Your only recourse would be to close the shear ram and get the hell out of the way, escaping, hopefully, with your life, but sending several hundred thousand dollars worth of pipe, a $40,000 drill bit, and whatever valuable well-sensing equipment was in use down into the hole.

Whether they're pistons or rams, the valves of a blowout preventer on a modern drilling rig are operated hydraulically, using a series of pipes that run from the preventers to the rig's accumulator system. A special mixture of oil and water called harmony fluid is pumped from the accumulator, through the pipes, to the blowout preventers, where about three thousand pounds per square inch of pressure is applied to close the valves. The accumulator is located as far from the wellhead as possible on a drilling rig, because if the well blows out or catches fire, those people responsible for closing the blowout preventers would be less likely to run away than if they were up next to the wellhead. But back in 1940 when Red Adair started out in the oil patch, blowout preventers were operated manually by turning a wheel attached to the preventer. This was a procedure that required considerable strength and plenty of guts.

Between each blowout preventer on the preventer stack is a metal flange used to connect the preventers to one another. This flange is held in place by a series of nuts the size of bagels, threaded onto bolts as thick as broomsticks — a very secure set-up as long as someone takes the time to torque down the nuts. On the well in Smackover, Arkansas, that had not been done to the flange at the base of the annular preventer, and the pressure of the gas allowed those loose nuts to work their way up the bolts. The flange, and the annular blowout preventer, followed right behind the nuts, creating a six-inch space through which the well was blowing. Red Adair could see this, and could see, too, that only two or three turns of thread remained on the bolts before the nuts, the annular preventer, and the flange came off completely and rocketed up through the drilling derrick, guaranteeing a shower of sparks and an instantaneous explosion that would obliterate him, the rig, and several acres of neighboring woods.

The nuts, flange, and preventer were shaking wildly on the bolts, and Red realized he had only a few moments in which to act. But now that he understood the problem and its solution, a feeling of tranquillity settled over him, and even the blowing well's noise seemed to diminish. Moving as quickly as possible, he made his way through the ankle-deep mud of the cellar, then, once clear of the rig, he sprinted toward the Otis Pressure Control truck. By pure coincidence, he had spent several hours the night before cleaning every tool on the truck, so he knew exactly where to find the correct wrench. He hadn't done it in anticipation of any trouble, but merely to make the next day's work go more smoothly, but his good luck taught him a lesson he never forgot. From that day on, he never went to work on a well without knowing the precise location of every tool and piece of equipment he might need in an emergency. Red had also coated all the tools lightly with paraffin, a trick he learned in the railroad shop to make tools easier to clean. With this coating, the wrench would be less likely to cause a spark while he worked with it. He would have liked to coat each of the nuts as well, but didn't dare take the extra time.

The wrench, boxed at one end and open-ended at the other, was three feet long and weighed twelve pounds, but Red ran with it as though it were a butter knife. Back at the wellhead, being careful to stay out of the flow of blowing gas, he began tightening the flange's bolts, a task of considerable difficulty given the minimum visibility in the cellar and the wild vibration of everything near the wellhead, including his hands. Still, there was no question in his mind that he would do it, that he would win, that he *had* to win, for that's how he regarded his first encounter with a wild well, and every encounter after that: as a battle against a formidable adversary that would never show mercy, a war against an enemy he could lose only once.

When he was through, the silence of the rig was overpowering. He stood transfixed, listening to the movement of leaves, the hiss of wind through grass, the rush of water in the river far away. He looked down and saw an earthworm near his boot, and it seemed that he could hear it as it slithered through the mud. He coughed and spat and was startled by the sound. Then he walked from the cellar to the water cooler, got himself a drink, and waited for the others to return.

When the other men drifted back to the drilling rig at the

Smackover well, they looked at Red with a mixture of awe and incredulity, for no ordinary oil-field hand had ever been known to stay beside a wild well and shut it in before that day. In the tight-knit world of the oil patch, from Arkansas and Louisiana, through Texas, Oklahoma, and New Mexico, and even as far west as California, it wouldn't take long for word of what Red had done to spread. That December morning in 1940 the legend of Red Adair began, but at the time, his actions did nothing but infuriate a man named Red Lucas, the Otis Pressure Control foreman in charge of the Smackover job.

"What the hell's wrong with you?" he screamed at Adair, who was replacing the three-foot wrench he'd used to stop the blowout. "You some kind of damned lunatic? I ought to fire your ass here and now. Don't you know that isn't our kind of work to do?"

Red Lucas was an old-timer in the oil field, tough as a lumberjack's boot, who'd worked his way up from swamper — a man who washed the dirt and grease off trucks and made sure they were filled with gas and their tires had air — to a position of considerable responsibility in the Otis organization. Along the way he'd become known as a strict disciplinarian who ruled his crew with an iron hand, adhering to oil-patch protocol, the basic rule of which was this: a man did exactly what his superiors told him to do and kept his mouth shut. Red Adair, though a newcomer to the oil patch, knew this rule as well, but without the slightest connection to an insurance policy or workman's compensation other than what the other men might have gathered up in the hat they passed to help pay for his funeral, he had just risked his life against a blowing well and come out a winner. This was something none of the other men on the job, including Red Lucas, had ever done, and the strength running through Adair from that victory, and that knowledge, would not let him remain silent.

"Well, Mr. Lucas, I don't know whose kind of work it is," he said, "but there wasn't anybody left *but* me. Sure as hell somebody had to stop it. To tell you the truth, you'd be a whole lot better off chewin' out the ass of the jerk who left the nuts loose on that preventer flange than tearin' into me."

For a long moment, Red Lucas stared at Red Adair, while every man on the rig stopped what he was doing and turned to look at the two of them, unsure whether Lucas would grab the hunting rifle he kept in his truck and shoot Adair where he stood, or simply kick Red off the site and make him hitchhike back to Texas.

"Son," Red Lucas finally said, "you got one hell of a set of balls, but you listen to me closely. When you're working for Otis you do snubbing and wire-line work, period. You want to fight wild wells, you go talk to Myron Kinley."

At first, in the years shortly following the discovery of oil at Spindletop in 1901, drilling rigs were driven by steam engines and made out of wood. Well control in those days was nonexistent; oil came spewing out of the ground and up through the derrick and was actually collected in huge pits or lakes. When one of these rigs caught fire (which they did with regularity), it generally burned to the ground. Sometimes drilling crews tried to fight the fires by using the steam powering the rig. Sometimes, if they were near a water supply, they tried fighting the fire as though it were a burning barn. Neither of these methods were particularly successful.

Then, slowly, through trial and error, well-control technology began to develop. Companies like Cameron Iron Works began manufacturing control valves with chokes, which evolved into more sophisticated blowout preventers. Drilling companies started experimenting with additives that raised or lowered mud weight. Drillers began installing drill-pipe floats in their drill pipe. These floats, which operate like check valves, allow mud to be pumped downhole, but keep anything from coming back up. But rigs still blew out, and they still caught fire, and all the men who tried to specialize in dealing with those fires and blowouts either died or quit. All, that is, but two: H. L. Patton and Myron Kinley, the kings of wild-well control, both out of Houston, the only men through the late 1920s and 1930s to fight burning, blowing wells and succeed.

It seemed as though Myron Kinley and H. L. Patton were cut from the same bolt of alligator hide. They were big, tough, outspoken men, afraid of nothing, and they hated each other's guts. Both of them pioneered the method of killing a well fire by directing powerful streams of water against the rig and then blowing the flaming wellhead out with explosives. They were also the first and only wild-well men to stay on the job after the fire was out in order to control the blowout by capping the well.

There were differences in the way they worked. Kinley operated alone, hiring helpers as he needed them on a job-to-job basis, while Patton had a kinfolks outfit that included seven or eight brothers, nephews, and nephews-in-law who followed him through the oil patch from well to well. For ten years Patton and Kinley ran neck-and-neck, and an oil man would have been hard pressed to say which one was better. Then one day in 1937, misfortune struck H. L. Patton and all but ended his career.

It was on a gas well owned by the Texas Company, not far from New Iberia, Louisiana, at a place called Vermillion Bay. The well was drilled in four feet of water and was raised up on pilings set in the sand. A crew had been working the well over, tripping pipe out of the hole to clean it, when the well let go and blew the whole set of valves on top — the Christmas tree, as it's called, that's installed once the drilling rig is done and the well's producing — a half a mile into the swamp. Texaco called H. L. Patton, who drove over from Houston to deal with the well.

Patton's specialty was the stinger, a series of valves, or manifolds, as he termed them, that ran both vertically and horizontally in the shape of a cross. He'd devised a way, using turnbuckles and come-alongs, and cranes with strong cables, to pull the stinger over a blowing well (not at all an easy thing to do), and snug it down with a leak-proof seal between the flange of the stinger and the wellhead. The well would then blow up through the stinger, and Patton could begin closing the valves and eventually shut the well in. He tried all sorts of things to fortify the seal: various glues and gaskets, lead, and even welding, which was toying with death near the blowing gas.

Patton got the Hughes Tool Company to build him a stinger for that Texaco well, and Hughes made a good one that snugged down tight. Haliburton, a company famous for its pumping equipment, came out and mixed mud with the pumps on their trucks, tied in a line to the stinger once it was closed in, and began pumping mud down the well. The pressure dropped, then dropped some more, and it looked as though the well was dead, when suddenly it began to kick stronger than ever — too strong, in fact, for the pressure limits of the stinger.

Patton asked a couple of the roughnecks on his crew to crawl out on the platform where the well was and open a couple of valves to relieve some of that pressure. They climbed out into the bay, into the water, and then those two men crawled right out onto that manifold and started opening the valve, and just as one of them put his hand up to the valve to open it some more, the whole thing blew up. They found one of the men in ten or fifteen minutes, but the other had been blown so far into the swamp it took them three days to find him. H. L. Patton was standing on a mud barge fifty yards away. A length of turnbuckle chain came flying through the air and nearly tore off his right arm.

A young man named Squirt Baker, fresh out of college, who was working for Cameron on the mud barge, got to Patton first and put a tourniquet on his arm, which was hanging by a piece of flesh no bigger than a thumb. They flew Patton to the hospital in a single-engine Texas Company plane, but it was too late; the doctors couldn't save his arm. That was on a Thursday.

Squirt Baker was already used to seeing tough men in the oil patch. He was sharing a hotel room with a hand named Fox Moses who'd lost a leg on a well but kept working in the oil field with another that he fashioned out of wood. The night before, Baker was sleeping when Moses came in drunk, unstrapped his leg, and threw it in a corner, where it landed with a crash. Baker jumped up and said, "What the hell was that?"

"Take it easy, son, it wasn't nothin' but my leg," said Moses, who then passed out. In the morning, he strapped the leg on, lit a cigar and went back to work.

All the same, Baker, and every other hand on the job, was speechless when H. L. Patton showed up at the well on Sunday morning. His right sleeve was pinned at the shoulder, his face was gray as lead, and the men could see the white hospital bandage showing at the open neck of his shirt. Patton stayed at Vermillion Bay until he killed the well that had killed his men, but he was never the same and soon left the wild-well business.

Myron Kinley had his troubles, too. On a burning well in northern Venezuela, near a town named Santa Rosa, he was loading his charges, packing solidified glycerine into containers, getting ready to shoot out the fire, when a welder, standing right behind him, lit his torch and blew them both into a ditch. The welder died. Kinley was far luckier, but his leg was mangled, and from then on he walked with a pronounced limp. Rig hands in the oil patch called him Board-leg, but never to his face, for once Patton retired, Kinley was the only man in the oil field who would walk up to a burning well, and the other men, no matter how rough, feared him and kept their distance.

Even Red Adair, who had backed away from no one in his life, was afraid of Myron Kinley at first. They met on an oil well in Alice, Texas, in the spring of 1941, three months after the Smackover job. In between, Red had further enhanced his reputation by single-handedly stopping another blowout shortly after New Year's on a well in Simonton, Texas, just west of Houston. Work with Otis had slowed again, and he'd picked up a job with a snubbing crew working for an oilman named Pat Corey. When the well let go, it blew the whole set of control valves known as the Christmas tree clear off the wellhead.

While the other rig hands raced from the blowing Simonton well, Red grabbed hold of a length of cable, wrapped it around the Christmas tree, and somehow managed to maneuver the tree over the wellhead by himself and bolt it back down. Unlike Red Lucas, Pat Corey said nothing to Red about doing someone else's work, but instead put an extra fifty-dollar bill in his pay envelope.

In Alice, Texas, Red was back snubbing with an Otis crew, when once again the well came loose, only this time it didn't just blow out, it caught fire, and Myron Kinley was brought in to put it out. Kinley climbed out of his shiny, new 1940 Ford pickup truck, lumbered over to the rig hands and the Otis crew who were clustered together two hundred yards from the well, and curled his upper lip back in a feral snarl. "I need somebody to walk up there to that well with me to check it out," he growled. "Is there one of you got the nerve for that?"

"I'll go with you," Adair told him. Kinley, who hadn't noticed Red in the crowd, turned and stared at him. He had heard about what some little redheaded guy had done on the Otis job up in Arkansas, and for Pat Corey in Simonton, but he said nothing about it.

"Son, you got any idea what you're stepping into?" he asked instead.

"Yes sir, I do," Red answered. "I been there before, only the other times it wasn't burning. At least with this one I know where the fire's gonna be."

"You do," said Kinley, "but what you don't know is how hot it is. You see that truck?" He gestured with his head to an old flatbed Chevy ablaze fifty feet from the well. "That truck's gonna be nothing but molten iron before I get this fire out," he said. "Most of the rig's already melted. That's how hot it is. You still want to go up there with me?"

Red nodded.

"Well, let's not waste any more time," said Kinley.

It took them two days to get the fire out and kill the blowout. During that time, the only words Kinley spoke to Red were terse orders, shouted over the roaring of the well. When they were done, the two of them sat on an empty case of dynamite, drinking a beer. Neither one had gone to bed the previous night; their eyes were red from smoke and lack of sleep, and they were covered with oil and dirt. Kinley was forty-five, twenty years older than Adair, with twenty-five years of experience working on wells. He stood a head taller and outweighed Red by eighty pounds, but in his heart, he knew his young helper was his equal.

"I heard about you," Kinley said. "You're the one stayed with the blowout up in Arkansas, and that one Pat Corey had, too. I'd heard you don't run from a blowin' well."

"No sir, not yet," Red said.

"Well, you work for me it has to be never. First time you do, just keep on goin' and don't come back." Then Kinley took a hundred-dollar bill out of his wallet and gave it to Red for his two days' work.

Myron Kinley didn't hire Red full-time until five years later, in 1946, but he began using him on jobs as often as he could. Secretly, he believed Red ws the man he'd been waiting twenty years to find, someone with the courage and intelligence to learn what he knew about wild wells and take it even further, but outwardly Kinley remained as gruff and irascible as he was on the day they met.

Because the blowing wells so often spit bushels of rocks and gravel into the air along with the gas and oil, Red took his standard-issue, tin, oil-patch hard hat and bolted it onto a football helmet to protect his head when he worked near a blowout. To get Red's attention, or to show his displeasure, Kinley would come up and hit Red on his custom-made headgear with a large crescent wrench. "I swear to God, Kemmie," Red would say when he got home, "I can't tell you if the dents in this hard hat are from rocks or from the Old Man's wrench." But in spite of Kinley's wrench and his reluctance to praise Red to his face, the bond between them grew, until finally a job came along that proved to Myron Kinley that not only was Red Adair a talented, hardworking man, he was blessed.

EDINBURG, TEXAS — 1941

It was a gas well twenty-five miles north of the Mexican border, and a week before Christmas, the day after the Otis snubbing crew got there to run wire-line tools downhole, it began to kick. The men could feel it, shaking the rig just a little from time to time, causing the ground all around it to tremble, and they would pause in their work and glance quickly over their shoulders the way a person does when he thinks he is being followed down a dark street. Then it would stop, and the men would go back to what they were doing. The kick stayed with them though, coming and going for five days, and though the weather was cold, you could see the sweat beading up on their foreheads and running in rivulets down their necks.

The gas pressure at the surface was 3,000 pounds per square inch and they had 5,000-pound preventers on the well, so it seemed things were under control, for a while anyway. On Christmas Eve, Red Adair and a man named Luke Long were working the preventer chokes, opening them by hand a little at a time to bleed off some of the well's pressure, but not so much that the mud in the well bore would drain through the gas and let the well come loose. Another Otis hand named Moose McMullen was with them, down in the cellar, underneath the rig floor.

This well was owned by a man named Paul Kyser, an oil field pioneer who founded the El Paso Natural Gas Company, one of the biggest gas companies in the United States. Kyser, a graduate of Baylor University, was known in the oil patch for his intelligence and attention to detail, and when his well in Edinburg started kicking, he brought Myron Kinley to the location on a standby basis, just in case. Kinley was fifty feet from the well, standing with the tool pusher and the company man, watching the rig and the three men crouched around the preventer stack in the cellar, and he would remember what he was about to see for the rest of his life.

By opening the chokes, or rams, on the preventers, Red and Luke had bled off well pressure, letting gas escape down pipes, known as low lines, that ran from the preventers out onto the prairie near the rig. When enough gas had been released, Red knelt beside the bottom preventer and quickly spun the wheel that closed its rams. He then picked up a wrench to lock the wheel in place, when the pressure surged upward like an underground tornado and tore the preventer stack from its threaded seat on the casing head.

Red could feel himself rising on the column of gas, his arms wrapped around the preventer, up through the cellar, past the draw works and the swivel, into the center of the derrick. Everything in the cellar went with him, and amazingly, he could see all of it, spinning, splintering, banging off the derrick's girders and flying every which way through the air like an exploding house: enormous metal valves and collars, chains and tools, the hundred two-by-twelve boards, each ten feet long, that lined the cellar, the other men down in there with him, all twisting and turning, higher and higher through the derrick, obscured, in part, by the swirling stream of dust-laden gas. He let go of the preventer and continued up, and when he neared the apex of his flight, a two-by-twelve smacked him in the ass and sent him even higher. (He must have risen eighty feet, passing his whirling friend Luke Long on the way up, then passing him again on his descent.) But he never touched a girder, and in his wild, careering trip the only thing that struck him was the single two-by-twelve. When he landed on the floor of the rig beside the shredded remains of the rotary table, he was on his feet, with the wrench still in his hand. He hopped lightly fifteen feet to the ground, looked at Myron Kinley, the tool pusher, and the company man, and drew his sleeve across his brow. "Holy shit," he said. "That was some ride."

Of the six other rig hands blown into the air, two died. Luke broke his arm and neck, and Moose was in the hospital for a month. Only Red was able to come to work the next day. It took him and Kinley more than a week but they finally got the well shut in.

KEMMIE

I remember that time he got blown out of the cellar very well, because that's when Mr. Kinley said he didn't want anyone else but Red working with him anymore. Still, Mr. Kinley didn't have enough jobs to put Red on full-time. I remember Red tried real hard to get that well finished in time to be home on New Year's Eve, but he didn't make it. When he did come home, he was real upset about the men who'd been killed. "That was a mean, mean well, Kemmie," he told me. It was like it had a personality as far as he was concerned. Like he had to get it before it killed anybody else.

He had changed by then. Something about him was different from the time he went to work for Otis. Before that, he always worked hard, but he was happy-go-lucky too. Then he got into the oil field and that changed. Maybe he realized he'd found his destiny, but he became . . . I was going to say obsessed, and I guess that's true, because forever after, no matter what else he was doing, or where he was, his mind was on the oil patch. His soul was there too. That's where he always was.

There was another reason for the change in Red's temperament. On October 6, 1940, Kemmie had given birth to their first child, a boy they named James Paul. The baby was at least a month early, the doctor said, and suffered from hyaline membrane disease, a respiratory distress syndrome characterized by the inability of the baby's stiff, immature lungs to function properly.

Hyaline membrane disease is one of the most common findings in premature infants. Today, treatment would probably begin before birth by giving the mother steroids to prevent respiratory distress in the newborn baby. At birth, the baby would then most likely be placed on a respirator through which additional, recently developed drugs, used to counteract any infections accompanying the lung problems, could be administered as a spray or mist. If carried by the mother for thirty or thirty-two weeks, as Jimmy Adair was, the newborn's chances for survival in a modern medical facility would be seventy to eighty percent. In 1940, however, when the only treatment for hyaline membrane disease was to place the baby in an oxygen tent and hope for the best, chances for survival were close to zero, and on the morning after the night Jimmy was born, the doctor came to Red and told him he didn't think his son would live.

To make matters worse, Jimmy's delivery — a Caesarean section — had been long and very difficult and left Kemmie so sick that at first the doctors were afraid neither she *nor* the baby would make it. For two days Red stayed in the hospital, sleeping in the waiting room, drinking black coffee, and eating an occasional sandwich brought to him by his sisters or Kemmie's sister, Jonilee, and dividing his waking hours between bedside vigils for his wife and son.

On the evening of the second day, he awoke with a start from a brief nap. "Something's not right," he thought, and rushed through the swinging doors into the maternity ward. Before any of the hospital personnel could stop him he found his way to the small treatment room where his son lay in a shallow bassinet. The doctor and two nurses in the room turned in surprise from the baby as Red burst into the room. "I'm sorry," said the doctor. "It's hopeless. He's dead."

Red leaned down over his tiny son. Jimmy's skin was blue from lack of oxygen and felt cold and clammy to Red's touch, but as he stared intently at the baby, concentrating with all his might, he still sensed the presence of life. "He isn't dead," he screamed. "I know he isn't. I can feel it. Don't let him go! Please, don't let him go!"

The doctor had already left the room to fill out a death certificate and one of the nurses followed him, but the second nurse, who was also a nun, was so moved by the intensity of Red's plea she stayed and began working on the baby, breathing into his mouth, pressing gently on the frail chest, over and over, until finally he began to breathe. "I told you he was alive," Red shouted at the incredulous doctor, who had returned to the room. "Now you stay with him, because he's gonna make it."

Jimmy did make it, but even after he was brought home from the hospital he was frail and sickly with respiratory and stomach problems, and the medical bills for him and Kemmie ran up into hundreds of dollars — far more than the Adairs could afford. "We'll pay 'em, don't you worry. You just get yourself well," Red said. "There won't be any problems, you'll see." But when he and Jonilee came to the hospital to take Jimmy home, the nun in charge of the desk told them they couldn't remove the baby from the hospital until all the bills were paid.

Jonilee tried to reason with the nun. "We're honest people," she said. "All the bills will get paid. But you have to let Jimmy go home. The doctor said you can't hold a human being hostage for a debt." Her arguments were to no avail. The nun sat impassively behind the desk and just shook her head.

"Jonilee, let me take care of this," Red finally said. "You go into the nursery and get Jimmy." Before the nun could get out of her chair, Jonilee went into the nursery, scooped Jimmy from his crib, and returned to the reception area where Red was waiting. The two of them began walking toward the door, Jonilee holding Jimmy, Red walking purposefully in front of her, his narrowed eyes daring anyone in the reception area to stop them. Just before they reached the door, Red stopped and turned to the nun, who was still sitting behind her desk, and snarled, "I wish you were a man, because if you were I would beat the hell out of you."

Soon after the blowout at the Smackover well, Red's reputation brought him plenty of work, enough to pay the doctors, nurses, and all the hospital bills incurred by Jimmy's birth and ensure that he and his family would never be penniless again, for a man who can save a company a ton of money is a sought-after commodity in any business, and in the ultra-high-risk petroleum industry he is a treasure second only to the riches lying under the ground.

CHAPTER TEN

Even with all the modern geological advances at its disposal — sonic surveys of the earth's rock layers, or seismology, the use of infrared photography to locate hydrocarbon traps, laser probes of the continental shelves — a petroleum company is rolling the dice every time it drills a hole. Consider this irony, for example: The first successful oil well in the United States, the Drake well, drilled just outside Titusville, Pennsylvania, in August of 1859, bottomed out at sixtynine and a half feet, to the delight of the unemployed railroad conductor who owned it, Edwin L. "Colonel" Drake. The colonel had been prepared, he told anyone who would listen, to drill as deep as a thousand feet if he had to. In comparison, the record depth for a well in this country is held by Loffland Brothers Drilling, who drilled a hole in southwestern Oklahoma for Lone Star Producing Company in 1974. Loffland's Rig 32 spent 504 days to go down 31,441 feet, 239 feet shy of six miles, at which depth they struck not oil, nor gas, but molten sulfur, for which they had no use at all.

The gamble becomes even more pronounced when you take into account the complexity of the drilling process and the dozens of people needed to accomplish it. The relationships between one group of these people and another in the oil patch have varied and shifted over the years, but one thing has remained constant: each has always been dependent on the others for a successful conclusion.

In the early days, back when Red Adair was starting out in the oil patch, the major oil companies such as Texaco, Mobil, Shell, and Gulf owned their own drilling rigs, and every man on one of their wells worked for them. But there were many independents in those days, small oil companies or individuals betting on a dream. Some owned property or had a lease on land with proven oil reserves. Others, known as wildcatters, were willing to drill in territory where no oil had previously been discovered. These independents were called oil-field operators, or operating companies, the same name used for the major petroleum producers. They had to have someone drill a well for them, and so gave rise to the independent drilling contractor.

When the great oil boom of the 1950s arrived, the major oil companies had so many wells to drill they didn't have enough rigs of their own to do all the work, so they sometimes hired drilling contractors as well. Then legislation was passed that gave an oil company a tax write-off if it hired an independent contractor to drill its well. Once that happened, the majors figured they were crazy to own their rigs and keep drillers, roughnecks, and mechanics on the payroll when they could have a giant tax deduction instead, so they got rid of their drilling equipment and the men who ran it. This produced a windfall for drilling contractors, who began charging more and more money to drill wells for the majors. The majors naturally objected to rates they considered exorbitant, so several, such as Chevron, bought their own offshore and land rigs and went into the drilling business once again. Nevertheless, about 98 percent of all drilling in the United States today is done by independent drilling contractors.

At any rate, once an operator, major or independent, decides where he wants to drill a well, the first thing he does is write a program, a recipe book that details exactly how he wants this well drilled. Every drilling company, in turn, has a catalogue listing its equipment and capabilities, and using these catalogues as guidelines, the operator submits his program to a number of drilling companies for bids. The eventual contract to drill the well may not be given to the lowest bidder, because oil-field operators place as much weight on a driller's integrity as they do on his price.

There are several kinds of contracts between operators and drilling companies in the oil patch. The driller may be contracted for a set fee to drill a particular well and be paid by the day, according to the number of feet he drills, or he may be paid a flat day rate regardless of the number of feet he drills. There is also an agreement known as a "turnkey contract" in which the drilling contractor is given a drilling program and then sent out to drill the well without any supervision by the operator. The drilling contractor, under this arrangement, supplies all the equipment that's needed to drill the well in exchange for a set, one-time fee. In these cases, when he's finished with the well he turns it over to the oil company, supposedly having fulfilled all the requirements of the company's program. A turnkey deal can be very risky for an operator if he doesn't have a scrupulous drilling contractor working for him, but it is often the only way a small, independent oil man can go.

Down in South Texas they tell the story of a rancher who had some land just north of the Rio Grande where he was convinced there was oil. He hired a drilling contractor on a turnkey basis, but he only had enough money to pay the driller for a 3,000-foot well. The driller went down 3,000 feet and found nothing.

"Listen," the rancher said. "I *know* there's oil down there. I can feel it in my bones. But I'm plumb out of money. Keep goin' another thousand feet and I'll give you a piece of the profits."

"Uh-uh," said the driller. "I ain't drilling another *ten* feet unless you pay for it."

The rancher tried some more to persuade the driller, but to no avail. The driller cemented over the hole, took his rig, and left.

Now there are some drilling contractors as willing as an operator to gamble. These men *will* drill a well for a part interest in it. Though this can reduce a driller to poverty overnight, there are a number of drilling contractors who have stayed in business through the current slump in the oil patch because they took deals for a percentage of the profit and wound up with producing oil wells and a steady income when nobody was drilling any new wells. The rancher found one of these men who had an added incentive. He had once been in business with the first driller and now hated his ex-partner's guts.

"I'll give you a half interest in the well if you'll drill it 2,500 feet further for me," the rancher told him.

"Hell, for a half interest and a chance to show that ex-partner of mine up I'll drill the son of a bitch to 10,000 feet," the second driller said. He towed his equipment onto the rancher's land, rigged up over the 3,000-foot well and went to work. At 3,200 feet he struck enough oil to eventually make him and the rancher $10 million each.

Once a deal has been struck between an operator and a drilling contractor, the driller builds a location to fit the size of the rig he intends to use. Drilling rigs are generally rated by their depth capabilities, not the amount of space they occupy, but to get an idea of how big they can be, one Parker rig, transported by barge to the North Slope of Alaska, measured 300 feet long by 300 feet wide with a derrick 280 feet high. At the other end of the scale are lightweight "helicopter rigs" less than half that size, constructed of smaller, more maneuverable sections that can be airlifted to remote locations by helicopter. Obviously, there is a great deal of difference between a location's requirements in West Texas, where you just have to level the ground and move in the rig, or "rig up," and the Sumatran jungle, where roads have to be cut, swamps filled or drained, and supplies flown in from thousands of miles away.

Offshore drilling requires an array of drilling rigs completely distinct from those constructed on dry land, and is generally more expensive than land drilling because of the cost of transporting everything across the sea. (It is also more dangerous, since there's nowhere to run if there's trouble.) There are jack-up rigs, which can be used in water up to about 350 feet deep, built so that they float when being moved to the location. Once at the drilling site, their legs, which look like sections of a giant erector set, are cranked down until they hit the ocean floor. Then the hull is raised, or jacked up, above the water's surface, and drilling begins.

Submersible offshore rigs have hulls on which the rig floats while it is towed through the water. Once on site, these hulls are flooded and come to rest on the bottom. The drilling deck, or Texas deck as it's often called, is constructed on long steel columns extending upward from the hulls. As in the case of a jack-up rig, a submersible rig can only be used in relatively shallow water.

A semisubmersible rig, like a submersible rig, has hulls used to float the rig to a location, but these hulls are designed so that when they are flooded they sink only a little below the surface of the water instead of all the way to the ocean floor. They can be used in water of any depth and, because of their stability, are considered an excellent choice for drilling where rough, stormy conditions, such as those in the North Sea, will be encountered.

There are also drilling-equipped, ocean-going vessels known as drill ships that are highly mobile and often used to drill exploratory wells in very deep water far from land. There are inland barge rigs — large, flat-bottomed barges outfitted with drilling apparatus and used in marshy areas such as the Mississippi Delta where the soil is not firm enough to support a land rig. These barges are towed to the drilling site, sunk to the bottom of the marsh, and held in place by pilings driven deep into the earth.

After an exploratory offshore well drilled by one of these methods has proven there is a significant hydrocarbon formation at a location, an offshore platform — similar to Piper Alpha in the North Sea and, like Piper, usually constructed on land — is floated or towed in sections to the site. There, using huge barge-mounted cranes, its pieces are assembled and then anchored to the seabed, making the platform a permanent installation until the formation below it is depleted.

Once a deal has been struck between an oil-field operator and a drilling company to drill a well on land, the site is prepared. The drilling company levels the area with bulldozers, runs pipe to a water supply — a river, a lake, a reservoir they had to dig — cuts a road over the prairie or through the woods, or builds a landing strip if necessary, sets up generators to provide electrical power, and puts a chain link fence around the location. In the center of the leveled ground, directly above the spot the operator believes there's oil, a large hole is dug, say, forty feet square and ten feet deep, which will be the cellar below the floor of the drilling rig.

At this point, the operating company sends its field representative — the "company man" — to the location, where he will stay in a trailer or some other temporary dwelling, on call twenty-four hours a day, until the well is completed. The company man is in charge of the operation at the site. He buys all the drill pipe, the mud, the cement, and all other supplies necessary to drill the well, and he makes sure that the drilling contractor is drilling the well the way the operator wants it drilled. He also makes sure that everybody on the job gets paid.

The top man on location for the drilling company, known as the "tool pusher," will also live on-site while the well is being drilled. Like the company man, he has a copy of the program, and every morning he will give a report to his boss back in the main office concerning the progress made on the well, the maintenance of his company's equipment, fuel costs, and any additional costs for equipment he's had to rent. These extras may include mud-servicing equipment, safety equipment, or electronic devices known as logging equipment, needed to monitor what's going on down in the hole. The tool pusher is also responsible for the drilling crew working on the rig: the driller, who controls the bit drilling at the bottom of the hole; the derrickman, who handles the lengths of drill pipe coming out of the hole from his perch up on the monkey board; the roughnecks and other floor hands, who screw or unscrew (make up or break out) individual lengths of pipe on the rig floor and keep equipment there clean; the motor man, who keeps the engines powering the rig running; and the rig mechanic and electrician, who assist him. The company man supervises the tool pusher, the tool pusher tells the driller what to do, and the driller oversees the floor men and other rig workers.

Then there are the service companies involved in the well — the drilling-mud company, for instance, and the company supplying the cement used to secure the casing pipe; or companies such as Otis Pressure Control doing valve or wire-line work on the well. Whether each of these is responsible to the operator or the drilling company depends upon the terms of contract between the oil man and the well driller, but in either case, the work of the service company crews is invaluable and has to be integrated into the overall drilling operation.

The Red Adair Company is also a service company, working almost always for the oil-field operator — the oil company — but when Red comes on a job the situation is dire, often a matter of life and death, and though he is responsible to whoever hires him, he takes over control of the location. Nevertheless, there are occasions when several parties, each with his own interest, are pulling on him at the same time.

What Red wants to do is get the job done as quickly and safely as possible. If he can, he'll save the drilling company's equipment and leave the formation intact so the operator can resume production, but the fire may be so intense he has to pull the rig over and drag it out of the way to kill the blaze. If this happens, the insurance company has to pay the drilling contractor for a rig, which of course they'd rather not do. On the other hand, if the rig is severely damaged, the drilling contractor would just as soon declare it a total loss and collect from the insurance company, a situation analogous to wanting your car declared a total loss after a bad accident, instead of having your insurance company insist that a body shop piece it back together.

In the early stages of drilling a well, however, when the location has been prepared, the cellar dug and lined on all sides with boards, and the company man and tool pusher on site, the last thing anyone is thinking about is a blowout or a fire. At this point, a pile driver is brought in, and right in the middle of the cellar it pounds a piece of pipe, two feet or more in diameter, into the ground. This pipe, called conductor pipe, is driven down until it hits a seal — a thick shelf of rock — usually occurring at a depth somewhere between twenty and one hundred feet. The pile driver is removed, the drilling rig is brought in and assembled above the cellar, and the actual well-drilling operation begins.

The principal structure of the rig is a large, rectangular steel floor, fifteen to twenty feet in the air above the cellar, supported by a framework of steel beams. In the middle of this floor, right over the hole being drilled, the derrick, or mast, is erected. This skeletal derrick is constructed of long, vertical steel beams cross-braced every twelve to fifteen feet by horizontal steel supports known as girts.

Red Adair was blown up through the derrick a second time back in the early 1940s at a gas well near McAllen, Texas, when a pipe on the wellhead known as a drilling spool exploded. This time, Red's flight was one way, because somehow he managed to hook an arm over the derrick's fourth girt, between forty-eight and sixty feet above the rig floor. For a few seconds he hung there, waiting until all the debris in the air fell back to earth. Then he climbed down the derrick. His arm was sore, but not sore enough to keep him from going back to work.

At the top of the derrick, ordinarily about 150 feet high, sits the crown block, an anchored set of six or eight pulleys. Below the crown block, halfway up the inside of the derrick, hangs the traveling block, a similar set of pulleys that can move up or down. Below the traveling block, and attached to it, are an enormous hook and swivel that in turn are attached to the components that drill the well.

Bolted to the swivel is the topmost of these components, a piece of pipe called the kelly. The kelly runs through a large steel plate, known as the rotary table, that is flush with the rig floor. As the kelly passes through the rotary table, it can be grabbed and released by a strong bushing — the kelly bushing — located in the center of the table. Unlike all the other pipe and bushings used in drilling a well, the kelly and its bushing are square, so that when the rotary table spins them at high speed the kelly will not slip. The kelly is threaded onto a piece of round pipe in turn threaded onto the drill pipe running into the hole. At the bottom of the hole, connected to this drill pipe, is the drilling bit.

At the back of the rig floor, or underneath it on some installations, are a number of eight-cylinder Caterpillar diesel engines, which provide the rig's power. These engines drive the draw works, a large piece of machinery shaped like the back end of a garbage truck, positioned near the rotary table on the rig floor. Inside the draw works is a large revolving drum around which hundreds of feet of heavy steel cable is spooled. This cable, or drilling line, runs up into the derrick, around the pulleys of the crown block, around the pulleys of the traveling block, and down under the floor, where it is hooked to an anchor. There is also a chain inside the draw works linking it to the rotary table, along with several gears, clutches, and a main brake to bring the draw works to an instant halt.

Next to the draw works is a control panel with dials, gauges, and levers, and in front of this control panel stands the rig's driller. By moving one of the levers, he can spool or unspool the steel cable in the draw works, thereby raising or lowering the traveling block. That, in turn, raises or lowers the hook and swivel, all the drill pipe in the hole, and the drilling bit on the bottom. Another lever activates the chain drive running from the draw works to the rotary table.

When the driller wants to drill, he unspools some cable. This lowers the square kelly into its square bushing and drops the string of drill pipe and the bit to the bottom of the well. Then the driller engages the clutch of the draw works' chain drive. The chain spins the rotary table, the rotary table spins the kelly, and the kelly spins the drill pipe and the bit. Moving the levers in the opposite direction stops the spinning rotary table and raises the kelly out of its bushing. The driller does this if he wants to put more pipe in the hole or remove lengths of pipe, or if he has a problem.

Drill pipe is threaded together in thirty-foot sections known as joints of pipe. When more joints are added to the string in the hole (tripping in), or joints are removed (tripping out), the upper end of the pipe is handled by the derrick man high above the floor on the monkey board. The bottom end of the joint is threaded or unthreaded by rotary helpers, on the floor, using huge wrenches called tongs.

The gauges on the control panel tell the driller about conditions downhole, and by closely monitoring them he knows whether or not he has trouble. The gauges tell him about formation pressure, mud circulation, resistance against the drilling bit, and the weight of everything hanging in the derrick.

Say, for instance, the weight gauge registers 130,000 pounds. The driller drops the bit onto the bottom of the hole and the gauge then registers 120,000 pounds. That means he has 120,000 still hanging in the derrick and 10,000 pounds resting on the bottom of the hole. That 10,000 pounds is the weight on the drilling bit. You need weight on the bit in order to cut further into the formation — to "make more hole" — but too much weight will tear the bit up. You can apply 4,000–5,000 pounds per inch of the bit's diameter, and since the driller knows the size of the bit he's got in the hole, he knows how much weight the bit can withstand. If he needs more weight to make hole than his bit will stand, he pulls the drill string out and installs a larger bit.

If something in the hole starts to grab the pipe, or the bit encounters excessive resistance, he can stop drilling before he ruins the bit or breaks the pipe. If the rate of mud circulating up out of the hole suddenly increases dramatically, indicating an unforeseen surge in formation pressure — a kick — he can respond by increasing the mud weight to counterbalance this pressure, or, if necessary, by closing the blowout preventers.

Once the conductor pipe has been hammered into the ground, and all the rig's machinery put in place, the actual drilling can begin. Assuming the conductor pipe is twenty inches in diameter, the driller starts work with a 17½-inch bit connected to drill pipe that fits inside the 20-inch conductor pipe. He starts drilling, pumping mud downhole as he goes. The mud circulates back up the outside of the drillpipe, is cleaned, gets picked up and pumped downhole again. This drilling continues until the driller drills through a freshwater zone, which can be anywhere from 200 to 3,000 feet down. The freshwater zone must, by law, be protected from contamination.

When the driller reaches this level, say, 1,000 feet down, he pulls everything on his drill string out of the hole and puts joints of sixteen-inch pipe — called casing pipe — inside the twenty-inch conductor pipe all the way to the bottom. Then cement is pumped down that sixteen-inch casing pipe. The cement runs out the bottom, and when enough has been pumped so that it comes back to the surface, the pumping stops and the cement is allowed to set. When it does, the driller has sixteen-inch pipe cemented from the surface to a depth of 1,000 feet. On top of that pipe he installs the bradenhead — the large blowout preventer flange — and his stack of blowout preventers.

Next, the driller puts a smaller drill pipe and a smaller bit —probably 14¾ inches in diameter — on the end of the kelly, runs it down inside the sixteen-inch pipe, and continues drilling, all the while increasing the mud weight to hold back the pressure from inside the formation. But now the driller must be very careful. He must watch his pressure gauges like a hawk, as well as the gauges monitoring fluid return to the surface. If he drills into a hydrocarbon pocket — a zone in the formation with lower pressure than the zones above it — the heavy mud will drain through that low-pressure zone, creating a disastrous state of affairs known as "loss of circulation."

It happens all the time. Upward pressure in a well supports ten-, twelve-, or even fourteen-pound drilling mud down to fifteen or twenty thousand feet. Suddenly, the driller hits a subnormal zone — one without even enough upward pressure to support a column of water. The drilling mud in the hole, which weighs nearly twice the amount of a similar volume of water, can't be supported by the subnormal zone, so it goes south, right through the low-pressure pocket, leaving nothing behind to counteract the high-pressure zones further up the well. If the driller is lucky, he can get his blowout preventers closed and pump fluid mixtures through them and into the hole to remedy the situation. If not, he's got a blowout on his hands and he calls Red Adair.

What Red must do in a situation like this is form what is known as a bridge — a plug, actually — between the low-pressure and high-pressure zones of the well. This bridge can be anything in the world that will form a seal over the low-pressure zone. Then heavy mud can be pumped into the well, the seal will stop the mud from draining through the low-pressure zone, and the upward pressure of the blowing high-pressure zone will be counterbalanced.

Over the years, Red has pumped all manner of things into wells to form bridges, grabbing whatever he could lay hands on quickest. He's pumped in rags and ground-up automobile tires from junkyards near the drilling site, or chicken feathers and peanut shells from nearby farms. He's used panty hose and sanitary napkins by the trailerfull, and golf balls or marbles by the ton.

The idea, though, from the drilling contractor's point of view, is not to have to call Red Adair in the first place, so each time the driller stops drilling and trips out of the hole — whether to install a fresh, sharp bit, or to add joints of pipe, or for any number of other reasons — he sets a new string of casing pipe, taking care to get a good cement job. Then, if he does encounter low pressure, nothing will come blowing up the outside of the pipe and he is much better protected, because the only way out of the hole is through the blowout preventers.

The driller continues decreasing the size of the drill pipe as he goes further and further into the ground, because every time he trips out he has to trip back in with smaller diameter casing that will fit inside the previous string. There is a whole science in the petroleum business devoted to pipe design — people have Ph.D.'s in the subject — but basically an oil man wants the biggest size pipe possible downhole so he can bring more oil or gas up quicker. Generally speaking, the size of the casing at the well's final depth ranges from $9\frac{5}{8}$ inches to a narrow 4 inches. If the driller is successful, if he's drilled the well to the depth agreed upon in the drilling program without blowing the rig into the next county, he pulls all the drill pipe out of the hole, leaving casing almost to the bottom. Below that casing he leaves open hole — hole with no pipe in it — down into the formation. That open hole is filled with mud, which sits, like heavy cream on top of skim milk, holding back the oil or gas in the formation.

Now, a wire-line company comes in and runs electronic tools down the well that tell them at what various depths the pockets of oil and gas are located, what the rock formations look like, the condition of all the pipe, and what kind of cementing job the cementing company did. All this information is logged on the surface. There's even a recently developed tool called a ring laser gyro that goes downhole and measures every twist and turn, every directional change, and every alteration in density of the entire formation. This information is relayed to a machine aboveground that uses it to draw a detailed picture of the entire underground landscape in the vicinity of the well.

When all the wire-line work is completed, a final string of casing pipe, slightly narrower than all the rest (seven-inch pipe would be an average size for this), is run from the surface all the way down to, and then through, the open hole, through the mud and through the formation below it, and *that* casing pipe is cemented. Next, a scraping tool travels the length of the seven-inch casing, cleaning all the cement, mud, and any other residue off the inside, and then the well is perforated.

Perforation, the blowing of holes in the well's casing, is necessary in order to let oil or gas exit the formation and come up the well bore. There are all sorts of perforation guns, the most advanced of which shoot specially designed bullets through all the layers of casing and cement into the formation at speeds up to 150,000 feet per second. (By comparison, the muzzle velocity of a .357 Magnum revolver firing factory-loaded ammunition is slightly more than 1,400 feet per second.) Some perforation guns still in use were originally developed to shoot holes in German tanks during World War II. Some, made from a ceramic material, or metal alloy, literally disappear from the force of the explosion, leaving only a little piece of wire behind. Others fire a stream of molten ions with such intensity they can put a hole the size of a dime in a wine glass and leave the rest of the glass intact.

But no matter what kind of gun is used, the principle is the same: A charge of very high explosives is packed behind one or more projectiles, and the device is lowered into the well to a point where the wire-line log has determined there is oil or gas. The charge is electronically detonated by a wire leading from the gun to the surface of the well. The projectile perforates the well bore, bringing in the formation, and the oil company is in business.

That's the modern way. In the early days, back when Red Adair was roaming from job to job in the oil fields of the South and Southwest, perforation was done by men known as shooters.

RED

I knew a number of shooters, and one of 'em was crazier and wilder than the next. There was a time in the early forties, when I took any kind of work I could find in the oil patch, that I did some shooting myself. What you did was drive from well to well with the trunk of your car or the bed of your truck filled with nitroglycerine. Once you got to the well, if you got there, you took a bottle and filled it with some of your nitroglycerine, lowered it down the final casing string to where they thought the production was, and dropped a rock on it, or dropped this metal device called a go-devil down the hole, until the nitro went off and just blew the shit out of everything.

Soon as I could, I quit that kind of shooting, 'cause the roads to those wells were hardly roads at all and gettin' to 'em was just too dangerous, since nitro's about the most unstable stuff ever invented by man. It's strange stuff too. I heard about one guy who drove from Beaumont, Texas, all the way to Mexico to shoot a well, takin' dirt roads all the way 'cause they wouldn't let you travel on the main highway with nitro. He must've hit three or four thousand bumps and nothing happened, but when he got out of his car at the well and slammed the door that nitroglycerine blew him, the car, and the whole damn oil rig back across the border. That was about the way it went for a shooter. They had a real short life span and when they died they were vaporized.

Sure, it was dangerous back in those days, but you kept your eyes open and that's how you learned. I once saw a length of pipe — a lubricator, we call it — that you put above a valve on top of the casing head or tubing head to seal off the well's pressure so you can run your wire-line equipment into the well bore . . . I saw one blow up and kill three men over in Louisiana. See, they'd run that line into the well and pulled it out and run it in again, over and over, and that lubricator was worn thin by the line running through it until, wham! The well pressure blew it apart in a million pieces, like a giant hand grenade. So after that, I'd keep track of how many runs that wire line made through the lubricator in my little notebook I carried, and I'd make sure that son of a bitch got changed in plenty of time.

Later on, when I went to work for Mr. Kinley full-time, I'd keep notes on all that kind of equipment and have it magnafluxed after a while to make sure there were no weak spots or hairline cracks you couldn't see with the naked eye. Guys would tease me about it and say, "Hey Red, what the hell you doin', writin' love letters?" I'd say, "Well, Buddy, I've ridden a drilling spool sixty feet in the air. I rode a blowout preventer higher'n that, and I've seen a lubricator kill three men. You laugh, but it might be your ass I'm savin'."

See, people call me a daredevil, but they don't understand. A daredevil's reckless, and that ain't me. The devil's down in that hole and I've seen what he can do, and I'm not darin' him at all. I'm a beware devil, that's what I am.

In the early 1940s Red scrambled, picking up work in the oil field wherever he could, when he wasn't on a job with either Otis Pressure Control or Myron Kinley. He did wire-line work — snubbing, drilling under pressure, pulling pipe out of the hole to clean it — for any oil-field service company that would put him on. He worked for Pat Corey on rigs all over South Texas, and for Schlumberger, Lane Wells, Cameron Iron Works, and Otis Pressure Control throughout the East Texas oil field; from Baytown, where years before he'd watched Bill Williamson chase the pig, up to Madisonville, across to Sour Lake, and further east, into Louisiana, sleeping on the ground, or on the rig floor, or on a sheet of plywood underneath a truck. If there were no other jobs to be had, he'd swamp for Haliburton, washing the mud and oil off their pumping trucks, tearing the machinery apart to clean it, then drawing sketches of it before he put it back together.

He worked in the Goose Creek field, where the wells stood side by side as far as the eye could see, their flares lighting up the sky at night so that a man could drive for a hundred miles without headlights, and there was so much oil it ran down the streets and clogged the sewers. Rig hands lived in a tent city there, along with speculators, gamblers, and whores, and often, in that great human stew, seething and scrabbling in the ankle-deep black ooze, the only way you could tell the difference between a millionaire wildcatter and a penniless roughneck was by the wildcatter's ten-gallon hat and the bourbon whiskey that he drank (the roughneck making do with a tweed cap and a can of beer). It was there, in 1942, that Red capped a well spouting oil so thick the houses nearby looked like they'd been coated with chocolate cake batter.

Still, there were times when neither the service companies nor Myron Kinley had any work in the field. On those days, Red and Kinley would take Kinley's old 1940 Ford pickup truck with the large reel of cable in the bed, or his 1939 Ford panel truck crammed full of blasting caps, primer cord, and solidified nitroglycerine, and drive out along Sage Road, on the west end of Houston, where now the vast Galleria shopping mall stands but where, in those days, there was nothing but prairie and woods. Out there, the two of them would dig deep holes or tunnels in the ground, set their charges, and practice, over and over again, trying to perfect the explosive devices they used to perforate well bores and bring the well in, to jar loose lengths of twisted pipe stubbornly threaded onto collars far down-hole, or to blow out the fires on burning wells. They experimented by changing the concentration of nitroglycerine, by lowering the charge into a hole with different sorts of tubing and setting it off with various detonating devices, and eventually, by altering the con-figuration of the charge itself — by molding the explosive to direct its force.

Their first attempts at this were primitive. While Kinley balanced at a good distance on his one good leg and a long-handled shovel, Red would climb down into the hole he'd just dug and point the charge one way or the other to see if he could get the explosion to spin a threaded collar right off a joint of pipe. At first, all he'd ac-complish was to blow the pipe up in the air, so he began using several smaller charges placed at different points in the hole, reasoning that forces coming from different directions would create a spinning ef-fect. For months and months that didn't work either, and all he and Kinley managed to do was use up lots of nitro, make a hell of a racket, and blow up a number of hapless trees.

But Red had the touch when it came to explosives. Kinley could see that right away, though he didn't tell his helper, shaking his head instead and saying things like, "What the hell you gonna think up next?" or, "I know if we keep this up you'll blow us both to hell, boy," but by now Red was used to it. He knew, too, that Kinley was proud of him and his innovations and bragged about him behind his back, so Red kept on experimenting, and sure enough, one day in the spring of 1943, his directional explosion finally worked: the charge went off, and when the smoke cleared, a collar had been spun off a pipe without even stripping a single thread.

Eventually, Red would further refine this technique, developing shaped charges — the famed Adair flying-saucer charges — that enabled him to orchestrate enormous detonations with surgical precision. But that would not take place for several years. Within weeks of his breakthrough blast on Sage Road, Red went to work for Otis Pressure Control full-time, and even though Otis agreed to let Adair join Myron Kinley whenever Kinley went off to fight a wild well, there was almost no more free time for the two of them to practice setting off experimental charges in the woods. The next experience Red had dealing with unusual explosives came not while he worked with Myron Kinley (though of course they continued to blow out well fires), but while he served with the United States Army in Japan.

JAPAN — SEPTEMBER 1, 1945

It was still dark when the squad — the 139th Bomb Disposal Unit — started up the mountain that rose above Tokyo Harbor, and by dawn they had reached the top. There were eight men in the squad attached, for the moment, to the Eighth Army Ordnance. Later they'd work with the Eleventh Airborne Division, then with someone else, but those connections were only official, for the records. In fact, they took their orders directly from G2, army intelligence, and worked alone, a wild bunch, a band of outlaws, who would be sent out to roam the Japanese countryside, hunting for unexploded bombs to defuse, caches of ammunition and weapons, and Japanese soldiers who hadn't heard their country had surrendered two weeks earlier, or didn't care.

The squad was originally part of America's Japanese invasion force steaming north from Okinawa when the atom bomb was dropped on Hiroshima and Nagasaki in early August. They had landed in Japan the day before, on the morning of August 31st, and been immediately briefed by a major from G2. "Men, you see that ship in the harbor?" the major had said, gesturing out over the water with the sweep of an arm. "That's the battleship *Missouri*. Tomorrow, General MacArthur is going to accept the official documents of surrender on that ship from Japan's military leaders. You see that mountain up there?" The major had pointed with his other arm in the opposite direction. "We understand there may be a bunch of renegade Jap soldiers up there with some pretty heavy artillery fixing to disrupt the proceedings tomorrow on the *Missouri*, which, I don't have to tell you, would be extremely unfortunate. What I want you men to do is go on up that mountain, and if you find that my information's correct I want you to take care of the situation, and don't waste any time doing it."

Red Adair, a member of this elite unit, lay on his belly in high, wet grass, behind an outcropping of boulders at the top of the mountain, waiting for the thick, early morning fog to lift, waiting with the others to advance on a promontory covered with heavy brush that seemed the logical placement for any enemy guns. Adair was thirty years old now, the oldest man in the squad, older even than the only commissioned officer, a twenty-seven-year-old lieutenant from the Midwest.

Red had volunteered for the bomb disposal unit during his infantry training at Ft. Hood, Texas, early in 1945, knowing full well it was treacherous duty, but convinced the experience with munitions would be invaluable when he returned to the oil patch, *if* he returned. He had been welcomed into the unit because of his previous work with explosives, and because of the leadership he displayed as an infantryman. As with everything else he did, he was determined to be the best bomb disposal man the army had ever seen, especially since it had taken him so long to get into the service in the first place.

Red had tried to enlist shortly after the bombing of Pearl Harbor, but was advised at his physical that he had a hernia and was rejected. He told the doctors he felt fine, but they said they were sorry, he was unfit for duty, so, unable to afford an operation, he went back to work in the oil patch.

Months went by, then a year, then two, and Red became more and more distraught. Not only was America now fully embroiled in World War II, but the results of the fighting had begun to touch him and his family personally: Kemmie's brother Bill was killed when the plane he was flying was shot down over the Adriatic sea; her brother Lionel was a marine fighting in the Pacific, and Red's brother Bob had joined the navy. Spot Gaines, Red's old roommate and friend from the railroad shop, had been killed by a German buzz bomb, and it seemed that a week didn't go by without some young man from the Heights either dying in the war or coming home badly hurt.

"Kemmie, I don't care what they said," Red finally told her. "I'm goin' down and enlist again." This time, the doctor told Red his condition could be corrected by a simple operation. Red, determined to serve his country, immediately had the surgery done and several months later was inducted into the army.

On July 28, 1944, Kemmie gave birth to their second child, a daughter, Robyn, who was immediately nicknamed Bobbie Lou. With two children to feed, Kemmie was wondering how she was going to get along on her army allotment check of $103 a month. After basic training, Red was sent with other members of the bomb disposal unit to Oklahoma, Florida, and Ft. Ord, California, for special training in disarming and detonating all kinds of ordnance at different climates and geographical locations. Then one night, at midnight, the squad shipped out across the Pacific.

"This unit I'm in's a crazy bunch of bastards, believe me," Red told her when he called shortly before he put out to sea. "We look out for each other and don't take crap from anybody, so don't worry, I'm gonna be all right. Soon as I'm back home, we'll have some real money, you'll see."

CHAPTER ELEVEN

The fog still hung in patches on the mountaintop above Tokyo Harbor, but it was getting late, so the squad fanned out and advanced on the bluff, staying close to the ground, their weapons ready. Once or twice they heard noises in the brush and the lieutenant stopped them with an upraised hand, but when they reached a flat open section with a clear view of the harbor, whoever had been there was gone, leaving only footprints beside two loaded, sixteen-inch cannons trained on the *Missouri* far below. The lieutenant deployed most of the squad to guard the rear and either flank while he and Red unloaded the cannons. Then Red quickly placed a shaped charge over the breech of each gun, set fuses on both charges, and moved back to join the others. The men had only moments to wait; the charges, molded to direct their force up the guns' barrels, had been perfectly set, and both cannon barrels blew up, thwarting the sabotage of the surrender proceedings aboard the *Missouri* on September 1, 1945.

RED

The war was over, but those damn bombs we dug up were still alive and there were plenty of them. The countryside was full of live stuff, Japanese and American, and the mission of our squad, and others like it, was to find 'em and disarm 'em, or blow 'em up. We went into caves in the mountains that the Japanese had worked on for hundreds of years — enormous, beautiful caves — where they'd stored thousands of feet of explosives. We went up to Hokkaido, where five hundred B29s had come in on a bombing mission one night, and let me tell you, that place looked worse than Hiroshima did. There were hundreds of unexploded bombs there. They'd impacted so hard their fuses had been torn up, so they hadn't gone off. What you'd do is listen with a stethoscope as you backed the fuses out of 'em and took 'em apart. All the time you were working you'd tell the guy in the hole next to you what you were doing so if it blew up, he'd know how far you got defusing it, and then the other guys could use that information later on. It was dangerous work; squads like ours were lost all the time. But I enjoyed it. It was a lot of fun, and man, we lived good while we were doing it. Anyway, I always figured if one went off, I'd never hear the son of a bitch.

JAPAN — JANUARY 1946

The squad had been in a dozen or more caves and underground caverns, but there was something different about this one, set into the side of a mountain in the central part of the northern island of Hokkaido. For one thing, the doors were thicker and more heavily armored than the others. They were large, too, as though the opening of the cave had been made to accommodate trucks bearing massive pieces of machinery as well as munitions. Red set his charges cautiously; he had no idea whether there were explosives right behind the doors and didn't want to blow up the entire mountainside along with his squad when he took the doors down.

The doors blew open without incident. The squad moved carefully inside and saw that, in addition to tons of explosives stored in a large cavern, the cave contained a network of smaller rooms. There was a power-generating system, scientific equipment, and several large steel chambers. It was as though they had walked into a secret, abandoned factory. The men couldn't say what went on there, but they agreed it was not a standard hiding place for arms and ammunition.

Red radioed the squad's discovery to headquarters. The following day, a G2 unit joined the bomb-disposal squad, took one look inside the cave, and gathered Red and his men for a briefing. "You are to tell absolutely no one about this," the G2 commanding officer said. "As far as you are concerned, this was a routine munitions cache. Now you guys climb down outa here and see what else you can find. And by the way, good work."

Weeks later, Red was told in strict confidence by another G2 officer that his bomb-disposal unit had uncovered a secret Japanese military research laboratory. "What are you boys gonna do with that lab?" Red asked him. The officer smiled. "Even I can't tell you that," he said.

In the spring of 1946, when Red's time in the army was almost over, he was moved north to the city of Otaru on the coast of the Sea of

Japan. There was a large ammunition dump there, mostly .105- and .50-caliber shells that had been made in Sapporo. Red, and an officer from another bomb disposal unit, had been instructed to blow it all up. The ordnance, thousands and thousands of pounds of it, had been loaded onto a convoy of a dozen trucks. It was to be hauled offshore several miles and dumped overboard. On the evening before the morning the convoy was supposed to roll, the officer, a young lieutenant from New Jersey, went looking for Red to finalize the details of their mission. He found Adair in a tiny restaurant on a narrow street near the water.

Red had learned a great deal during his tour in Japan. Instead of the bitter hostility he'd expected, he found the Japanese people — even most of the Japanese military patrols he and his squad encountered — to be friendly. Red had early on decided that even though he was part of the occupying forces, it was still not his country, and had treated the local people with respect. In turn, he had been given much valuable information that had been inscrutably withheld from less sympathetic army personnel. At first, he had told these other men they'd get much further being kind, then he'd given up, assuming they were just too dumb to understand. As for himself, he never forgot this lesson, using it over and over again in later years when he fought wild wells around the world.

HOUSTON — 1946

Kemmie Lou could sing. From the time she was a little girl, when she performed with the choir at church and the chorus at school, everyone who heard her recognized that she'd been blessed. Her parents, thrilled by her talent, encouraged Kemmie. "Who knows how far she'll take it?" her singing teachers said. "A voice like that comes along only once in a very great while." So music became Kemmie's life, but when her mother died and her father moved away, although she'd sing for Red and for their family and friends, and later to her babies, the dream of a singing career receded like the whistle of a speeding train.

Then one day in 1943, when Jimmy was two years old and Red was working for Otis, Kemmie met two women — Leatha Hoff and LaVelle Godby — at a party next door to the house she and Red lived in on Avenue O in east Houston. Leatha and LaVelle could sing too, and the three of them entertained everyone at the party with show tunes, Duke Ellington numbers, and even some country and western, which Kemmie didn't ordinarily sing. When the party broke up at two in the morning, Kemmie, Leatha, and LaVelle made plans to get together and sing again, and soon they were practicing together regularly.

Before long Leatha and LaVelle, who were both a little older than Kemmie and single, were after her to form a trio and start performing professionally. This was the heyday of women's trios such as the Andrews Sisters, and people who heard Kemmie and her new friends kept telling them they were every bit as good as the groups they heard every day on the radio.

"No way," said Red, when Kemmie asked him if she could do it. "If I go in the service, then you can sing with them, but not until then."

"But Red," Kemmie said, "what's the difference whether you're in the service or not? That doesn't make any sense at all."

"Well, it makes sense to me," Red told her, and walked out of the house, thus ending the discussion.

Maybe he didn't really believe the army would ever let him in. Maybe he thought that if they did, once he *was* gone she wouldn't have the courage to go out and perform on her own. Maybe he believed that if he was away and didn't see it, then it would be as though it weren't happening at all. (This latter notion occurred to Kemmie years later when she realized that even though Red would never walk away from physical danger, he routinely turned his back on conflicts in their personal lives, pretending they didn't exist.) Whatever his reason, the fact is Red did go into the army, and when he left, Kemmie, Leatha, and LaVelle formed a trio and immediately met with success.

They got an agent, a woman who lived in Houston, who first booked them at local conventions — Shriners, Elks, groups like that — and at a number of social functions at a large Jewish temple in town. They sang every Monday night on a local radio station, and then began to tour all over Texas, playing for veterans at army hospitals in a series of variety shows sponsored by the Hughes Tool Company. They did mostly big-band shows: numbers like "Moonglow," "Mood Indigo," and "Whispering," and two of Kemmie's favorites that she sang solo — "My Man" and "The Man I Love." The soldiers loved them, people in the clubs they played loved them, and the radio audience wrote bushels of mail to the station raving about the trio's class and style.

Kemmie wrote to Red about it: "You can't imagine how much I

love singing with the trio," she told him. "It means so much to me. The music lifts my spirits, and when I sing, I really feel like I'm somebody, like this is something God meant for me to do in my life. And when I sing those two solos, all I think about is you."

Red did not approve; he made that plain to her in his letters. It seemed to her that he just couldn't understand why she wanted to sing, but Kemmie had never felt such a sense of accomplishment and was determined to keep doing it anyway. Then one day, not long before Red was due to come home, their agent called the trio together. "Girls," she said, "we've finally got the break we've been waiting for. I've got you booked into a hotel in Mexico City for six weeks on the same bill with Cantinflas. This is it, the big time. There'll be all kinds of publicity and if you do well, which I know you will, I guarantee you the next step's a recording contract."

Kemmie never went to Mexico City. She agonized about the trip for days, lying in bed at night, seeing the trio on stage in a succession of beautiful new outfits, singing in front of elegant international audiences, traveling to exotic places, then coming home and launching a successful recording career. But she wasn't single like Leatha and LaVelle, with nobody but herself to consider. She had two children now, and she knew she wouldn't have a moment's peace in Mexico City thinking she'd left them for six weeks with her sister or a friend. And besides, Red was coming home. She and Jonilee were going to drive over to San Antonio in a week to pick him up, so how could she go off traveling with the trio?

Later on, when Red was gone two hundred days a year fighting oil-well fires and she was home alone, being both mother and father to Jimmy and Bobbie Lou, she would think about what might have happened if she'd made the trip, if the trio had become famous, if she had hung onto her dream, for in effect it died when she chose to stay in Houston instead of going on the road. True, she performed with the trio a few more times. Red even came to the last of the benefit concerts they gave and acted like he was proud, but she could tell underneath he was furious, watching her standing up there with the other two girls while all these guys out in the audience were cheering and whistling, and she never sang publicly with the trio again.

When Red came home from Japan, he knew he was going to work for Myron Kinley full-time. The postwar oil boom was in full swing, Kinley had more work than he could handle alone, and he had already written to Adair telling him there was a job waiting for him as soon as Red returned. But first, before he joined Kinley, Red wanted to take a little time and twist off.

Twisting off is an oil-patch term, derived from the fact that when a drilling bit gets hung up, or stuck, at the bottom of the hole, and torque continues to be applied to it, it will snap, or twist off, from the drill pipe. After that, the drill pipe spins free, without the bit, grinding and cutting its way through dirt, gravel, and rock to slow it down. So, too, with a man working hard and long in the oil field, or anywhere else for that matter, where there is tension, or pressure, or the constant threat of injury or death. The time comes when he too wants to spin free like a drill pipe disconnected from its bit, to cut loose from any constraints, to twist off.

When Red Adair came home to Houston from the army to his wife and his son and his baby daughter, who was a year and a half old, he twisted off for a month. At first Kemmie tried to be understanding. "He's been through an ordeal," she said to Jonilee one day when her sister came to visit and asked where Red had gone. "He doesn't mention it, but you know, he could have been killed any second working with those bombs all the time. He needs to unwind." But after a while it seemed to Kemmie the stream of old buddies he had to see would never end, and when he was at home he began bringing up names of men Kemmie had never even heard of, suggesting that maybe she'd been dating them while he was gone. None of it was true, but even to be accused of infidelity shocked Kemmie and hurt her deeply, and she would lash back at Red, who would then get angry and go out once again with the boys.

She kept trying to get him to sit down and talk to her. She wanted to tell him how she had changed, how she was more self-sufficient and sure of herself than she'd been before he'd gone away, and most of all, how important singing was to her, but he refused. She couldn't understand why he resented the trio so much, and why he was so insanely jealous for no good reason. "It's like he wants to wipe out the time when he wasn't here and go back to how it was," she thought. "It's like he is trying to deny who I've become."

It was summer now. The afternoon was hot and very humid, without a trace of breeze to ruffle the curtains she'd made for the window that overlooked the narrow, dirty alley outside their house. She was twenty-four and he was thirty-one, and she remembered thinking, "We aren't children anymore; we have two of our own who depend on us, but it feels like I'm in this all alone." He was going

May, Red, Bob, and
Mrs. Adair.

Red (third from left)
with some of the
"Heights Gang."

Above left: Red's mentor, Myron M. Kinley.

Above right: Jimmie, Kemmie, and Robyn (Bobbie) sent these pictures to Red while he was in the Army to show him they were okay.

Red and Kemmie shortly after their marriage.

Devil's Cigarette Lighter,
1961–1962. We call this
the dragon picture.
Note heat wave on left.

Jimmy and Red, Carlsbad,
New Mexico, January 1964.

Red with friends and
Russian cosmonauts in the
late 1960s. The young Paul
Wayne is on Red's left.

Red in Kuwait, 1965.

Secret job in 1973
when all equipment was
painted gray.

Dubai, 1973.

On the set of *Hellfighters*
in Baytown, Texas, 1968.
From left to right: Coots,
Red, John Wayne, and Boots.

Gaylord, Michigan, in 1977.

Libya, late 1970s.

Sumatra, 1980.

Mexico, 1980.

Ixtoc, Mexico, 1979–1980.

Ixtoc, Mexico, 1979–1980.

Canada, January 1982.

Red and best friend Rush
Johnson. Note the collar
and tie on Rush. He dressed
very well, just never
quite finished the job.

Indonesia, 1984.

Robyn and Sunny today.

Candy and Jimmy Adair today.

The "Rojo Grande" averaging almost 100 mph in Miami.

Kemmie and Red today.

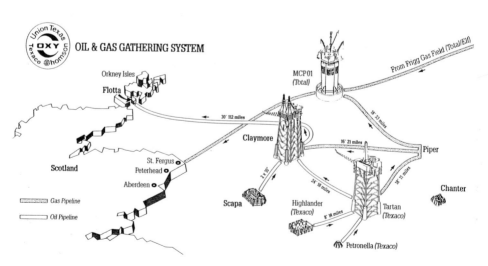

Oil- and gas-gathering system.

PIPER 'A'
PRODUCTION PLATFORM

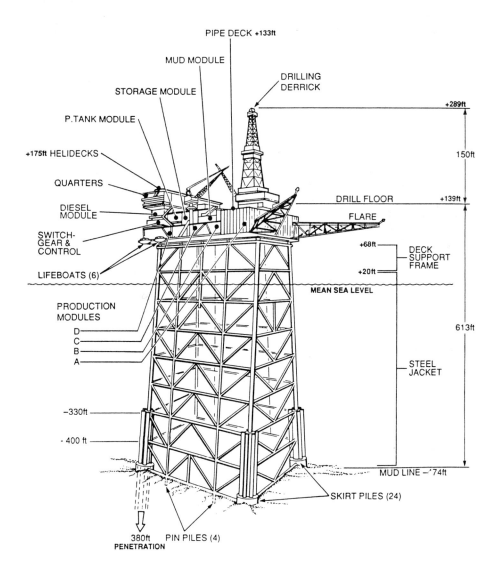

PIPE DECK +133ft

MUD MODULE

DRILLING
DERRICK

STORAGE MODULE

+289ft

P.TANK MODULE

150ft

+175ft HELIDECKS

QUARTERS

DRILL FLOOR   +139ft

DIESEL
MODULE

FLARE

SWITCH-
GEAR &
CONTROL

+68ft   DECK
                     SUPPORT
+20ft   FRAME

LIFEBOATS (6)

MEAN SEA LEVEL

PRODUCTION
MODULES

613ft

D
C
B
A

STEEL
JACKET

−330ft

- 400 ft

MUD LINE −'74ft

SKIRT PILES (24)

380ft   PIN PILES (4)
PENETRATION

Piper Alpha production platform.

Piper Alpha platform before.

Piper Alpha after.

Opposite: These three pictures were taken in a span of 5 seconds and show the second and most destructive explosion.

The Rotary Rig
and Its Components

CIRCULATING SYSTEM
1. Mud pits
2. Mud pumps
3. Standpipe
4. Rotary hose
5. Bulk mud components storage
6. Mud return line
7. Shale shaker
8. Desilter
9. Desander
10. Degasser
11. Reserve pits

ROTATING EQUIPMENT
12. Swivel
13. Kelly
14. Kelly bushing
15. Rotary table

HOISTING SYSTEM
16. Crown block and water table
17. Monkeyboard
18. Mast
19 Traveling block
20. Hook
21. Elevators
22. Drawworks
23. Cathead
24. Brake
25. Weight indicator
26. Driller's console
27. Substructure
28. Drilling line

WELL-CONTROL EQUIPMENT
29. Annular blowout preventer
30. Ram blowout preventers
31. Accumulator unit
32. Choke manifold
33. Mud-gas separator

POWER SYSTEM
34. Power-generating plant
35. Fuel tanks

PIPE AND PIPE-HANDLING EQUIPMENT
36. Conductor pipe
37. Surface casing
38. Drill pipe
39. Drill collars
40. Drill bit
41. Annulus
42. Pipe racks
43. Catwalk
44. Pipe ramp
45. Rathole
46. Mousehole
47. Tongs
48. Tong counterweights

MISCELLANEOUS
49. Doghouse
50. Walkways
51. Cellar
52. Casinghead
53. Stairways
54. Hoisting line
55. Gin pole

 Petroleum Extension Service
The University of Texas at Austin
Balcones Research Center
Austin, Texas 78758

Telephone (512) 835-3154

Red, Brian, and Raymond setting up water flow.

Men in basket being taken over from the *Tharos* to the Piper Alpha before "Stairway to Hell" was constructed.

◀ The rotary rig and its components.

Scenes from the Adairs' fiftieth anniversary party, December 1989. *Top:* the surviving Adair brothers and sisters, left to right, back row, David, Red, and Bob; front row, the twins, Faye and May. *Bottom,* left to right: Jimmy, Candy, Kimmie, Red, Sunny, Robyn, and Paul Wayne.

out again, with a couple of his friends, and suddenly she couldn't stand it any longer and began to cry.

"Red," she said, "if you leave me here today again by myself I'm not going to be here when you get back."

He turned at the door and looked at her, and she could see by the expression on his face he didn't believe for a minute she would do it, and so he walked out without saying a word. When he was gone, she got boxes and put all her clothes and the children's clothes in them and took Jimmy, who was five and a half, and Robyn, who was not yet two, and left. Her girlfriend Olive Evans, who had loaned Kemmie a nightgown for her wedding night, had a mother who ran a nursery where she kept twenty children. Kemmie asked Mrs. Evans if she could come over there with Jimmy and Bobbie Lou, and Mrs. Evans said yes. Kemmie stayed there for nine months.

KEMMIE

I didn't know how to do anything to support myself, but Olive was a keypunch operator, so I decided to do that, too, and went to IBM. They didn't have an opening in their school, but the lady there gave me a book and said I could come in every day and practice on a machine that wasn't being used, and I taught myself. I passed the test and got a job at the Texas Company, who hired through IBM like all the companies back then. I left the kids with Mrs. Evans. I worked all day and then I went to school at night so I could advance at my job. I worked until five in the evening and started school at six-thirty, so I had an hour and a half alone. I couldn't afford to eat out, so I'd just walk around downtown window shopping. I felt free during that time. That was *my* hour and a half, the only time all day I had to myself.

Now, Red was back home, and he started calling at Olive's mother's saying things like "get your ass back over here where it belongs," but that approach was not gettin' it . . . uh-uh. Then he'd come over or call and say, "I want to take you out to dinner. I won't start anything. We'll just go out." I'd say OK, but before the evening was over he'd begin talking about wanting me back. I told him I just wasn't ready.

My sister was absolutely in shock. My friends were all in shock. Everybody in Red's family was in shock. Nobody ever knew we had any problems, because we'd never argued in front of any of them. One day, when I felt completely alone, cut off from the whole world, I took twenty-five of my hard-earned dollars and spent it on an hour with a shrink. I squawked. I cried. I told that man everything just like it was. I said, "Don't tell me to go back. I can't go back now." He said, "I'm not going to tell you to go back. I'm going to tell you to sing with the trio, and I'm going to tell you to go on and work at your job, and when *you* decide to go back, then go back. Don't let your family pressure you into it at all."

Well, after a few months, Red realized his hard-line attitude toward me wasn't going to work at all. There was no way in the world anyone was going to make me go back. I mean, I gave a guy twenty-five dollars to tell me I wasn't wrong, and this was 1946, a long time before the women's movement or anything like that. Red was making real good money now with Mr. Kinley, but I didn't ask him for a dime. A Christmas went by and he bought all this stuff for the kids — I couldn't afford any of it — but really, they were too young to know what was going on. I was saving ten dollars from each paycheck, twice a month, because I figured if anything happened I'd be in a heap of trouble.

When Red saw that I was going to make it on my own that worried him. I thought about divorce, but never really got serious about it, and then he started coming by and taking me out for dinner, not pressing me at all. He was just being nice, and it worked. Finally, I told him, "You find us a house and the kids and I will come back," and we did, early in 1947. Red bought us a house in Foster Place for $9,750, an older brick house that was within walking distance to the neighborhood school, and I gave my notice at work. I got together with Leatha and LaVelle a couple of times to sing, but then they got married and moved away, and that was the end of that.

It was different between Red and me from then on. I mean, for a long time, he still had the idea that he could do what he wanted and I couldn't, but during that nine months he realized I wasn't something that just sat around looking pretty. He realized I was a person, an individual capable of thinking for myself, of taking care of myself, and that changed us forever.

CHAPTER TWELVE

RED

I'll tell you this, it was a lot hotter in the old days. Now we have better pumps so we can get more water on a fire, and we have Nomex suits, which we didn't have back then. We'd wear an old cotton sweat-shirt and that sucker would get so damn heavy you could hardly walk. Nomex doesn't hold water and makes it a lot easier to work.

But it's not near as much fun as it used to be. I look back on some of those old jobs where you had to drag your water line in and stake it down by hand, and I think, "That's when you learned something from the men around you." You have to stake the line so it won't leap all around when the water runs through it under pressure. That can be dangerous as hell. We used to drive crisscross stakes into the ground with a sledgehammer to hold the lines down, and doing that near a burning well is one helluva hot job, believe me. Everybody on the location would pitch in and help.

Now they've got these big hydraulic mobile cranes to haul the line, and power-driven hole drillers instead of sledgehammers. Wham! Boom! They make a hole, stick in an anchor, chains come along, and that's it. Your line is held down. I'll admit it's quicker, but the cama-raderie is gone. These days, what you have are agencies checking on you, groups demonstrating against you, and engineers. There's engi-neers every place you look, always lettin' you know who you can use, how you can use 'em, and what you *can't* do. They've been to school, but they haven't been out bustin' their asses on oil rigs, so they don't know nothin' and you can't tell 'em nothin'. Arguing with an engi-neer's like wrestling with a pig. Everybody gets covered with shit and the pig's the only one who has a good time.

It used to be a bunch of guys doing it all together. You'd get per-sonal with everybody. You had a good time while you worked, no matter how hard the job. You didn't worry about whether someone was doing something that wasn't in their job description. Back then, roughnecks knew how to do everything on a rig. In the old days, when I wanted to know what was really going on, I'd go drink beer at night with the roughnecks, and they'd tell me what was what with that ol' well."

SOUTH TEXAS — 1949

"If I was you," Hugo Andre said to Red, "I'd wait a while to cap that well, 'cause the ol' sumbitch ain't through unloadin', not by a long shot it ain't." It was quarter to one in the morning, and the two of them were sitting in a bar in El Campo drinking tequila and listening to a Mexican violinist play the blues. The Mexican launched into a languid, mournful version of "All of Me," and Red sipped thoughtfully, watching Andre across the table, waiting to reply.

Hugo Andre was a roughneck, as hardworking and tough as they came, with hands like two rusty coal shovels and a face as craggy as the bottom of a dried-out river bed. Thirty years before, he'd been a pilot in World War I, and every so often he'd get drunk, don his old leather flight jacket and aviator's scarf, drive out onto the prairie and steal a crop duster's biplane, which he'd fly in as hair-raising a manner as anyone in South Texas had ever seen until it ran out of gas. Then he'd glide to a landing, leave the plane, walk over to his car and go home. Now and then, Andre would run out of gas far from his automobile, but someone would always give him a ride, and no one ever turned him in.

In 1941 Andre achieved immortality of sorts when he looped a brand new bridge across the Brazos River just north of Richmond, Texas, in a stolen plane during the bridge's dedication. The previous night he had been entertained by a beautiful young Mexican woman in Rosa's Café, the oldest whorehouse in Texas, over on Mud Alley in Richmond, and to show this woman his gratitude, Andre offered to take her for a plane ride. He stole a particularly agile airplane for the occasion, since the woman had never flown before, and Andre wanted her first flight to be particularly memorable. They brought along a bottle of wine, just to keep the party alive.

The bridge was crammed with dignitaries, local politicians, and members of the media, all primed for a momentous ceremony, when Hugo Andre came at them over the water at full throttle in an open-cockpit Stinson, scarf stretched out behind him, face fixed in a broad, toothy smile. You can still see the smile, and the horror-stricken look that crossed the young woman's face just as Hugo

Andre roared under the bridge, pulled the nose of the plane sharply up, and whipped smartly into the first of two cleanly executed loops, because even though the dignitaries and politicians hit the deck in unison, the newspaper photographers stayed on the job. They even got the bottle of wine, dropped by the young woman, and frozen for eternity in the instant before it hit the roadway, christening the bridge and spattering a dozen politicians with blood-red droplets of Thunderbird.

The Mexican finished his number, bowed, and sat down at the bar. Red set his glass on the table and rested his chin on his fist. "What makes you think that well's still gonna unload?" Red asked.

"When it first kicked, I told the driller not to pull the pipe out of the hole," Hugo Andre said, "but the sumbitch was nervous as a bride and he didn't listen. When the bit came out of the hole it had a swab on it the size of a baby elephant, and of course it brought the well right along with it. Naturally, that driller ain't about to tell you nothin', 'cause then he gets the blame for this mess we're in. When the well let go it blew the swab, the bit, the pipe, and half the derrick to kingdom come, so there's no proof, but I saw that swab, and it was full of rocks and gravel. It was the same kind of shit that come out of those two other wells you and Kinley did down here, and remember what happened with both of them."

When a well kicks — when there is a surge of formation pressure — an inexperienced driller, in a moment of panic, may pull his drill string — all the joints of drill pipe and the drilling bit in the well — out of the hole. This is a mistake, as Red and Hugo Andre well knew, because if there is a large ball of mud — a swab — on the end of the bit, it will create a vacuum as it comes out of the hole that pulls everything below it up the well bore. Then you no longer have a kick, you have a full-power blowout on your hands.

Hugo Andre bought two pints of vodka every day. He'd drink one early in the morning to get him going and stash the other in his pocket to keep him going. Every once in a while, he'd stop what he was doing and take a drink, but when he was sixty-five years old he could still outwork any man of twenty-five on the job, and Adair knew he understood an oil well. "I'm tellin' you, Red," he said, "don't cap that well yet. It ain't through blowin'. Go on up to it in the morning. You'll see what I mean."

Red didn't wait for morning, but drove straight from the bar thirty miles to the well. The night watchman opened the gate for him; he parked by the watchman's trailer and began walking up toward the wellhead, which was lit by a single spotlight hooked to a generator that hummed in the dark.

Jim West was an old Texas wildcatter who didn't feel dressed until he buckled on two chrome-plated, long-barreled, .45-caliber revolvers. He had a mansion in River Oaks, the same exclusive Houston subdivision where Myron Kinley lived. Several times a year, West would throw lavish parties at his home, but you had to be careful if you went, because every time he'd lure one or two unsuspecting guests into an all-night poker game and have his men paint these guests' cars blue while they were parked out in his yard.

When Jim West traveled around to his blue drilling rigs in his blue car or blue plane, he carried with him sacks of silver dollars. He enjoyed holding contests for the rig hands with the sacks of money as prizes. He'd place the sack on the ground at the drilling site and have the men race to see who could get to them first. Sometimes, he'd make the races more exciting by throwing large firecrackers at the sacks just as the men reached them. Sometimes, he'd fire his .45s into the air instead, or fire them at the ground. You could never be sure. But West was a generous man, as well as a crazy one, and he gave sacks of silver dollars away to men who did a good job on his wells.

This well in El Campo had killed three men when it blew up, and it burned for thirty days before Red and Kinley put it out. West gave Red $500 at the time and promised him another $500 when he capped it. When it blew, a piece of the drill pipe was left sticking up out of the rotary table, canted about forty-five degrees, so that the flame shooting from it went off at an angle. This made it extremely hard to get in close to the fire and drive the flame up into the air with a stream of water from a hose, so after clearing away as much of the debris as possible, Kinley called in an artillery team from an army base to see if the fire could be shot out with a bazooka. That didn't work, so Kinley turned to Adair and said, "Well, Red, I guess the only way to get this one is with your fancy stuff."

The "fancy stuff" was Red's shaped charges. He first used them on a Continental Oil Company well near Jennings, Louisiana, in 1947, where he'd been bragging to Kinley and the men from Haliburton — the pumping company — about how good he'd gotten with explosives in the army.

"Well, Red, if you're so good, how about you moving that slab we've been killin' ourselves over all morning?" Kinley said to him. The slab was the concrete floor of the blown-out Continental well. It had to be removed so that Red and Kinley could work on the wellhead, and they'd been working from dawn until noon breaking it apart with small charges of dynamite Kinley inserted in cylindrical holes he had Red drill with a jackhammer.

"Mr. Kinley, you go on and take these men to lunch, and I'll see what I can do," Red told him.

As soon as Kinley and the others left, Red made four shaped charges, placed them at the corners of the slab, set them off, and reduced the slab to a thousand chunks the size of dinner plates. When Kinley returned, Red had just finished hauling the whole mess away with a bulldozer. "You and your fancy stuff," was all Kinley said, but from then on, he let Red set the charges and blow out all the fires, and it was a molded charge, carefully shaped to accommodate the angle of the drill pipe, that had finally put out the blazing El Campo well.

While Red was away in the army, Kinley had been severely burned at a well fire in northern Venezuela and broken his bad leg at another fire in Goliad, Texas, and by the late 1940s, his mobility was probably less than a third of what it had once been. On a job in Mexico in 1948, he was close in to a well that cratered, or caved in, because of the force of the fluids escaping from the well, and he began to flounder in the sea of oil and mud, unable to get himself out. Red quickly jumped into a truck with a winch on it, drove up as close to Kinley as he could, and waded toward his boss, carrying a thick rope.

"You do that to me and I'll never speak to you again," Kinley said, embarrassed to be so helpless in front of the onlooking Mexican crew. But Red paid him no mind. He tied the rope underneath Kinley's arms and winched him out, the Old Man fuming at Red the whole time. After that, Red would wave Kinley off from the really hot wells as often as he could, taking care that no one else on the job saw him do it, for fear of hurting Kinley's pride.

The two of them had become inseparable after the war, and many people assumed Red was either Kinley's son, or his son-in-law, married to Kinley's daughter Joyce. Kinley did have a son, Jack, but he wanted nothing to do with the oil patch and stayed, instead, in his father's office, managing the books. Still, as much as Kinley treated Adair like a son, he demanded that Red work for him in the manner of the old school. This meant that if Red was not off fighting a fire, he was expected to be at Kinley's shop fixing equipment, cleaning it, or, if there was nothing else to do, sweeping the floor.

When Red went to work for him full-time, Kinley, feeling the effects of his injuries, was doing only eight or ten jobs a year, turning down wells that had cratered. "There's no way we can get that one," he'd tell Red, but Red was still hungry and, moreover, became possessed when someone told him there was no way he'd be able to do something. As far as he was concerned, the well didn't exist that he couldn't kill.

"Hell, Mr. Kinley," he'd say, "I'll take care of it," even if the well was completely submerged under a lake of fire. Then he'd go in, set up a relief program, drill a directional well, pump mud in, and kill the cratered well, so that production could resume.

Before long, Kinley's company was doing thirty jobs a year, then forty and fifty. Red did one job back then, in Alice, Texas, that the drilling company, the operator, and the insurance company had given up on, saying it was impossible to get to the drill-pipe casing because it was submerged in a sea of muck.

"Impossible?" Red said. "Nothing is impossible. Get me a damn bulldozer." Then he worked all night, all the next day, and the following night, until he managed to tie a cable onto the casing, pull it out, and run a new one down the hole, which all the while was blowing oil. Before he went back to Houston, he killed three more blowing wells in the same field that the drilling companies had written off. These were wells that had cratered so badly they'd sucked trucks, cars, huge mud tanks, and generators into the ground along with the drilling rigs. No one wanted to go near them, so Red did the capping jobs by himself.

Red was making good money now, more than $25,000 a year. He had recently bought his second new car, a 1949 red Plymouth convertible that he gave to Kemmie as a present. (He kept the new Oldsmobile for himself. He had painted the '39 Ford coupe red and pulled the back seat out of it, and that vehicle was crammed with tools and explosives.) Red also told Kemmie to start looking for a better house, which she found in a subdivision called Idlewood. But he was working almost all the time, and when he wasn't, he would hang out at the local stock-car tracks or go drinking with his friends, so he was almost never home. His children barely knew who he was in those years, and Kemmie had resigned herself to raising them alone.

*   *   *

At three in the morning he came up on the El Campo well, the well that had killed three men, and when he got near it, twenty feet away, he could hear it breathing, making chuffing noises like a lion in the bush. Then, for a while, it was silent. Then it breathed again. The day before they had pumped mud into it and it had ceased to blow, but still it breathed, like a giant, wounded beast, he thought, lying deep inside a cave, waiting, waiting for the moment to attack. When the well breathed, everything around the wellhead trembled — the mud truck, a pickup, the rack of pipe — and the ground underneath his feet rose and fell as though it were a chest. Hugo Andre's right, he thought, this well's not finished talking to us. If we cap it, and it comes to see us, some more people may get killed.

In the morning he told Kinley, and while they kept everyone else away, Red put his helmet on, the one with a tin hard hat bolted to it, and strapped on shoulder pads under his hooded sweatshirt. (He didn't wear coveralls yet; they would come a year later, after the flow of a well got under the tail of his shirt and flipped him into some prickly mesquite fifty feet away.) The pads were for the rocks he felt were coming up the well bore, for that's what was predicted by the swab that Hugo Andre saw before the well let go.

The well kept breathing on and off all morning while he worked around it, tying in his lines, so that when it quit for good, they could pump the mud in once again and he could close it in. Then the breathing quickened. This is it, he thought, I can feel it, I know this damned well, and he began to run, finally taking cover behind a steel-plated shield he'd built in Kinley's shop and set up a hundred yards from the hole.

The rocks came, some small as marbles, some big as basketballs, mixed with dirt and drilling mud, flattening the pickup truck and almost all the pipe. They came from far below the surface where the pressure had been great, and when they hit the atmosphere, they expanded so rapidly many of them exploded like grenades. The well spit them in the air for half an hour, coughing and rumbling as it did, like a consumptive bear. And then it stopped.

Now that bastard's through, Red thought. Now he's got no more to say and I can cap him. Now he's dead.

CHAPTER THIRTEEN

EUREKA SPRINGS, ARKANSAS — 1988

Far from town, out where it is so quiet you can hear the crunch of tires on gravel in a driveway a mile away, sits Jimmy Adair's house, at the top of a hill overlooking a valley and a low, thickly wooded mountain that rises abruptly from a meadow on the valley's other side. It is a long way from Houston, a long way from the oil fields and the hard-drinking, hard-living, hell-raising life that Jimmy Adair turned his back on in 1983, when he was forty-two years old and nearly died of a heart attack.

The house is huge, a well-proportioned, three-story fortress with a natural wood exterior, designed by Jimmy to be energy efficient despite its size. He sits in the kitchen one morning in July looking out the wide picture window at a spiraling hawk that has flown off the mountain and caught a thermal rising from the valley floor. He watches the hawk for several minutes, his arms folded across his chest, his face reflecting a weariness all the rest in the world won't cure.

Jimmy Adair is a short, sturdily built man, with the same powerful forearms and hands as his father, and even some of Red's toughness in his face, but his green eyes and pensive mouth are soft and sensitive like his mother's, and in personality he is closer to her than to Red. He is a thinker, a reader, a dreamer, a man with analytical intelligence but not a man of action — not Red Adair the Second — though he tried to be that for many years. He has red hair and a sparse red beard, turning gray along the edges, and like certain red-headed, fair-complexioned men, would look almost childlike were it not for the deep lines at the corners of his eyes and on his neck.

He didn't need to shave every day until he was thirty. At thirty-five he still looked like a kid. This youthfulness, and the fact that he was Red's son, made it terribly difficult for Jimmy in the oil field, despite his expertise. He'd go on a job and for the first three or four days everyone there would hassle him wanting to know when Red was going to show up. Trying to convince them that he knew what he was doing would drive him nuts. "If we need Red, he'll be here," he'd say, "now let's just go ahead and do this job." He was smart, a good fire fighter, but he wasn't Red, and there was no way he was ever going to win, at least not fighting wild wells in the oil patch. If he had it to do all over again, he'd have finished college and become an engineer, which was what Red and Kemmie had hoped he'd do.

"Jimmy, come quick, you have to see this," Candy Adair calls. "You have to see this. It's your daddy on TV. There's a terrible fire over in the North Sea and he's going to fight it. They've got a camera crew with him in Houston."

She is in the long, high-ceilinged living room that looks like the inside of a north woods hunting lodge. At one end is a giant-screen TV set, and at the other, thirty feet away, a couch where Candy sits. She is Jimmy Adair's fourth wife, a pretty woman, thirty-seven years old, with kind, understanding eyes, and a soft, musical voice. When she speaks to her husband, her tone is at once deferential and calming. "Don't you think so, Jim?" she'll often say at the end of a statement, or "Isn't that right, Jimmy?" and when she says it, the sound is like a lullaby.

Once, five years before he married Candy, in a drunken rage after a fight with his former wife, Jimmy ran from his house carrying several guns from his gun collection. He was confronted by two policemen, one of whom thought that Jimmy was pointing a gun at him. The officer was about to fire at Jimmy when his partner recognized that it was Red Adair's son, intervened just in time to avert a disaster, and instead disarmed Jimmy and carted him off to jail. At that time in his life he needed calming, no question about it, but not now, not any more.

Jimmy crosses the room and sits beside Candy, and she lays her hand on his arm. They have been married for eleven years and give every indication of remaining together for good. Their wedding was held by the swimming pool at Red's house in Houston and was the first of Jimmy's four that Red attended. For some reason that remains a mystery to his son (and to Kemmie, too), Red went out and bought white shorts and red and white striped sailor shirts for him and Jimmy to wear to the ceremony. It was the only time Jimmy ever saw his father in shorts. Kemmie and Candy wore blue jeans, and Candy threw her bouquet to two ducks floating in the pool.

Eureka Springs is a small, lovely resort town of winding, hilly streets and old wood-frame houses, set in the foothills of the Ozark Mountains, in northern Arkansas, not far from the Missouri border.

At the turn of the century, tourists went there for the restorative spring water, which they bathed in and drank. Now, religion is the big draw, followed by foot-stomping country-music variety shows and stores selling Ozark crafts. Tourists come in droves for the famous Great Passion Play, a number of religious revivals, and the Ozark Folk Festival, but all that takes place during the summer. The rest of the year Eureka Springs is inhabited by a handful of locals who argue about such things as whether a young woman who plays guitar and sings folk songs on the patio of one restaurant is disturbing the clientele inside the restaurant next door. To bring a little year-round publicity to the place, a local entrepreneur offered Jim and Tammy Bakker a job running his hotel after they were kicked out of the PTL's enclave in North Carolina, but the Bakkers turned him down.

Jimmy and Candy like living near Eureka Springs. They belong to a small church there, not to one of those preaching hellfire and brimstone, but to a peaceful, sedate congregation where there is much singing. They have purchased the historical, four-story Flatiron Building in the center of town. They plan to rent out the bottom floor to a variety of shops and run a bed-and-breakfast hotel upstairs.

This, too — the church, the bed-and-breakfast hotel, the small-town politics — is a long way from Houston, a long way from the oil fields, a long way from the quart or more of Crown Royal Jimmy drank, not every day, but several times a week, for years and years until he finally met Candy and had the sense and the fortitude to check into a rehabilitation clinic and quit, cold-turkey, for good. But it's not far enough to escape the long shadow of Red Adair that hangs over Jimmy every day of his life.

Red is there while he labors over renovation plans for the building he and Candy bought; he takes care not to leave out a single detail because when he shows the plans to his father, on a rare trip to Houston, he knows Red will look for something he has done wrong. Red is there when he talks to his mother once a week, checking in, and hears about how his father refuses to slow down — and thinks, "Had I stayed down there I'd probably already be dead," knowing at the same time that if things had worked out differently the fire-fighting business would one day have been his. "He was my hero," he thinks. "I wanted to be just like him, so when I grew up I wanted to go to bars. That's what he did, so that's what I did." (Thinking, too, "He did it and handled it, but I couldn't.") And Red is there when he goes to town and someone he knows introduces him to someone else, saying, "You've heard of Red Adair, the famous oil-well fire fighter. Well, this here's his son." And now, in Jimmy's dark, cool living room, Red is up there on the giant TV screen, big as life, packing his aluminum Haliburton suitcase, riding to the airport in the company's red Chevy Suburban, saying something to the reporters at the Houston airport about the awful loss of life on the Piper Alpha rig in the North Sea.

"Well, there he is," Jimmy says. "He's never gonna quit. Not the Old Man. He wouldn't last two weeks if he did, and besides, there isn't anybody, still, to this day, who can do what he can at an oil-well fire. I suppose that's why, after all the bullshit and the fighting and the stress of being his kid for forty-eight years, he's still remained a hero for me and always will.

"I mean, who else at seventy-three years old acts like he's nineteen and gets away with it? He was sixty when the family got together and screamed and hollered at him to get him to quit racing boats. Even then, he only stopped because in his last race (which, by the way, was a one-hour marathon which he won by driving one hundred miles) they had to literally pry him out of his race boat and carry him to his trailer. He still parties. He still drives fast cars and fast boats. Just blowin' and goin'. That's Daddy. Always was, always will be."

JIMMY

When I was a little kid, I couldn't talk to him about problems and things because he wasn't there. I have absolutely no memory of him. He'd show up and it would be a sackful of toys, and then he'd be gone for another month or two. Jobs took much longer back then — equipment was more primitive, and Daddy was in the process of refining his techniques — so he and Kinley'd be on a fire six, eight weeks at a time. Hell, I think once or twice they were on one six months or more. I remember going to father-son banquets with my mamma. He was either working or he was out playing. When he was off from a job he played, going out with the boys to bars or car races and then, much later, to boat races.

I remember that when we started going places together — when he started having a little time — was around 1950 or so. That's when he started having a couple of extra dollars so he could take me places, and we started going to the race track — the stock car track. He'd always had the car bug, from the time he was a little kid riding on the back of the race cars his daddy fixed, and then I got the car bug from him.

Well, anyway, Daddy bought him a stock car, even though he wasn't really doing well enough financially to afford one. (Mamma had some choice things to say about that, as I recall.) He drove some himself and he was pretty damn good, but then he got other drivers to drive for him. So, like everything he did, he had to win, and if you were going for most season points — the track championship — you had to be there every week to race, which he often wasn't because he was away on jobs. He had quite a few drivers — the best of 'em was a guy named Willy Williams — and if his car didn't win it was torn down and rebuilt, immediately. His first car was a '37 or '38 Chevrolet with a six-cylinder motor. That car was just all right. Then he got a '34 Chevrolet coupe with a '49 Olds V-8 engine in it. That car was a winner. He got trophies with it and all.

I'd sell popcorn or soda in the stands because I was too young to go in the pits during the races. The main place he raced was Arrowhead Speedway on Old Spanish Trail in Houston, which had been a horse-racing track, but he also ran at Channelview, Texas, on a dirt track, and then at Playland Park, which was asphalt. They're all gone now. Playland Park's where A. J. Foyt got his start. Foyt's father, Tony, was a real good friend of Daddy's.

Daddy was truly in his element there. The only way he could let off steam was by involving himself in a situation that created tension. If he can't create tension he's not happy. The adrenaline has to pump, which is why he got release from fighting well fires by going to the race track, by driving, and when he couldn't do that, by getting down in the pits where it was wild and greasy and loud. That's what turned him on.

HOUSTON — 1951

By the time Red's plane touched down in Houston on Saturday evening he'd been traveling for fourteen hours, first in a single-engine Cessna from the thickly wooded mountains of northern Colombia, up the Magdalena River Valley to Barranquilla; then on an oil company's DC-3, 550 miles across the mountains to Caracas; then up to Miami on one commercial flight, and finally back to Houston on a second.

In Barranquilla he took a shower, but still the smell of smoke and hot oil and drilling mud hung on him the way the smell of gamblers' cigarettes, whiskey, and cologne hangs in a hotel room the morning after an all-night card game. Not that Red was overly concerned. He had escaped from Colombia with his skin, an outcome that for a time had been in question.

It wasn't the well that almost cost Red his life, though the fire had been a bad one. The location for the drilling rig had been cut into the side of a mountain, and when the rig blew out, the cascading oil took half the mountainside with it, leaving a quagmire of mud and boiling petroleum intermixed with boulders and large trees at the mountain's base. Gas bubbled continuously up through this mess, and a mist of distillate fell like fine rain for two days, until an actual tropical rainstorm came down off the mountains, accompanied by lightning that set the well and everything around it on fire.

Red and Kinley could see the devastation, the billowing smoke, and the flames as the oil company's Cessna banked for its descent onto a rutted, grass landing strip, but they knew, as soon as they hit the ground and a hail of arrows peppered their taxiing plane, that the burning well was only half their problem.

They had landed in the middle of a local guerilla war between rebellious Indians and the Colombian government, which, as far as the Indians were concerned, was represented by anyone with white skin. The Indians, armed with machetes and blowguns through which they fired long, poison darts, had been launching hit-and-run attacks on farms and small settlements up and down the Magdalena River Valley. The fighting would rage for several days, then it would stop and life would continue as it had before the war, the Indians trading at the various outposts along the river, the settlers dealing with them in a state of continual unease. Then, without warning, trouble would start again.

RED

Both sides were chopping each other up with machetes. We were working right near the river, which was good because we had plenty of water to pump on the fire, but while we worked we'd see bodies floating by. It was a spooky place out there in the middle of nowhere, like you were a million miles from civilization. We were camped next to the landing strip about a mile from the well, and the first night one guy with the oil company offered me a gun. I'd already decided I was never going to carry a weapon on a job, especially outside the United States, because I don't care how good a shot you are, you're never gonna shoot your way out of a whole country, so I said no, but I thought about it. What the hell good would it do me anyway? With all the noise from the well, one of those Indians could've snuck up through the jungle and put a poison dart in my back if he'd felt like it, and I'd never have known it.

They were a bunch of mean bastards, those Indians, let me tell you. One day they'd be friendly to you, the next day they'd kill you. There was one farmer near the location who got along well with them. He had a garden, and he let 'em take what they wanted from it. Then one time we went up there and that poor farmer was all shot full of arrows. They'd killed him.

We worked day and night for a month to get that well done and be out of that place. Well, we got the fire out and had it pretty nearly cleaned up, but we never finished because one morning these military guys came rushing in and told us the rebels were coming and we had maybe twenty or thirty minutes to get the hell out. They had several little planes in there, and Kinley and I and a few other men who worked for the oil company said, "We're leaving," and away we flew. The rest of the crew there thought it was a false alarm and decided they'd stay, and right after we took off those Indians came through and killed every last man left in the camp.

Death and destruction. Oil, 400 degrees hot, flowing down a mountainside, gurgling over your boots like black lava, burning the bottom of your pants (and your legs, too, if you step away from the spray of the hoses), while bloated bodies drift in the river at your back. Nearby, poison darts and hostile Indians lurk in the bushes. You can hear them at night, outside the camp, calling to each other, like demented birds. A month of that would make any man yearn for a week of hot baths, home cooking, and long naps in the shade, but not Red Adair. Not him. He hits the ground in Houston on a dead run, makes a quick call to Kemmie to tell her he's fine, but has to go over to the track to make sure his race car's OK. Kemmie's used to it by now. She knows she might see him that night, or she might not.

Into the parking lot he trots and over to his car, a red '51 Cadillac coupe, first Caddy he's owned. It's a beauty, and boy, is he proud of it. Drove it to his folks' the first day he had it and everyone came over — sisters, brothers, wives and husbands, kids and friends — all wanting a ride, and naturally Red took them, five and six at a time, all over the Heights and out South Main to the drive-in for burgers and shakes, saying over and over to each carload, "Isn't she somethin'? Listen to that motor. Doesn't she ride nice?" ("What do you think, Daddy? My very own Cadillac.")

Eighty miles an hour out to Arrowhead Speedway, barrel-assing through the gate, past the security guard ("Yeah, Red, you get that ol' fire?" "Yes sir, got her good.") and into the pits, four-wheel drifting to a halt just in time to see his race car finish at the back of the pack in the feature race.

"That's it," he says. "I'm gonna get rid of this damn Jimmy and get me a car that'll haul ass."

"Red, I hear that '34 Chevy with the '49 Olds V-8 motor's for sale," Red's driver, Willy Williams, said.

"You mean that number-nine car?" Red asked.

"Uh-huh," said Willy.

"Well now, that piece of machinery can run," said Red. "I'll buy it." Which he promptly did, right then and there.

When Red Adair bought car number nine, he got two cars for the price of one. The second machine, car number eleven, a lesser race car, came with a man who had driven the car in several races. On the night Red bought car number nine, as he was preparing to leave the track with a group of friends, this driver came up to him. "Red, I'd like to drive your second car for you," he said.

He was a short, stocky young man of twenty-six, ten years younger than Red, who walked with a rolling swagger, his head tilted back slightly, like a surefooted sailor on a ship who wants his mates to know he doesn't need to watch the deck. His name was Asgar Hansen, but everyone who knew him called him Boots. He was a sign painter by trade who worked with his father, the two of them supplementing a rather meager living by painting numbers on race cars at the track. He stood in front of Red with his hands on his hips, a faint smile on his face, sure of himself, almost daring Red to turn him down. "I'll do a real good job for you," he said. "That number-eleven car don't look like much, but I can make it run."

It was a night of great joy for Red. After a year and a half of owning a clunker, he was finally in a position to get his hands on a real race car, a car he knew could win him a championship, and he was filled with excitement. He was also still buoyed by the wave of elation he'd been riding since his escape from the renegade Indians in Colombia, and it was in his nature, at times like that, to want everyone around him swept along as well. "Sure," he said to Boots. "You drive the number-eleven car for me. C'mon, let's get both of 'em over to the garage."

A few months later, Boots came to Red and told him he needed a job and wanted to become an oil-well fire fighter. At first, Red put Boots to work in the small wire-line company Adair had started as a sideline business. Then, when Red decided to sell the wire-line company, he spoke to Myron Kinley on Boots's behalf, and Kinley agreed to hire Boots as a helper under Red's tutelage. It was an association that was to last for twenty-five years.

From the first, Adair treated Boots like a son. Many people wondered what chord Boots Hansen struck inside Red Adair, but nobody really ever knew. It may have been that Boots was the first man Adair hired (even though he was still not in business for himself). Perhaps Red secretly enjoyed the intrigue and controversy Boots's presence constantly provided. Red wasn't above that; he once admitted to Jimmy's wife Candy that he sometimes put volatile things and people together just to see what would happen. Or it simply may have been that Red met Boots when he got the Oldsmobile-powered race car and somehow associated Hansen with a feeling of youth, speed, and freedom from any restraints. Certainly as a stock-car racer Boots was no great shakes — as far as Jimmy Adair can recall he never won a race. Eventually, he drove the number-eleven car through a fence and wrecked it — and though he did have the grit to get out into the oil patch and work on wild wells, and did become, in time, a competent hand, he was a constant source of friction for Red.

RED

Boots doesn't realize it to this day, but I saved his life about three dozen times in the oil field. He never got in a fight, but he'd mouth off to guys — call 'em names, tell 'em they were no-good screw-ups — which you just don't do in the oil patch. I know at least a half dozen dozer operators that would have killed him, beat his head to a pulp. I know some Haliburton hands that would have killed him. I had to keep my other men off him a number of times 'cause they wanted to whip him.

Boots tried to go into one side business or another a dozen times, and every time I had to bail him out. I bailed him out when he got in trouble with his taxes. I even had to help him one time when they repossessed his Cadillac, and he was making damn good money at the time, a couple a hundred thousand a year. Why'd I keep doing it? Damned if I know. Who knows why they do all the things they do?

Kemmie Adair, who never had much use for Boots, and who eventually grew to despise him, was particularly perplexed, especially when, in later years, Red sent Boots and Jimmy on jobs together and Boots gave her son a really rough time. She spoke to Red about her feelings, about the fact that she thought Boots was causing trouble by blaming one or another of Red's other men for any mistake he made, but Red either didn't seem to hear her, or didn't care. "The Fair-Haired Boy" the other men called Boots, or "Golden Boy."

A newspaper reporter came over to Red's house one time to interview him and looked around in amazement. The driveway was filled with souped-up cars, race boats, and motorcycles. This was when Jimmy and Robyn were teenagers, and about a dozen kids were engaged in a battle with some of Red's friends from the oil patch and some neighbors, one group attempting to throw the other into the swimming pool. When the reporter arrived, Red, wearing dress shoes, a suit, and a silk sport shirt, had a death grip on the diving board, while three of Jimmy's friends who were high school football players, all over 200 pounds, tried in vain to pry him loose. It was 1958. Red was forty-three years old and had just returned from the swamps of Louisiana where, in the August heat, he killed a blowout for the Fifteen Oil Company. "You little farts," he shouted. "You ain't about to get me wet."

"Why do you do this?" the reporter asked Red. "Why do you buy all this stuff and run and party and carry on all the time? Why don't you sit back and take it easy?"

"When I go out on a job, I never know if I'm gonna come back or not," Red answered. "So when I do get home, I like to enjoy myself."

Maybe, deep down, that was why Boots, in spite of his shortcomings, appealed to Red, because when all was said and done, Boots Hansen knew how to raise hell, how to keep the party rolling. The continuous turmoil that hovered around him at work — the friction that grated on the other men — was nothing more than seasoning for the bubbling pot that Red Adair never took off the stove. In any case, all this controversy was years away when Red's number-nine race car was tearing up the stock-car tracks around Houston and Red's fame as a fire fighter was just beginning to make front-page news.

Red may have had no time to drive his stock car for the

championship at Arrowhead Speedway, but that didn't mean he quit racing. He simply stopped doing it on the track. Instead, he would have his personal car set up as a race car, then, when he came in from a job, he'd compete on the street against his friends. Two of the men in this group were named Carroll Miller and Gerald Jones, both of whom at one time held records at the Bonneville Salt Flats in Utah. Miller and Jones were professional engine builders, and Red would have them build him an engine just as though he were going to Bonneville, too. Then, along with his racing buddies, he would go out to Stewart's Drive-in on South Main Street, where the gang would fire up their machines and head southwest to Sugarland, or further out into the country to Richmond-Rosenberg, at speeds reaching 130 or 140 miles an hour. They would pick a spot, twenty, thirty, or forty miles away, generally some drive-in restaurant or filling station they were familiar with, race to it, grab a bite to eat, tinker a little bit with their cars, and then race back to Houston. If Red didn't win, he either had his engine rebuilt or got another car.

He rarely lost, at least against any of his friends, but that was not the case when he drag raced against his wife. Over the years, in dozens of cars, with hundreds of high-speed mechanical modifications, he tried, but not once could he get through the quarter mile quicker than Kemmie. What made this even stranger was that unlike Red, who'd trade cars once a month if he thought his new one would go faster than the old one, Kemmie was content to hang on to the same automobile for several years.

Red and Kemmie had moved out of Houston proper by the time this competition began, out to a subdivision called Jersey Village that in the mid-1950s was only sparsely populated. Just outside the subdivision was a stretch of deserted country highway called Britmore Road where some local teenage street-racers had marked off a quarter-mile drag strip on the asphalt. Every time Red got a new car, or had a hot camshaft, bigger carburetor, or tuned exhaust system added to the one he was driving, he'd come looking for his wife.

"Kemmie, you gotta see this new car," he'd say, pulling her from the kitchen to the driveway to look at his new Cadillac, Lincoln, or Chrysler. "It's just a beauty. I'll beat you with this one for sure."

"You won't, Red," she'd tell him. "You know you won't but your new car sure is pretty, I'll give you that."

So, off they'd go out to Britmore Road and line up side by side, engines screaming, hands vise-gripped onto steering wheels, eyes fixed on the finish line a quarter mile away. Neither of them would be smiling, for Red Adair cannot stand to lose at anything and this racing was dead serious. At the signal from one of their kids they'd take off, tires smoking, rear ends fishtailing, and the result was inevitably the same. Kemmie might beat him by a car length, the length of a fender, or by only a bumper, but she always beat him.

The competition continues to this day. Maybe they'll be having dinner with one of their grandchildren, or maybe they'll be alone, at her house on the lake or in a restaurant nearby. They'll be talking about something far removed from fast cars when out of the blue he'll grin at her and say, "I can beat you this time, Kemmie. I know it."

She'll shake her head and say, "Well, let's go then."

On a deserted stretch of road, they'll line up side by side, Mercedes against Mercedes now. They hold the steering wheels even tighter than the old days, and squint a little harder at the road, and when one or the other of them yells go they're somewhat slower off the line, but they're still doing ninety miles an hour or better at the finish, and Red hasn't beaten her yet.

CHAPTER FOURTEEN

WEST TEXAS — 1952

West Texas. Odessa was its hub. Enough oil and gas stuffed beneath the Permian Basin to keep America humming for fifty years, maybe a hundred, maybe more; and just enough tough, ornery ex–saddle tramps, desert desperados, and itinerant Cajuns from the Louisiana swamps to pull it out of the ground. Wells running all the way south to Ft. Stockton and Pecos, north to Brownfield and Lubbock, east to Sweetwater and Abilene, and west into New Mexico, to Jal and Eunice and on up to Hobbs. Wild country, West Texas, wild and open and free, the least civilized of all the oil fields in North America, where you thought twice before crossing a man, especially an oil-field hand; even in the 1950s and early 1960s men settled scores with double-action .45 long Colt revolvers outside roadhouses that appeared suddenly over a sand hill or behind a clump of trees after a hundred miles of hot dust, mesquite, and lonesome cattle.

"Always had my Colt at my side," an old West Texas Cameron Iron Works hand named Wiley Hodgens says. "So did everybody else. It was that kind of place. What I'd do is ream the cylinder out straight through, then put about seven and a half grains of Unique gunpowder in the casing, a quarter-inch wad, and fill it flush with number seven and a half birdshot. Makes a commendable cartridge. Nothing long-range, mind you, but put a darn fine hole in whatever's directly in front of you."

Got towns out there called Notrees, Tarzan, Tokio, and Wink, with nothing around them but space. Distances that elsewhere loom like moon voyages were insignificant in West Texas even in the early days, once they discovered cars. Rig hands thought nothing of driving 120 miles each way to work, toting delicacies such as fried squirrel and fried rattlesnake sandwiches in their lunch boxes. In a hot car on a long, straight road it only took them an hour and a half anyway, sometimes less if the wind was right. They'd work like dogs, these West Texas rig hands, and when the day was over they'd get in their cars and there'd be five of them in one vehicle to save on gas. They'd have a gallon of whiskey — white lightning, best stuff west of North Alabama — and before they set out they'd take the lid off and throw that lid out the window because there was no way they were about to save anything from that bottle for when they got home.

The fastest car Red ever owned he drove out to West Texas, wide open from Houston all the way to a well in Coyanosa, to break it in. It was a 1953 Lincoln coupe he got early in the fall of 1952. It had two four-barrel carburetors. Its engine was bored and stroked. Its cylinder heads were extensively modified, and when it idled, its racing camshaft caused the hood to jump up and down. The exhaust headers dumped into straight-through pipes so when you sat in the car it sounded as though someone were playing a bass drum in the trunk. The car's suspension had been beefed up with special shock absorbers, antisway bars and heavy-duty springs; it had an extra-heavy-duty cooling system so it wouldn't boil over, and on a long, flat stretch of Texas highway it would do an honest 140 miles an hour for as long as a man cared to keep his foot on the floor.

Red was running close to that, hour after hour, coiled like a spring behind the wheel, priming himself for the well in Coyanosa that was as nasty as they came, even for West Texas. It hadn't just blown out, it had blown up. People standing half a mile away saw the entire rig lift straight up in the air and then come back down again on the same spot where it had been, engulfed in a fireball that could be seen eighty miles away across the plains. When it blew it killed four men, whose bodies were never found, and sent 130 others to the hospital in Monahans with burns.

In the car with Red was a man named Rush Johnson, head of Rush Johnson Associates, an independent loss-adjustment firm that worked with Lloyd's of London, underwriters for nearly every oil-well rig in the world. If an oil rig blew out, if it caught fire or turned over, or if a drill ship sank to the bottom of the sea, Rush Johnson was the man — for many years the only man — who determined the amount of the drilling company's insurance claim. It was his job to save the underwriter money, and in this regard he valued Red Adair more than anyone else in the oil patch, for no one saved equipment at the site of an oil-well disaster the way Red did.

The oil company or drilling company hired Red, who billed them for his work. Lloyd's of London, through Rush Johnson, settled the insurance claim of the oil company or driller, who in turn paid Red's bill. Over the years, Red's techniques for pulling drilling rigs away from blazing infernos rather than simply jerking them over onto the ground or letting them sink into the ocean, his willingness to walk up to a burning well to determine exactly what the situation was and what could be salvaged, saved Lloyd's of London millions of dollars, and so Rush Johnson never argued when Red Adair told him what he was going to charge for his work. Whether Red sent in a bill for two million dollars, or whether he did a job for nothing for an independent oilman in danger of going under, Johnson knew Red was worth whatever the insurance company paid him.

Rush Johnson was also Red Adair's best friend. He was a brilliant man, probing and incisive, with a wry sense of humor and a biting wit, and Red respected his intelligence. They met in the late 1940s, and through the years, until Johnson died of a stroke in 1980, he was the one man who could influence Adair's decisions.

Rush stood two or three inches taller than Red. He was stockily built, but with tiny feet, and though he dressed in very expensive clothes, something in his attire would invariably be awry, so that he never looked perfectly turned out. His silk shirt wouldn't be tucked completely into his pants, for instance; or if it was, his tie would be wrinkled or there would be food stains on the lapels of his custom-made suit, or a cigarette burn on one of the cuffs. Still, he was a striking man — a better-looking Mel Torme, Kemmie was fond of calling him — with large, piercing blue eyes, a broad smile, and the kind of continental charm that appealed to certain women. He was married at least five times.

Rush Johnson was the only person Red felt comfortable confiding in. He was the man he would talk to about his parents, about Kemmie and his children. He revealed his fears for their safety, fears that bordered on obsession because of Jimmy's brush with death in infancy and his own brushes with death almost every day. Rush was the only man to whom Red revealed his own feelings of mortality. "You try not to think about dying on a job," he'd say, "but you know death's there, maybe in a year, maybe in ten years, maybe waiting for you at the next well."

"When I do die," Red once told his friend, after narrowly escaping an exploding oil well on the coast of Mozambique, "I'd like to be remembered as a man who gave everybody an even break. If I ever did gyp anybody in my life, I didn't do it intentionally. I'd also like to be thought of as somebody who respected his fellow men — who respected another man's work — too many people don't do that, Rush. They all seem so cutthroat nowadays, and they shouldn't be."

That was much later, after Red had fought wild wells for twenty years. Now they drove west, into the night, toward Coyanosa, and it was Rush who was talking, trying to persuade Red to go into business for himself. This was a sensitive subject, for while Red was by this time handling most of Myron Kinley's jobs on his own, his devotion to his old mentor was deep. He could not bring himself to even think of leaving Kinley, and he would not do it for another seven years.

The discussion waned. One hundred and twenty-five miles an hour through the darkness and it was silent in the car, save for the whistle of wind and the rumble of exhaust. Rush Johnson smoked, one cigarette after another. Ahead, too distant yet for them to see its glow, the oil well burned, and a man waited for Red Adair. Red hadn't met this man before, but he would come to trust him, not with his deepest thoughts, but with his life.

The man's name was George Curry, and he sat chain-smoking in a watchman's shack a mile from the well, his chair tilted back against the wall. He was six feet tall, weathered and tough as a piece of bullhide nailed to the side of a West Texas barn. All of two fingers and part of a third were missing from his right hand. He lost them in 1932 when he crimped a fuse too close on a stick of dynamite he was using to blast a tree stump and it went off in his hand. The explosion also lodged some shrapnel in his ribs. There was no penicillin back then, no antibiotics. His wounds were treated with iodine and turpentine, and it took eighteen months for him to heal.

George Curry chain-smoked Chesterfield cigarettes and was well on his way to a case of emphysema. He walked with an awkward, disjointed gait, but no one worried much about that because his virtuosity was accomplished sitting down. He drove a Caterpillar bulldozer — a tractor, he called it — for Shorty Hall, a trucking contractor who moved drilling rigs, and he had come to Coyanosa from his home in Odessa because none of the eight bulldozer operators already on the job was willing to drive up next to the burning well. Someone asked George Curry if he'd do it. "Hell, yes," he said. "No problem about that." He had a twenty-one-year-old wife and her mother to support, and he needed extra money.

As soon as Red met George Curry at that well in Coyanosa, he began calling him Three-Finger George, or sometimes just Three-Finger. The name stuck, and over the next thirty years, in oil fields around the globe, it would become synonymous with wild West Cat skinning supremacy. So revered was Three-Finger George Curry as a dozer operator in the oil patch that when he died in 1984 a Caterpillar tractor led his funeral procession in Odessa.

The bulldozer operator is crucial on a wild-well job, since he is the man who first has to pull all the metal debris away from the wellhead. This is necessary so that during the period when the fire is out but the well has not been capped, oil, or more likely gas or distillate, won't hit a piece of hot iron and reignite the well. The bulldozer operator is also the one who hauls up to the wellhead the explosive charge Red Adair uses to blow out the fire. He always drives in reverse, his back to the well, enabling Red or one of his men to face the fire and direct him with hand signals at the same time. He is shielded from the fire by a three-sided metal enclosure on his Cat, staying with the wind to keep as much heat and smoke away from him as possible.

Driving a bulldozer around a burning oil well takes incredible skill, because a man not only has to skin his Cat in reverse, he must jockey an athey wagon that is hooked to it as well. The athey wagon, a bulldozer-operated crane designed and put to use fighting well fires by Red Adair, began life as a two-wheeled steel cart with a long boom mounted on it. Red first built one on a job in 1941 when the rig hands at a well fire told him there was no way to get near the blazing wellhead to remove a twisted valve. Red spied a two-wheeled wagon on the location, got a length of drill pipe and a large hook, and had the welder mount the pipe on the wagon and the hook on the end of the pipe. Pushing the wagon by hand, he then worked his way up to the wellhead and basically went fishing until he snagged the valve. Over the years, Red refined his original design considerably, substituting tracks for wheels and adding remote controls that allow a dozer operator to maneuver the boom and the hook from his seat atop the Cat, but the driver still has his hands full.

To get some idea of what he's up against, imagine hooking a trailer with a thirty-foot cabin cruiser on it to a pickup truck and then backing it across a hundred yards of mud two feet deep toward a burning barn. When you get near enough to the barn so the paint on the boat begins to peel and the skin on your face feels as though it's shrinking, you drive back to the place where you started. Now imagine doing that over and over again, twelve hours a day, for a week. Imagine doing it with a 550-gallon drum of dynamite lashed to the bow of the boat. And remember, a burning barn is like a campfire compared to a blazing oil well.

A D-9 Cat, the largest bulldozer made by the Caterpillar Tractor Company, is twenty-seven feet long. It stands eleven feet high and weighs more than 100,000 pounds, and end to end its blade measures close to fifteen feet. The first time Red Adair saw Three-Finger George Curry drive a D-9 Cat he knew he was watching the best Cat skinner he'd ever meet. Three-Finger George could make a D-9 Cat pirouette like a ballerina. In reverse, he could run it up fifty times in a row to within six inches of a gaping pit filled with boiling oil. From his perch high above the ground, he could back it toward a blowing well, back it for a quarter of a mile parallel to a length of high-pressure water hose leading to that well, keeping the Cat's track and the wheels of an attached athey wagon an inch from the hose, and never puncture it.

Chevron once had a well catch fire on a platform in the mouth of the Mississippi River. There was no way to get a barge-mounted crane in close to it, so Brown & Root, a construction company that builds offshore oil platforms, built a second, cantilevered platform that hung out over the water, sixty feet high, next to the one that was on fire. The cantilevered platform — more like a bridge, actually — was 200 feet long and 40 feet wide, and when Brown & Root's most seasoned Cat skinner looked at it he said, "I've driven a tractor for years and years, but I'm not that hard up. There's no way I'm gonna get out there with a tractor. Get somebody else."

"What are we going to do now?" said Chevron's engineer to Red Adair.

"I know an old boy out of Odessa, Texas," Red said to him. "We call him Three-Finger. He'll be here."

So they called Three-Finger George, and sure enough, he was there, working his dozer and the athey wagon back and forth on the bridge, which was slick with oil and swayed from side to side in the wind. Forty feet is not very wide in conditions like that, not even for the world's best Cat skinner, and there were times one of the dozer's tracks hung partway over the edge. There were times, too, when smoke from the fire had Three-Finger working almost blind, but he had the tractor's balance point implanted in his soul and wouldn't quit. He thought about it once or twice, but didn't want to let Red Adair down.

When the fire was out and the well was capped, a reporter asked

Three-Finger George why he did it. "Was it the excitement?" the man asked. "Did you do it for the thrill?"

"Thrill? Son, are you crazy? I did it for the money," Three-Finger told him. "I don't like sleepin' with a hungry woman!" This was in 1978, when Three-Finger George was sixty-eight years old.

Back in West Texas, on the Coyanosa well, it didn't take Red long to test Three-Finger George's skill. The fire was so hot that part of the rig floor had become molten and the floor had sunk, causing a large diesel motor on its far end to slide next to the wellhead. If Red put the fire out without first removing this motor, he knew the spouting oil and distillate would spray directly onto the motor and reignite the fire. Three-Finger George backed up to the well, swung the boom above the motor, and several times hooked onto it, but each time, as he slid it toward the edge of the floor, the motor would fall off the hook.

Red signaled George to drive away from the well to a spot where they could hear each other speak. "Three-Finger, can you put me up there on the floor?" Red asked him.

"Yeah, I can put you up there," George said, "if that's where you're aiming to go, but man, you're gonna be hot."

"I'm aware of that," Red told him.

They used high-volume fire monitors, or nozzles, three of them pumping 5,000 gallons per minute, but at low pressure so as not to knock Red down. George Curry could see him through the spray, in his coveralls and hard hat, stooped beneath a sixty-pound length of log chain he had draped across his back. Slowly, hand-over-hand, Red crawled up onto the wet and slippery boom, which would shortly be as hot as a steam pipe on a January night. He wrapped his legs around it and signaled with one hand, pointing to the motor.

Three-Finger George could see all of it. The athey wagon was hitched to the front of his Cat, and he was facing the well this time, not backing up to it, since there was no one else but Red who could direct him, and Red was on the boom, twenty feet off the ground, slowly being lowered toward the motor and the fire, like a marshmallow preparing to be roasted. Three-Finger knew that if he bucked the Cat, or jerked the boom, Red would go tumbling to the floor, perhaps right onto the wellhead, where he would surely die. Then Red was on the sunken floor of the rig, under a deluge, wrapping the chain around the motor, working quickly but not in panic.

"Jesus Christ, it must be hot," Three-Finger thought, because in spite of all the water, Red's shoes began to smolder and his pant legs caught on fire. The water put the flames out. Three-Finger looked away for just a moment in order to hook the chain, and when he looked back the pants were burning once again. "Can't worry about that," he thought, "gotta think about that motor. Gotta ease it off that floor." Smoothly, carefully, he slid the motor toward the floor's edge, thinking "What will Red do now? How will he get off?" And then he saw him, almost hidden by the spray and by the flames, hanging from the boom by one arm, pointing with the other toward the sky.

"You got it, brother. Up we go," Three-Finger shouted, lifting the boom as he yelled, backing the dozer through the crevassed mud as though it were an iceboat on a lake of glass.

Three-Finger George did 225 more jobs for Red Adair. He saw him walk up on fires, walk around them and into them, calmly as a mother cradling a sleeping child. He saw him with an air pack on his back, working in Alaska at seventy below zero, on poison gas wells, wells spewing H_2S (hydrogen sulfide) — sour gas, the rig hands call it. Breathe it for thirty seconds, you're dead. George saw Adair come away from wells like that with his eyes so red they seemed to glow; he saw him carried unconscious from one H_2S well, watched him come to, take a long drink of water, and go back to work. He saw all of that and more, but he never forgot the job in Coyanosa, in West Texas. "That's the *most* courageous thing I ever saw him do," he'd tell people, "'cause he wasn't on the ground. He didn't have a way out. He was swinging up there in the air, at the mercy of that fire and of my Cat. Now that's a brave son of a bitch, you better believe it!"

The 1953 Lincoln was painted red, as were all of Adair's cars. People assumed this was because of his name, and while in later years that may have been true, the original reason had more to do with communication. Back before car telephones, Red and Myron Kinley would often have to be located while they were on the road for home, so they could change direction to deal with an emergency. There weren't very many red cars on the road in those days. In fact, for many years car makers supplied them only to fire departments, and anyone else wanting a red vehicle had to special-order it. Having a red car made Adair and Kinley easy to spot as they sped along the rural highways of Texas, Louisiana, Oklahoma, and New Mexico.

Say, for example, Kinley's office knew that Red, who had just put out a fire at a well in Ardmore, Oklahoma, was driving due south to Houston, and a call came in for help at a blowout in Mineral Wells, a hundred miles to the west. The office would call the sheriff's office in Gainesville, Texas, or the highway patrol in Denton, and ask the lawmen to be on the lookout for Adair's red Cadillac or Lincoln, which would be coming through town any time, and the cops were more than happy to oblige. For one thing, they all knew about Red by now and enjoyed being thought of as part of his team. For another, Red and Kinley had taken to donating twenty-five dollars a year, and later fifty, to dozens of police department benevolent associations spread along the Gulf Coast and throughout the Southwest. It cost them a few thousand dollars a year, but the practice paid them a whole lot more in the time it saved.

It took the highway patrol an hour and a half to catch up with the '53 Lincoln heading east out of Coyanosa, and they had to use a plane to do it. "Jesus, Red," said the pilot, who had flown alongside him six feet off the ground for ten minutes in order to get Adair's attention, "what the hell you do to that engine? You were doin' a hundred and thirty . . . hell, at one point I think one thirty-five. Ain't a highway patrol car in all of Texas can run like that. Anyhow, you best turn around. Got another well back where you just came from blowin' like crazy."

So Red went back, and the following day while he was mapping out his plan of attack he got a visit from the sheriff up in Monahans, Texas. "Heard about your car," the sheriff said to him. "Heard it'll run faster'n anything on the road."

"It's a fast one, sheriff," Red said. "Fastest thing I've ever driven, on the street."

"Well, Red, I was wondering whether you might be willing to let me give it a try," the sheriff said.

"Help yourself," Red told him. "Time I rig up and get this well capped it'll be four, five days 'til I need it again anyway. Here's the keys. Have yourself some fun."

Now there were some bootleggers out near Coyanosa, making moonshine somewhere in the mountains to the south and selling it in Midland and Odessa, and even as far east as San Angelo. This sheriff had been after these bootleggers for over a year, but they had always given him the slip because their cars were faster than anything his department had. Two days after Red loaned him the Lincoln, the sheriff brought it back with a smile on his face as wide as its grill. "Yes, indeed, that car is quick," he said.

Unless there is great loss of life at the location, tradition calls for a celebration on the night a wild well is controlled. Sometimes, when the fire rages for weeks or months and killing it is truly like a drawn-out military campaign, or even if it can be controlled quickly but is near a center of population, the celebration will be elaborate, replete with entertainment, not unlike a state dinner, and will be attended by politicians, celebrities, local movers-and-shakers, and oil company officials. The atmosphere and protocol of these festivities varies, of course, from place to place.

Once, for instance, in Hanover, Germany, in 1970, after Red put out a fire on a poison gas well that was particularly dangerous because of its proximity to thousands of the area's inhabitants, the town fathers threw a party complete with costumed folk dancers, a brass band, and enough food and beer for hundreds of people. The folks in Hanover offered to buy him a new, red Mercedes but Adair turned it down and asked them instead to give the money the car would have cost to a hospital treating children with severe burns.

In 1964 Red successfully fought a well fire off the coast of Formosa. At the same time, he sold the Chinese Nationalist government some new fire-fighting and well-safety equipment he'd designed, but refused to charge them for putting out the fire. Red stayed on Formosa after the fire was out in order to provide the government there with some technical assistance for future well control. Chiang Kai-shek was so grateful he took Red on a tour of the country and then honored him with a traditional Chinese dinner of tribute where Red was given several pieces of antique Chinese furniture, including an ornately carved chair that now sits like an ancient throne in his Houston condo. At the dinner many toasts were drunk to Red Adair and his men, and to America in general. There was also a moment of silence in honor of the late President John F. Kennedy, who had been shot only months before.

In late 1979 and early 1980 Red did a job in Libya for Exxon. The well cratered, sucking most of the drilling rig, several vehicles, and a large mud tank under the sand, but leaving the flaming wellhead exposed. After Red shot out the fire, the ground all around it was lava-hot, bubbling like a percolator for a hundred yards in every direction, spouting oil and distillate and poisonous H_2S, which played havoc with Red's eyes in spite of the air pack and protective gear he wore. What with drilling a directional well under these conditions and dealing with armed Libyan militants invading his camp to harass him and his men, Red was on this job for six months.

This was during the period of fighting between Libya and Chad, and by the time Red finished the job, he, his men, and three Exxon employees were about the only Americans left in the country. During the last two weeks at their camp in the desert near the well — twenty minutes by air from Port Brega in a Twin-Otter aircraft — the fighting cut them off from resupply and they subsisted on instant coffee and melba toast, so Adair was good and ready for a feast once he finished with the well and had been flown, under cover of darkness, to Port Brega.

The 270-pound head of the country's secret police, who had been assigned to protect Red and his men during their stay in Libya, obliged by inviting the Americans to his house for a special dinner. The Libyans were dressed in their best robes, and everyone sat on the floor, barefoot, the men in one room, the women in another. As the bowls of food began to be passed around, Red noticed that his host was scratching his toes and then sticking his fingers into each of the bowls.

"I'm not really hungry," Red said.

The room grew silent. One of the Exxon executives coughed and became quite pale. He had noticed that the man directly to the right of the police chief had a long knife stuck in the sash of his robe and did not appear at all pleased with Red's remark. Neither did another man packing a nine-millimeter Browning semiautomatic pistol.

"What do you mean, not hungry?" said the police chief. "How could you not be hungry after what you've just been through?"

"Well, you see, Chief, that's just it," said Red. "All that melba toast and coffee shrank my stomach, and I'm afraid if I eat a bite I'll get sick, and see, I got this thing with my stomach that when it acts up I can't fly in an airplane, which reminds me, hadn't we better get goin' if we're gonna get on a flight out of here tonight? That well over in Australia I told you about this morning, you remember that, don't you Chief? I know this dinner's just gettin' under way and all, but Chief, they told me it's blowin' like crazy and they need me there real bad. It's like a matter of honor for me to get over there right away."

The police chief nodded gravely. "I understand," he said. "I'll drive you myself."

The police chief had an old Saab. Whether he was on a stretch of desert highway or a narrow city street he drove it the same at all times: flat out, foot to the floor, scattering whatever or whoever was in his path. Red had come to loathe riding with him, but now he had no choice.

"That's awful kind of you, Chief," he said. "Let's go."

In Coyanosa, back in 1952, in the land of Three-Finger George and tool pushers toting sawed-off shotguns, the celebration took shape as a West Texas poker game in which a faux pas could be just as dire as one made at a tribal dinner in the Middle East. The game was held at a hunting camp in the mountains south of Crane, and it began within two hours of the time the well went dead. Some of the players were clean, with perfectly creased Stetsons and fancy boots, and some were still coated with oil and drilling mud.

They'd been playing for nine hours. While they played they drank moonshine, and once they broke for a dinner of venison steak and beans. At midnight, when the game was almost over, a hand of five-card stud was dealt, and after all the cards were on the table only two of seven players stayed in the game. One was a driller from Kermit, near the New Mexico border, who showed a pair of queens. The other was Red Adair, who may have had a straight, though the driller didn't think so. There was $4,000 in the pot. It was Red's bet, the hand's last bet, and Red threw in five $100 bills.

"You're bluffin'," said the driller, "but I'm out of money, so I'll tell you what I'm gonna do. I'll bet you a night in the sack with my ol' lady against that new Lincoln that you're drivin' that folks claim is so quick. After that, you can keep her around for a week, if that's your fancy."

Nobody in the room moved except for Rush Johnson, who lit a cigarette and smiled. He was up two grand, but the game had gotten boring and he'd been itching to get started back to Houston. Now he was glad he and Red had stuck around. He looked at Adair, as did everybody else, and finally Red spoke. "I ain't never seen your wife," he said, "but I bet she's got more miles on her than my car does. It's cash or crash, partner."

Rush Johnson almost swallowed his cigarette. Refusing the bet was one thing. Insulting the wife of a West Texas rig jockey was something else again. The oil man from Midland who owned the hunting camp sucked on his diamond pinky ring and cast an eye at the far wall, gauging the time it would take him to reach the gun rack hanging there. The driller's best friend, the man he commuted 180 miles a day with, was the six-foot-eight-inch tool pusher. He'd left his shotgun in his car and had spent the evening laughing uproariously at Adair's jokes, but he was still wearing his knife, and the oil man noticed that he was no longer smiling.

"But I tell you what I'm gonna do, since you stuck around and helped me rig up to fight that fire," Red said, pulling four of his hundred back from the pot. "I'm only gonna charge a hundred to find out whether I got the straight or not."

Forever, from the time he got extra food from the cook at the Faith Home when he was six, until he walked away from a well in Indonesia three minutes before it blew up when he was sixty-five, people called Red Adair lucky. They'd listen to him ramble, listen to his slightly slurred, stream-of-consciousness monologues that made them feel as though they'd been patched into three telephone conversations at once, and find it impossible to believe that Adair knew exactly what he was doing all the time. Sometimes, even after they'd seen the precision with which he operated around a wild well, they considered him an absentminded daydreamer, one of those fortunate few for whom things just seemed to fall into place. They didn't realize that his high-speed Texas drawl, delivered like bursts of automatic gunfire, was the verbal equivalent of speed-reading. While they were trying to make sense of one paragraph, he had already galloped ahead three chapters, assuming his listeners were on the same horse. Even Red's best friends would chuckle when he cut loose with one of his oral barrages. "How the hell could someone who manages to fuse past, present, and future into one all-encompassing tense be anything but lucky to survive in the places Red ventures?" they'd wonder. "How can such a person really plan out every single move he makes?"

For twenty years Red packed a fifty-foot length of rope with his gear in case the hotel he was staying in caught fire and he had to shinny from his window down to safety. Fortunately, he never had to use the rope, but if he *had* used it to escape a conflagration, people would have called him a lucky dog, which is exactly what Rush Johnson called him for the first three hours of that trip toward home.

"You're a lucky son of a bitch, Red," he kept saying. "Never mind the guy lost to ya. If he hadn't had that hundred stuck inside his boot to call your hand we'd'a had to shoot our way out of that place, and neither one of us had a gun! Please don't ever do that to me again."

"Hell no, Rush. I won't. I promise you that. You got my word on it," Red said. "I sure was lucky on that one, wasn't I?" He never did tell his friend he'd seen the driller stick the hundred there before the game began. If those around him refused to keep their eyes open that was their business. For him, never closing his eyes was crucial. It was the only reason he was still alive.

CHAPTER FIFTEEN

I was never scared about Red being out in the oil field, probably because I didn't know enough about what went on to be scared. Nobody outside the oil field did in those days because the wells were usually in the middle of nowhere and the jobs were not as publicized as they are today.

I did know that people got hurt. I knew the business was dangerous. I knew men were killed. Red had a steel hat with a chunk knocked out of it where it was hit by a falling wrench. What I thought about most, I guess, was that if he got hurt it would be his leg, probably because of what had happened to Mr. Kinley's leg, so when Mr. Kinley called me in 1953 — when Red got hurt in California — I immediately thought, "He lost a leg." That isn't what happened, but that's what I thought.

Kemmie Adair

ENGLEWOOD, CALIFORNIA — 1953

It was New Year's Day. Red and Kinley were thirty minutes from finishing with a gas-well fire across from Hollywood Racetrack. They had been there a week, cleaning up the location, putting out the fire, and taking the old wellhead valve off. All they had left to do was put the new valve on and they were through. Thirty, maybe forty minutes at most, was all it was going to take them, even though the mud around the well was knee deep and the well was blowing more mud, along with sand and rocks, into the air.

Red waded through the mud, pulling a steel cable that was attached to a crane — a drag line, as it's called — up to the wellhead. Then he walked over to the crane operator to explain what he wanted the man to do. The crane operator had been drinking since early on New Year's Eve. Red knew it. He could smell the whiskey on the man's breath, but Adair wanted to be done with the job. Once again, for what seemed like the tenth time since he'd begun working in the oil patch, he was away from Houston for Christmas and New Year's, and he wanted to go home, so he disregarded this breach of behavior at a wild well.

The crane operator leaned down out of his cab to hear what Red was saying, and when he did, he kicked the cab into gear. Instantly, the cab spun and caught Red between it and the base of the crane, crushing his pelvis and jamming his chin back until his head touched his shoulder blades. An engineer who witnessed the whole thing began to scream and the crane operator finally heard him and kicked the crane back in the opposite direction, turning Red loose and sending him flying into the mud. Had the crane operator waited another couple of seconds, Red's neck would have been broken, killing him immediately.

RED

I was conscious the whole time. I was mad as hell, and the first thing I was going to do was get up and whip that crane operator. I was cussing at him and trying to get out of the mud, and that's when I realized how badly I was hurt, because I couldn't move. My pelvis was shattered. My hip had popped out, and that crane had ripped me up the spine. Luckily, I had just emptied my bladder or it would've been ruptured and I'd have died.

When they got me in the hospital, they popped the hip back in and sewed me up. Then I suffered delayed shock. I started having the shakes and my fever went sky-high. I was delirious, I felt myself slipping, but I could hear everything that went on in the room. The nurse said, "Oh, we lost him. He's dead." The doctor bent over me, and that's the last thing I remember.

When I woke up, they had me all taped up and full of IVs. I looked at the doctor, who said, "Boy, you really fooled us. We thought for sure you were dead." I said, "Doc, I can tell you everything that went on in that room." He said, "Baloney." I said, "Well, the X-ray technician was a dark-haired German girl." The doctor could hardly believe it, while telling me I was right. Then they broke the news that I'd never walk again. I said, "Well, I fooled you once, and I'll fool you again."

Kemmie had flown to California as soon as she'd heard about the accident from Myron Kinley, who called her and began crying over the phone. She had never seen or heard Kinley cry before and remained absolutely petrified from the moment she left Houston. For two weeks she sat there in the hospital room watching Red, feeling helpless and completely alone. She was staying in a hotel near the hospital. She had never been in a hotel room by herself before. She had never been away from her kids like that before, where she couldn't get back to them the same day, even when she was singing. She might come home at four in the morning after a performance or a club date, but she had never stayed away from them overnight. When she left the hospital, went back to the hotel, and closed the door to her room she felt like she was the only person in the world.

The doctor had told her they were worried about infections and about Red's blood. They had been giving him transfusions, and for some reason, every time he received one he'd have a reaction and begin to shake. He was in terrible pain, and the more he shook the worse his pain became. This went on for days. Then, miraculously, Red's condition began to improve. He was still in great pain, but the fever had subsided and the doctors said that he would live.

Kemmie went back to Houston after two weeks. Red stayed in the hospital in California for two months. Finally, he was well enough to come home on a train with a nurse, but his personal physician and close family friend, Dr. Tuttle, insisted he stay in the hospital in Houston. At first, Dr. Tuttle put Red in a steel corset. Then he progressed to a walker. After he was released from the hospital, his friends built a ramp to the backyard so he could get outside and watch them tinker with his stock car.

This infuriated Kemmie, who had never cared much for the stock-car crowd to begin with. She found some of them to be crude and coarse, perfectly content to mooch off Red — take money from him, use his car and his tools, and eat his food — but never give anything to him in return. As soon as they heard Red was back in town, these stock-car buddies, their girlfriends, and their wives began coming around his house expecting the same old handouts, only now there was little or nothing to take.

Myron Kinley may have loved Red like a son, but he gave Adair no financial support when he was hurt. The only money Red and Kemmie had coming in to pay for hospital and doctor bills and survival for him and his family was a $40-a-week workman's compensation check. In no time, they went through what little money they had in the bank and were reduced to using the $1,000 nest egg given to Kemmie by her father.

The Adairs' financial crisis came to a head when they were almost out of money and Red spent most of what was left on a racing camshaft for his car. On the evening the camshaft was delivered, Kemmie took Jimmy and Robyn to her favorite fried-chicken restaurant for dinner because she wanted some privacy from the stock-car people running in and out of her house. When she came home, her kitchen had been wrecked, all the food was gone, and Red was asleep. Then she saw it. The infamous camshaft was leaning in the corner of the living room still wrapped in its cardboard shipping package. Kemmie stormed into the bedroom.

"Red, that's it," she screamed. "My kitchen's ruined, we don't have any food, and we don't have any more money. This thing, whatever it is, that you just ordered for your race car, is going back where it came from, because we're not paying for it, and furthermore, either the stock car goes or the kids and I go. And you know I'm not jokin'."

The stock car went. The stock-car crowd disappeared, and Red, four months after his accident and still using a walker, went back to work against doctor's orders. He was in great pain. In fact, the pain from the crane accident would remain for many months and the stiffness in his hips and back would stay with him for years. Red adapted to his condition though, and was soon bounding through oil-slick mud, snaking his body over and around the wreckage of fiery drilling rigs.

RED

I went to a job in Ganado, Texas, where a well was on fire. I had me some crutches, and I had that little basket thing, that walker, to get around with, and I managed pretty good. I could run a bulldozer, even. I put that fire out, shot it out, and capped the well, and they put a picture of me in the paper, y'know, crutches and all. That's how Dr. Tuttle found out, and he was some kind of mad at me, too. He said, "What the hell you trying to do, kill yourself?" I told him, "Dr. Tuttle, I have to work. I'm broke." He said, "Listen, you're not going to be any use to your family under the ground."

That's when he took my crutches away from me and stuck me back in the hospital. He got me working with weights and pulleys to build my strength. Finally, I said, "That's it. I'm gettin' out of this place and goin' to work whether anybody likes it or not." I went down to a job in Mexico in the mountains. I took a hatchet and chopped off the crutches at an angle so I could go up and down the mountain. It was real muddy there, and believe it or not, I could get around on that mountain better with my crutches than anybody else on that job could with just their two legs. Dr. Tuttle was still angry with me.

Thought I was nuts. I had to tell him, "Dr. Tuttle, my family has to eat. And maybe I *will* die, but at least it'll be while I'm doin' somethin' I love."

ROBYN

Intimacy, showing affection openly, is very difficult for Daddy, but that doesn't mean he doesn't feel it. You have to understand his background, where he came from. There was very little intimacy there, and they were so poor, dirt poor. He wasn't trained to be intimate. He was trained that you either work hard or you'll starve.

In 1980 mother had a stroke. Her sister, Jonilee (Aunt Sis, we called her), was dying of cancer so Mama was having a real rough time. Daddy called me in the middle of the night and he was crying. I was shocked. I mean this is the rough, tough, macho Red Adair we're talking about. "Bobbie, I don't think she's going to make it," he said, "and I don't know what I'm going to do without her." See, they don't stay together that much physically, but they're always together emotionally. They need each other to survive. I don't think either one of them would last very long without the other.

In a way they're the most incompatible people God ever created, they're like sand and silk, they just don't meld, but then on another level they make an incredibly dynamic working force. He's this big ol' ship on a stormy sea, and she's his anchor. It's a very bizarre relationship.

HOUSTON — 1988

Red Adair's offices, occupying the third floor of a building he owns along the Katy Freeway west of downtown Houston, are like the halls of a museum. Everywhere on the walls are mural-sized photographs of fires he and his men have fought, and these pictures, filled with towering flames and clouds of smoke, are riveting, enthralling, overpowering. You could stand in front of them for hours, moving from one to another, speaking in hushed tones. They are that spectacular.

His own cavernous office — with mementos from around the world; signed pictures from presidents, governors, and heads of state; shots of the family — is interesting enough, but it's the fires, as real in their way as a Rodin sculpture or a Van Gogh field of wheat, that pull at you like a primeval magnet. "He walked into those," you think. "He put them out." Even when Red isn't there, they remind you of his presence and of what he's done.

You feel his presence in his daughter's office too, the place where she handles financial matters and public relations for the Red Adair Company. It is set between her father's and the smaller ones occupied by Red's men and is a bastion of femininity in this man's world. It is light and airy with a decorator's touch — upholstered chairs in pastel tones around a glass-topped coffee table, a large, rococo desk and chair — but Red presides in a portrait on the wall behind the desk, formidable and in control.

For three days after her father left for Scotland to fight the Piper Alpha fire, Robyn Adair sat in front of this picture, listening to the constant ringing of the phone. Newspapers, magazines, and radio and television stations from around the world all wanted to know what was going on, where Red was at that very moment, how he was going to deal with the platform. Politely, she told all of them the truth. She didn't know any more about the disaster than they did.

It was at times like this she would wish that her friend Margaret Ochs was still around to talk to. Margaret worked for the Red Adair Company for almost eleven years. She started out as a receptionist in 1972 and ended up handling all the shipping and purchasing of the equipment orders for both foreign and domestic jobs. By the time she left in 1983 she had practically become a member of the Adair family. In fact, she even named her daughter after Robyn. Eleven years earlier the EKOFISK Bravo, another platform in the North Sea, had blown out and received considerable attention in the press. In Margaret's words, "EKOFISK was a media nightmare." Well, EKOFISK was a piece of cake in Robyn's mind compared to this.

Finally, late on Friday afternoon, she'd had enough. "I'm going for a ride," she told Paula Pearce, head of Red Adair's office staff. "If Daddy or one of the guys call in from Scotland, patch 'em through to me." She got up from her desk and before leaving the office turned and looked at her father's picture. He seemed so powerful in it, as though nothing could ever hurt him, but quite frankly, she was worried about his being over there on the North Sea. Two years earlier, when he was seventy-one, he'd had a minor heart attack. He'd recovered quickly, but his doctor had told him to stay away from oil-well fires, from the intense heat and the pressure. "Right," she thought. "Red Adair stay away from oil-well fires. Like telling a nun to stay away from church."

She took the elevator down to the ground floor and walked to her dark blue Mercedes 420-SEL sedan parked near the building's front entrance. Robyn Adair is a small, attractive, energetic woman with sparkling eyes and the same dark red hair as her father. She also shares his aggressive jaw, firmly set mouth, and determined, short-legged stride. Like Red, she has a quick mind and a burning will to succeed, but she lacks the instinctive, split-second decision-making ability that has kept him alive on the job and made him a successful businessman as well.

"Daddy has a knack that I don't have," she says. "I can get all the information together and make a decision based strictly on facts, and it'll be wrong. Daddy can do everything wrong in a decision-making process, and almost always it turns out right. There's a killer instinct in business he has that I don't have." Still, Red has great respect for his daughter's ability to persevere. "Robyn's a survivor," he says. "I don't worry about her making it when I'm not around. She'll do just fine."

She drove south toward Galveston, toward the beach house Red helped her buy, which sits in a field of sea grass fifty yards from the gulf. An Anita Baker tape played softly on the car's stereo system, and she drifted with the music, thinking, "When did he ever listen to a doctor anyway? When did he ever listen to anything but some voice deep inside him that seemed to always pull him through?" She was remembering now how he disobeyed Dr. Tuttle, way back when he was hurt.

It was one of the first memories she had of him, long ago in 1953 when she was nine. He was flat on his back when they wheeled him off the train and he turned and smiled at her. "Hi, Little Pig," he said. It was her nickname then and she hated it ("That's what everybody called me," she'd later tell her friends. "Is it any wonder I had a weight problem?"). But when he said it that day and smiled she felt warm inside. A few days after he came home from the hospital, she went up to his bedroom and sat on the floor next to where he lay and told him she loved him. "I love you too, honey." It was the first time he said that to her, and she never forgot it.

She had been a shy child when she was little, almost reclusive, and she talked in a strange way that sounded to Kemmie almost like a foreign language. Eventually the doctor found she had a problem with her ears. When it was corrected her speech became normal, and she came out of her shell. Then, in 1955, when she was eleven, they moved from the east end of Houston, out into the country where everybody knew everybody else. She learned to ride a horse, other girls began coming around to visit all the time, and Robyn blossomed. She took dancing lessons (her costumes were always the prettiest; Kemmie once sewed 7,250 sequins on one herself) and developed a wide circle of friends.

She remembered Jersey Village well, remembered it now in a flood of memories as she rolled on toward the beach. She thought about that time in the late 1950s when there was lots of work and Red was doing well financially, and when finally, in 1959, he went into business for himself. His company was small — just Red and Coots in the field and Joy Hamilton in the office, taking the calls from frantic oil companies, keeping things as straight and orderly as one human being could for Red Adair.

She thought about Coots. Edward "Coots" Matthews. The Cooter. The tall, slow, easy cowboy who listened a lot and talked only a little, and got along with everybody (but don't cross him — he could switch gears faster than a race-car driver, and he loved to fight). Coots, seven years younger than her father, worked for Haliburton, a company that made oil-field equipment. When Coots lost his job at Haliburton, Rush Johnson, who was married to Coots's sister, spoke to her father, who in turn talked to Myron Kinley about Coots. With his business growing, Kinley agreed that he could use an extra hand. He had already hired Boots. Now Coots joined the Kinley Company too, working under Red's command.

They were as different from each other as a goat is from an owl, Boots and Coots, but they had one thing in common; they were both wild hell-raisers of the first degree. Once, Myron Kinley told Red he was going to let both of them go, but Red pleaded with his mentor, saying he could turn them into first-rate hands.

"All right," Kinley said, "but they're your responsibility. You gotta teach 'em and you gotta control 'em."

"I promise you, Mr. Kinley," Red answered. "They're both loose cannons, but they both got guts. You won't be sorry." Red made good on his promise, and with his guidance, he and his two helpers became a unit, a well-oiled machine, for many years the only force combating wild wells around the world.

Robyn thought some more about those early days in Jersey Village, when the men would do a job, go home, or go out to one of the bars where the oil-field guys hung out, drink some beer, whoop it up, and then go back to work. Those were really the best times, before all the craziness started, all the notoriety that began with The

Devil's Cigarette Lighter, all the megabucks and megadeals and megacompanies. Then the oil boom of the 1960s hit, and there were chartered jets, and then Red's own jets — first one Lear and then a bigger one — and all the publicity: *Life* magazine and *Newsweek*, the Johnny Carson show, and all the rest.

It was simpler before that. The money was great, she'd be the first one to admit it. (As Kemmie once told her: "Bobbie, I've been rich and I've been poor, and believe me, rich is better.") But the closeness that had been there for those few years had disappeared. There were parties back then, out by their pool with high-school friends and oil-field hands, where her mother sang and her father cooked enough hot dogs and hamburgers to feed an army. There was the Red Adair spring fish fry: all winter long, Jimmy and Raymond would seine the creek for grass shrimp or small fish, which they'd throw in the pool and feed until spring. When it was warm enough to start swimming, Red drained the pool and shoveled out the fish. Then, while all the guys in the neighborhood scrubbed the walls and the bottom of the swimming pool, the girls would prepare food for the party. Once, there'd been enough food to feed a hundred people. There were the times her parents raced their cars and the time her father got his car stuck up in a tree.

She'd stopped singing and began to laugh. That was one she'd never forget. It had to be 1957 or '58. Red had a brand new Lincoln with a car phone — one of the first car phones in the state — and he'd gone down to the Bulldog Drive-in to meet some friends and show it off. These were buddies from way back in high school. The drive-in, named for the Reagan High Bulldogs, was owned by Al Hocker and run by Carter Puccio, both of whom had been friends of Red's for years. Naturally, he'd stayed later than he'd said he would, so before he left he called to tell them he was bringing home barbequed chicken for the family to eat. Everyone loved it when he brought home chicken for dinner. That would get him off the hook.

The weather that night was terrible, lots of rain and fifty-mile-an-hour gusts of wind. A giant oak tree had come down across the road that Red had picked to travel back to Jersey Village. It was dark, he was speeding, and he never saw the tree, not until he'd climbed eight feet up it with his car.

"Damn it, Kemmie," he screamed into the Lincoln's phone, "they ought to know better than to leave trees in the middle of the road. C'mon down here and get me, and bring a camera 'cause I want a picture of this. I'm gonna sue the city."

"Red, where are you?" Kemmie asked.

"I'm two blocks from my sister Faye's house," he said. "I'm in my new car. And I'm in this damn tree."

When they got there they could hardly believe what they saw. The Lincoln was stuck up in the branches of the oak, way up, so you could see all the way underneath it. As usual, Red had bought chicken in quantities normally associated with a kitchen purchase for a small hotel. There were pieces of it everywhere, all over the inside of the car, hanging in the branches, strewn across the street, all of it dripping with barbeque sauce. The police were there too, but they had no idea what to do, and Red was paying them no attention. Instead he was high above them, in his car, on the phone, yelling at the mayor of Houston, whom he didn't know but whose number he had found. "Damn it all, Mayor," he was shouting. "You got this tree here where it shouldn't be. Now I'm stuck up in it with my car."

They'd finally coaxed him down, and of course he never sued anybody. In the morning he'd traded the Lincoln for another one, and a short time after that, she remembered, he and the mayor had become good friends. Those were the days when the business was fun for him, before it got so big that he didn't know everything that was going on, before it got to be so big he worried all the time that things weren't being done exactly the way he wanted them done.

"Daddy knew he could trust himself," she thought, "but when the business got beyond where it could be totally controlled by one man, knower of all things, when it got to be such an enormous success, then he didn't have much fun anymore."

She drove down the road parallel to the beach, pulled into her driveway, got out of the Mercedes, and climbed the stairs to the deck of her beach house, a magnificent, two-story dwelling set up on pillars to protect it from stormy seas. This was part of the good side of being Red Adair's daughter — this house, the car, her furs and jewels — all those things that people envied, thinking if only they had them their lives would be perfect.

She knew it wasn't quite like that, for as she looked out over the water, tinted amber on the surface from the setting sun, she felt alone, and a mild wave of panic swept over her. That was the bad side, the feeling of abandonment that would overcome her if she had to meet someone at the airport and their plane was twenty minutes late, if her boyfriend didn't call her every day, if she took a long ride in her car and didn't call her father to tell him where she was. She was sure the feeling came because all her life — even during the good times back in Jersey Village, at picnics, before dance recitals, when the family was about to gather for Thanksgiving or Christmas, when things were really neat — what she remembered was her father always walking out the door. Mostly, he went off to work, but other times he just went off with his friends, to bars, or to work on cars, and later, when he raced boats, to the yacht club at the bay where there were drinks and jokes and maybe even women, but there wasn't any threat of true intimacy, of closeness. Maybe, she thought, that was why she'd been married three times and her brother four. Maybe that was why her mother had protected them so zealously it took them both forever to grow up, and when she and Jimmy were finally out of the house, why Kemmie had left for Austin.

Although the temperature was still almost ninety degrees, she shuddered from a sudden chill. She went inside the house, where she'd be near a telephone in case Red called, and sat for a long time, feeling torn, feeling pulled in two directions, by the two sides of her father's personality. She remembered a day in 1983 when she rode, also in a long Mercedes, with her parents, on a summer afternoon.

It seemed to her the ride had taken a week, even though the trip was only fifteen miles. Her father and mother were in the front seat of the car and she was in back, as nervous as she'd ever been in her life. The trouble her son, Paul Wayne, was having with substance abuse had gotten completely out of hand, and he'd been admitted to a rehabilitation center outside Houston. He'd been there for two weeks, and this was the first time they'd been allowed to go and visit him. Chemical abuse and rehabilitation centers were things that were totally alien to her father, something only criminals or hoodlums on TV got involved with, and she was scared of the way he might react.

She sat in back, in the deeply cushioned leather seat of the Mercedes, twisting a handkerchief in her fingers, remembering the way Red's face would turn almost purple when he lost his temper. It was as though half her life was spent anticipating the great presents he bought her and the other half spent walking on eggs, waiting for him to explode over one thing or another. Her father's temper. You never knew what might trigger it. Paul Wayne himself said jokingly one time that an employee could wreck a Cadillac one day and Red would laugh it off. The man could lose the keys the next day and be fired.

In the front, Red talked to her mother now about some new equipment he was designing, avoiding the issue of Paul Wayne. That could mean anything, and Robyn continued to worry. A station wagon full of kids pulled alongside the Mercedes. The kids saw the Red Adair Company emblem on the side and stared open-mouthed at her and her folks. Robyn thought about the mountains of little American-flag pins Red took with him wherever he traveled. He gave them out to everyone, cops on the street, the pilot of the airplane, presidents of giant corporations. He even gave them out in Russia when he was over there on a job. The Russian authorities must have loved that. And kids. He loved to give them to kids all over the world. "Are you really Red Adair, the oil-well fire fighter?" they'd ask. They couldn't believe a big-time hero would go around handing out little gifts to strangers. People were always so in awe of success and notoriety and money. They didn't realize that even heroes are just plain folks with hopes and fears and problems, the same as everyone else.

The Mercedes turned in at the hospital gate and parked, and the three of them went inside. Robyn was sweating nonstop. Then they were in the visiting room and Paul Wayne came in. "Don't let Daddy make a terrible scene," she prayed. "Please." She looked over and saw tears running down her mother's cheeks and realized she was crying too. Paul Wayne stood in front of them looking frightened. "God, he's so thin," Robyn thought. Red crossed the room toward him and suddenly Paul Wayne was in her father's arms and Red was hugging him tight.

"Now, Paul Wayne," he said, "you gotta face this thing like a man and beat it. But don't you ever forget that I love you. We all love you, and we're going to stand behind you and help you see this through. We're your family and that's what family is for."

"So he missed dance recitals," she thought. "So he missed family picnics and Thanksgiving dinners. So he got mad for strange reasons known only to himself, but at least he didn't stay mad long. So he didn't show emotion on a day-to-day basis and maybe even ran away from it, because maybe he thought if he gave in to it all the time that would mean that he was weak. So he did all of those things. But when push came to shove, when a friend needed him late at night, when a child who had been burned needed money for an operation to save his life, when hospitals for crippled children needed funds for special equipment, when her own son, whose father wasn't around when he was young, needed a man to hug him and tell him he loved him and would see him through his pain, Red Adair was there."

He always had an amazing rapport with kids. She remembered the time he went to a children's hospital in Canada. He was the grand marshal of the Calgary Stampede that year, and while he was there he went to visit the children in the hospital. There was a little boy in a room by himself who had been in a terrible accident and had stopped talking. The nurses had known Red was coming to visit and told the little boy, hoping to perk him up. The minute Red walked into the room, the little boy looked up and said, "Hi, Red." It was the first time he'd spoken in six months. Before Red left, he gave the boy the gold hardhat that had been presented to him by the Stampede officials. The boy put the hat on his head, waved, and said, "Good-bye, Red." Red told Robyn the memory of that boy would stay with him until the day he died.

"God, I hope he's safe," she thought. "Don't let something happen to him over in the North Sea."

CHAPTER SIXTEEN

Right after I started in business for myself I was riding in a car with Rush Johnson and John Mecom, Sr. Old Man Mecom was a wildcatter, one of the real pioneers in the oil field, and a great guy, too. He helped me out a helluva lot when I was first working in the oil patch. He got me jobs shooting wells, got me snubbing jobs, things like that. So we're riding along, and he's talking about buying this building and investing in that business, and we said, "Boy, all that sounds good, but it ain't us." Old Man Mecom said to Rush and me, "Well, when you guys get a few million dollars together it will be." I said, "A few million? I'd be plenty happy with one million." He said, "Red, you'll see. Once you get that first million the other ones come a whole lot easier."

Red Adair

HOUSTON — 1959

In June of 1959 Red Adair finally went into business for himself. There were many people in the oil patch who were surprised, not that he started his own company, but that he didn't *already* own it. They assumed Kinley had long since sold out to Red, since Myron Kinley's injuries had finally caught up with him, and by the mid-1950s, when the Kinley Company was called to control a wellfire or blowout, it was Red, with Boots and Coots as his assistants, who almost always did the job. This meant that Red was doing virtually all of the wild-well work in the oil patch, because until the 1970s he *had* no competition.

That Adair waited so long to buy Kinley out was a mystery, even to some of his good friends who only saw one side of him, the outer Adair, as it were: Red the Fearless, the consummate Texas wild-man, tearing up the countryside in his crimson Cadillac, his trunk filled with explosives. To them, he was the lone gunslinger with a high-powered hose, ready for a showdown at the well. He'd set that sucker straight and disappear in a cloud of dust, and always be ready for a good time when he was back in town, always be ready to pick up the tab, too. Good ol' Red. "Still workin' for the Old Man? Shit, Red, you crazy or somethin'?" They missed plenty, these people who thought they knew him well.

They knew this: He had just turned forty-four in June of '59, and had by then spent thirty years of his life working hard for someone else. For nearly twenty of those years he fought wild wells, from the equator to the arctic circle, and the continuous exposure to extremes of heat and cold, from the weather as well as the fires, had taken its toll. The skin of his face, neck, and hands was creased and blotchy, and in the next twenty years he would undergo numerous operations for skin cancer. Constant proximity to gas and distillate had left the tissue around his eyes puffy and red, and despite taking precautions by packing his ears with cotton soaked in vaseline, the noise of the wells had permanently damaged his hearing. He could hear every word of a conversation only if people spoke loud and slow.

He was considerably thicker through the chest, middle, and thighs than when he first started out in the oil patch, but there was nothing flabby about him. Instead, the lean, sinewy strength of his youth had been transformed into the kind of bulky power that includes deceptive quickness and is most often found in professional athletes. In Adair's case, this quickness was further enhanced by his intensity and high energy level, which had in no way diminished over the years.

Robyn was still in high school in 1959, and Kemmie spent almost all her time at home. Jimmy was in college. It was Red's dream that his son would graduate from college and become an engineer or scientist, but that was not to be. In two years Jimmy would get married for the first time, quit college for good, and go to work for his father. It was Jimmy's dream to become a fire-fighting legend like Red. Though neither Red nor Kemmie wanted their son to fight wild wells, they relented, and the stormy, on-and-off-again, twenty-year working relationship began between Red and his son.

Robyn also would quit school and get married in 1961. The year before, Red bought Kemmie her first lake house — a rustic cabin, actually — and in 1961 her withdrawal from Houston would begin.

Red's father had been dead for four years by 1959. Though he didn't live to see Red become famous, he did see him attain a measure of financial success that neither one of them had imagined possible when Red left school in 1929. Red was unable to spend much time with either of his parents in their later years, but he never neglected them. When his father was very ill with emphysema, Red made sure all the doctor bills were sent to him and paid for regular deliveries of oxygen to Charlie Adair's house.

Ironically, Red's mother, whose health was more fragile, outlived her husband by nine years. She *did* see her son achieve worldwide renown, but Red would never tell her when he was going to fight a fire so as not to worry her, and she learned about his exploits from newspaper and television reports. She cut out all the stories about him from the newspapers and kept them in a large scrapbook displayed on a coffee table in the living room of the house Red bought for her in the Heights.

In 1981, when Kemmie had her stroke, Red was putting out a fire at a well in East Texas. Kemmie didn't want anyone to tell Red about her illness while he was at the fire because she was afraid he'd be so worried he'd get hurt himself. By the time Red got back to Houston and found out about Kemmie, it was too late at night for him to visit the hospital, so instead he dropped over to his sister Faye's house in the Heights. Faye made him a sandwich, and the two of them talked until the early hours of the morning, reminiscing about their childhood. Finally, Red grew silent and sat staring off into space for several seconds.

"Do you think Mamma and Daddy would be proud of me?" he said, suddenly. To Faye, it was almost like the time, nearly fifty years before, that she'd found him crying in the backyard because he had to quit school.

"Oh, Red," she said. "I know they'd be proud of you. They *were* proud of you."

Rush Johnson said he talked Red into leaving Myron Kinley. Kemmie had tried subtly to persuade Red for years to leave, but she was too smart and not egotistical enough to assume she was totally responsible. Both she and Rush pointed to a night in the spring of 1959 as the moment Red decided to make the break. Rush and his wife Maureen had walked across the little bridge over the creek that separated the Johnsons' house from the Adairs' in Jersey Village and were sitting on the Adairs' patio with Red and Kemmie. Rush, Kemmie, and Maureen were all encouraging Red, each giving reasons why the time had come for him to go out on his own. The four of them had had the same conversation many times before, but on this night Red finally turned to them and said, "Yeah, I guess you're right. I'm gonna talk to the Old Man tomorrow morning and do it."

In fact, Red had decided to make the break from Myron Kinley years before that night, but his loyalty and love for Kinley had slowed his departure. While his wife and friends sat talking to him, he was thinking of a burning gas well thousands of miles away, in the desert of Iran, that he had fought three years before, in 1956.

The well was in the Ahvaz Field — Ahvaz #6 — fifty miles north of the Persian Gulf. At first Kinley went to control it himself, taking Boots along with him to help. After a week, Red received a call from Kinley, who told him to come over to Iran to join him at the well.

When Adair arrived at the location, he took one look at his mentor and knew Myron Kinley should not be fighting a wild well. A week in the desert had totally exhausted the older man, his usually florid face was ghostly white, and he could hardly walk. The well was still blazing a half mile away.

"Red, I've shot it out three times, and it keeps reigniting," Kinley said. "It looks like we finally met our match."

"Mr. Kinley, you go on back to the camp and get some rest," Red told him. "I'll see what I can do with it."

After Kinley left the location, Red grabbed a tin shield, instructed the men handling the water monitors to keep a heavy spray on him, and approached the fire. As soon as he got close to the wellhead, he saw the problem. Down at the bottom of the bradenhead — the heavy, flanged, steel fitting connected to the first length of drill pipe in the hole — was a little nipple through which gas was blowing under great pressure. The gas was hitting white-hot rocks and sand around the wellhead, creating a blowtorch effect that kept reigniting the fire. In the days when Red first began fighting oil-well fires with Myron Kinley, his boss would have been able to get in close enough to the blazing wellhead to spot this problem, but now the intense heat and noise were too much for his crippled body to stand.

RED

It took about a week to get that well cleaned up. I got me a bulldozer and dug a hole in the ground around the wellhead big enough to put a condominium in, and it was hard diggin'. That sand was like concrete, and the well was still burning so it was hotter'n hell to boot. After I got the wellhead exposed like I wanted it, I made a big horseshoe-shaped charge and I put it on the end of a long piece of drill pipe that we mounted on the bulldozer. I drove on up to that well myself and put the shot in there just right. Then I went back to the camp and told 'em I was sick. I said I had dysentery. There wasn't a thing wrong with me, but I wanted the Old Man to have the honor of shooting that thing out. He went out to the well and set it off, and man, you should have seen the happy expression on his face when he came back to camp. He said, "Red, I really didn't think we were going to get that one."

I knew right then he wasn't up to it anymore, but there was no way I was going to embarrass him by shooting it out myself. He'd been too good to me. He was such a fine old man. And anyway, you just don't do that kind of thing to someone you love.

After Ahvaz #6, it was obvious to both Red and Myron Kinley that Kinley's days in the oil patch were numbered and that the relationship between the two of them had to change. At first, they talked about restructuring Kinley's company in order to give Adair a share of the profits (he had never received more than a salary and a year-end bonus), but Kinley's son, Jack, wouldn't hear of that arrangement.

Jack Kinley and Red never got along. The younger Kinley spent all his time in the company office poring over the books, never setting foot in the oil field, and was known to be quite parsimonious. What bothered Red most, however, was not that Jack Kinley counted every dime that crossed his desk, but that Kinley's son, who never worked out in the oil patch, tried to tell Red how to do his job. Not only that, he wouldn't confront Adair face-to-face, but instead sent him notes. The problems between the two of them that had simmered for years came to a head just after Red fought the famous CATCO fire in 1958.

CATCO was a consortium of four major oil companies — Continental, Tidewater, Atlantic and Cities' Service — that contracted with a drilling company to build an enormous platform in the Gulf of Mexico off the coast of Louisiana. Eighteen wells had been drilled from the platform when it came loose, and every one of those wells began to burn. Offshore drilling was then in its infancy, and since this was the first major fire on an offshore drilling platform, there was no precedent for controlling it. When Red Adair arrived at the scene with Boots and Coots to help him, he was treading in new territory, fighting a familiar enemy on totally unfamiliar ground. There was no walking up on an offshore platform to check it out, no way to set your explosive charges and run for cover. Once you climbed up on that baby you stayed there until somebody plucked you off, and no one had ever climbed onto a burning offshore platform before.

Neither had anyone previously dealt with eighteen burning wells at once. On land, even in the case of multiple blowouts or fires, there was always plenty of working space between them — the setup on land was one rig, one well — and you could shoot them out and cap them independently. Not here. Not this time. These wells were so close together that blowing them out one at a time with a conventional explosive charge would only compound the wreckage.

The men in charge of the CATCO operation stood on a barge a hundred yards from the burning platform and asked Red Adair what he planned to do.

"I'm goin' up there and check it out," Red said. "It's the only way I'll be able to figure out how to kill it. You got a crane operator with a steady hand?"

"We have a real fine one, Red," said the CATCO company man.

"That's good," said Red, "because he's gonna have to swing me up there and drop me exactly where I tell him."

The crane swung slow and steady, with Red standing in a small basket made of steel grating that hung by a hook from the end of the crane's boom. Once or twice, as he lowered Adair toward the platform, the crane operator lost sight of Red, who was obscured by thick clouds of smoke and sheets of flame, but finally he saw Red's hand pointing down, motioning to a spot on the platform where there was no fire. He could see Red hop onto the floor without hesitation, then disappear behind a pile of iron debris. All the crane operator could do then was wait for Red to return and hope that the flames didn't fan out further to envelop the basket.

The rig floor was covered with oil, ankle deep and boiling hot, and was such a mess Red couldn't tell which of the eighteen burning wells had started the conflagration. As he crept from one side of the rig to the other, however, he could see that every one of the wells was burning and would have to be put out individually. Red moved from place to place on the floor, writing notes in his pocket notebook, eyeballing distances between the wells and various pieces of twisted equipment, moving as quickly as possible, since the hot oil was blistering his feet and legs. By the time he returned to the crane's basket, he had decided on a plan of attack.

The first thing Red did was get the drilling company to build another platform next to the one on fire to use as a base of operations. Then he brought in several large derrick barges and rigged them with pumps and fire monitors to spray thousands of gallons of water on the burning rig. Eventually, he would design his own offshore pumps — the famed "Red Iron" — with powerful turbocharged twelve-cylinder Detroit Diesel engines capable of hurling up to 5,000 gallons per minute straight up into the air. On this job, however, he had to make do with standard firefighting pumps, the sort you'd find on a fire truck. These had manifolds made of lightweight aluminum that were unable to withstand the kind of water pressure Red wanted to employ, but he had no choice; they were the only pumps available at the time.

Once Red had his water system set up, he confronted the problem of blowing out the wells. He had been experimenting for a number of months with various configurations of explosive charges and was convinced he had hit upon one that would implode rather than explode. It was shaped like a pizza, with the explosive material packed into a tube around the outer rim. He decided this CATCO job would be the perfect opportunity to find out whether his new concept would work; whether, in fact, he could shoot something from the outside in instead of the reverse. If it did, he could open up one wellhead after another without damaging anything around it, until he had the entire platform under control.

Using composition C-3 plastic explosive, Red made a stack of his pizza-shaped charges, each sixteen inches in diameter. When he was finished, he had himself lowered once more by crane onto the flaming deck, and while the fire hoses kept him soaked, he set the first of what would come to be known as Red Adair's flying saucers next to one of the burning wellheads.

The flying saucer charge imploded perfectly; the twisted blowout preventers and the warped pipe above them left the platform as cleanly as if they had been cut with a knife and sucked skyward by a passing tornado, yet the rest of the platform remained as it was before. Red capped that well, then blew out another the same way and capped it. By the time he was done extinguishing and capping all eighteen, the press had gotten word of Red's innovation and his success won him worldwide acclaim — the first major offshore oil platform fire controlled by the redhead from Texas and his flying saucer charge — but when he returned to Houston, things around the Kinley office were the same as always.

One day, not long after the CATCO job, Red received a note from

Jack Kinley reprimanding him for the way he had used the company's wire-line truck. Now, Red Adair knew his way around a wire-line truck the way a combat marine knows his way around an M-16. He could take all the equipment off the truck, disassemble and clean each piece, and put the whole thing back together again, in the dark. Jack Kinley, on the other hand, had never run a wire-line truck in his life. Red was given the note out in the field, and when he was through with the day's work he drove straight to the office, and confronted Jack.

"This here's the last note you're ever gonna send me," Red screamed, "'cause I'm gonna whip your ass so bad you won't have any strength left to write."

Myron Kinley somehow managed to calm Red down. "It doesn't mean anything, Red," Kinley said. "I know the kind of job you do. I know nobody's got any call to criticize your work, so please, let him alone."

The tone of his old boss's voice stopped Adair in his tracks. Never before had Kinley asked Red for something this way, and Adair's complexion turned from purple back to its usual weather-beaten reddish tan. He mumbled to Myron Kinley that he'd see him in the morning and left.

Red stayed on with Kinley for a few more months, but both he and the old man knew it was time for Red to go out on his own and that their days working together were over, so in June 1959 Red left to form the Red Adair Company. The split was amicable; Red and Myron Kinley never had anything resembling an argument in all the years they knew one another. Red took Coots with him, and Boots stayed on with Kinley. Kinley kept fighting fires for a short while, but one day he called Red on the phone to say he was through. "Red, I just don't want to do it any more, it's as simple as that," he said. Red hired Boots. Kinley sold him all his equipment, which wasn't much, for $125 and moved to Chickasha, Oklahoma, with his second wife, where he lived until his death eight years later.

A few years after he formed his company, Red ran into Myron Kinley at the Tulsa Oil Show, an annual gathering of everyone associated with the oil patch. "Red, you're the best there ever was at fighting wild wells, no doubt about it," Kinley told him. "Because of you the whole industry's changed. You made the oil field a safer place to work." As far as Red is concerned, that is the greatest compliment anyone has ever paid him.

*   *   *

To understand Red Adair, to appreciate what motivated him and kept him working for Myron Kinley for years after that connection no longer made economic sense, one has to understand how important loyalty, devotion, and a personal code of honor were to Red. Only then is it clear why, at age forty, he swept the floor at Kinley's shop, cleaned Kinley's tools, and gassed up his trucks when there was idle time between jobs, even though he was then making $50,000 a year and, for all practical purposes, was running the company. Only then is it clear why Red insisted on the same kind of absolute commitment from his own men and ran *his* company much the way a strong, demanding, yet benevolent father runs a large family.

As the boss, the general, the leader, his job was to take care of everyone in his kingdom. From them he demanded loyalty, obedience, and hard work. That's what he gave Myron Kinley, that's what his people would give him, no questions asked.

There was one other component of this system, unique to Red. He demanded to know where every one of them was, all the time. If you went to the movies, to get a haircut, to take your kid to a ball game or your wife out to dinner, you checked in. If you were on a job you checked in. If you were on vacation you checked in. If you were going over to your grandmother's house for Thanksgiving dinner you checked in before you left home and called again from grandma's.

Of course, there was once a practical reason for this. The Adair office had to be able to contact Red and his men immediately when a well blew out, and once upon a time, the telephone was the quickest way to do that. But in the age of beepers, when all Red's employees carry paging devices, there really is no reason for them to constantly call the company's answering service unless they are out of town, beyond the beeper's range. And what about the office staff? And Red's daughter? And his wife? They all have to check in, too.

"Part of it's a holdover from the old days before electronic communication was so good," Robyn says, "and part of it's just Daddy's need for control. He's afraid if he doesn't know where everyone is every minute of the day they'll all somehow run off and leave him, maybe because of being left himself when he was a young boy. Whatever the reason, though, if you're part of his family (and that goes for all the employees, because as far as Daddy's concerned they're his family too) you better check in. He pure and simple goes wild if anyone doesn't.

"Once, when Jimmy was on a job, he forgot to call in as often as Daddy wanted him to. When Jimmy came back to Houston, Daddy was livid. He screamed and cussed and called Jimmy every name in the book. Jimmy said, 'Hell, I called you every night. Isn't that enough?' Daddy said, 'No, it isn't. When you're on a job I want you to check in twice a day, morning, noon, and night.'

"That kind of became the company joke. Somebody would get hired and they'd say, 'What's this checking in all the time about?' We'd say, 'You want to last around here you better do it, twice a day, morning, noon, and night.' They'd look at us like we were nuts."

JOY HAMILTON

I came to Houston from Henderson, Texas, in 1959, when I was twenty-two. My sister worked there in a bank that was built around an old house. One day when I was visiting my sister at the bank, she said, "There's a man back there with an office in the library of that house and he needs help. He definitely needs a secretary because he keeps running in here asking me to type this and that for him. His name is Red Adair."

I had worked for an independent oil producer in Abilene so I recognized the name. I went over to Red's office and found him standing there with Coots and another man. I asked him if he needed a secretary. He said, "Oh, well, see, I'm waiting on my charter" and all this other stuff. I'd been out in the business world, so I considered that just a brush-off situation. I figured that was the end of it and went back to Henderson. The next day my sister called and said Red was storming around wondering where the hell his new secretary was, so I drove back to Houston as fast as I could, and that was how I started with Red Adair.

I'd always worked for typical company types — you know, chain of command, where everything goes down the ladder — so I waited for Red to tell me what to do. Little did I know he had no knowledge of the administrative end of things and even less interest in learning about it. He was waiting for *me* to take over and run that part of the company. So, I took over. He never asked me what I was doing, and truthfully, he didn't care.

I remember one job, early on, over in the Middle East. Boots and Coots went with Red and so did Rush Johnson. They landed in Beirut, where you need a visa, but since none of us knew that, they didn't have visas. The oil company hired one guy — a taxi driver — to keep track of the four of them the first night and keep them out of trouble. That poor soul spent the entire night chasing all over Beirut from one club to another. He'd get three of them rounded up and go back to the hotel, only to discover the fourth had taken off again, and he'd have to jump back into his taxi and try to find him. Finally he got all four of them back in the hotel. They made it as far as the lobby, sat down, and fell asleep. Red spent the whole night in a chair. The next day, the oil-company people picked them up and they went and put the fire out.

When Red came back to Houston he said to me, "Joy, we have to have visas when we go back to that country again." I said, "What's a visa?" So, you see, in the beginning, it was really the blind leading the blind.

Back in the beginning, in the early sixties and the midsixties, when Red began racing boats to relax, the jobs would come in so fast the boys went from airport to airport for months and I hardly ever saw them. They were just voices calling in the night. And then there'd be a lull and they'd hit town. Then everyone would get together and raise hell here in Houston or down at the bay, partying and boating and laughing it up, and then they'd be gone for months again. You have no idea how much work they did, how many jobs. Hundreds. He and Boots and Coots would have to split up, there was so much work. They'd be flying through so many different time zones they'd lose track of what day it was. Coots once flew back and forth across the Atlantic three times in twenty-four hours checking on jobs and lining up equipment.

I remember one time Red went from fighting a fire in the desert somewhere in the Middle East where the temperature *away* from the well was a hundred and twenty degrees, to a job in the ice and snow in Alaska, to another one in the jungle in South America, then back up north to Canada where it was thirty below zero, and finally to one blowout in West Texas and another one in a Louisiana swamp — all in less than a month. How that man didn't catch some strange disease or get pneumonia and die is beyond me. How he managed to kill every one of those wells is beyond me, too. Red wasn't a young man by then. He was pushing fifty, and then some. I don't know how he kept it up. Energy. He was pure energy.

He never wanted to be a big-time millionaire. He wanted everybody to be happy, to get along with each other. He was good to his employees, all of them. They were his children, his second family.

Really, I was like a daughter to him. I remember one time I went with Kemmie and Coots's wife Mickey to Indianapolis for the Indy 500. We went a week early and took two weeks driving back. Finally, Kemmie called Red from Baton Rouge where we were cavorting about and he said, "Isn't it about time y'all came back to work?" He wasn't mad, he just missed us, is all. It was work hard, play hard in those days, but it was fun.

But then it got too big. It got out of control. The closeness was gone and so was the fun. That's why I left. I miss it though. That old feeling could still be there. It could. Just like a family. It grows apart and with luck it comes back together again. I hope it does, for Red's sake. He deserves it.

RED

I think it was real important to start out working in the earlier days of the oil patch, when a man's handshake really meant something. You'd go do a job and you wouldn't have to worry about being sued or signing a whole bunch of papers. Then, after you finished, everybody went and drank a beer and was friendly with one another. You shook hands and they said, "Well, we hope we never see you again under these circumstances, but if we ever get in trouble we'll be sure to call you." They knew you'd done your best and treated them honorably. So you left with good feelings all around.

Today, the oil companies are run by accountants and lawyers, and it's all business. First thing they want to know is how much it's going to cost. In the old days, they didn't worry about that. No one ever asked, "How much do you charge?"

Mr. Kinley charged the oil companies according to how long the job took and how dangerous the situation was. I'd go out and do a job and go back to the office. Kinley'd say, "What'd you do, Red?" I'd tell him I did this and that, and he'd say, "Was it a real bad one?" I'd say, "Mr. Kinley, it was a real son of a bitch. It was worth more than the usual rate." So he'd charge them accordingly, and everyone knew what he charged was fair.

It worked the other way, too. I remember one job I did for Tidewater Oil near Venice, Louisiana, when I was still with Kinley. It was back in the swamp where it's real tough to move around, blowin' gas and oil all over the place, and of course any second it could have exploded and they never would have found me. I sent 'em an invoice, and that ol' boy sent it back and he said, "Red, you guys didn't charge enough." I doubled the bill and sent it back. He wrote me a note and said, "You're still too cheap for the kind of work you do. You risked your life out there. You deserve more money."

When I went into business for myself, I did things the same way. If the job was real dangerous, if it was offshore, or if it was a poison gas well, or if it was in the middle of the jungle where there were hostile Indians or tigers or something, of course I charged more. I'd have been a damn fool not to. And I charged 'em more if I didn't get any cooperation at the location, because that jeopardized the safety of me and my men. But there were plenty of times I didn't charge anything.

I remember one well . . . Ol' boy who owned it was just some wildcatter who'd found some oil where nobody thought there was any, like a lot of guys in the oil patch willing to gamble on a hunch. He wasn't rich, but he was a decent person. He'd had a heart attack and he was laid up in bed when his well blew out. He called and said, "Red, I've got a real problem on my well, but I heard all these things about how much you charge and I don't know if I can afford you." I said, "Listen, you worry about gettin' better and let me worry about your well, and don't let either one of us worry about money. You'll be all right." Gave me a real good feeling when I wrote a big fat zero on the bottom of that man's invoice.

That was part of Red's code, too. In 1982 he made over a million dollars controlling an offshore well owned by the Indian government. In 1979 he made more than $2 million working on the Mexican government's offshore Ixtoc I well, and in 1980 and 1981, $1 million each for controlling two wells in Sumatra — and these sums didn't include his expenses or the purchase of extra equipment. There were many others that paid him handsomely as well, but if an independent oil man was in financial distress, Red billed him accordingly. Red knew that when he was the only game in town, a man with a wild well had nowhere else to go *but* to him. Honor dictated that he never hurt a man by taking advantage of that situation.

KEMMIE

Living with a man who works in the oil patch is like living with a gambler. Sometimes it's chicken and sometimes it's feathers.

When Red Adair went into business for himself he had $10,000 to his name. He had an office, a secretary, one helper (Coots), two cars and a truck (all painted bright red), four sets of red coveralls with his name logo — "Red Adair Company, Wild Well Control, Oil Well Fires, Blowouts" — on the back, and great expectations for immediate success. Then the bottom fell out of the oil business, and for three months he had absolutely no work.

The oil industry is like that, booming and busting in cycles that make men rich overnight and penniless just as fast. In 1956 Red went eight months without a job, but then he was working for Myron Kinley and still received a salary. In the early 1970s it happened to Red again, and because he had been imprudent with the money he made prior to the '70s slump, he almost went broke. That brush with monetary doom was Red's last. He and Kemmie promised themselves they would be careful from then on, and when Red's business soared in the middle and late 1970s they began putting more money aside than they spent. When the latest oil-field crunch hit in the mid-1980s, Red was able to weather it with almost no financial stress.

"When things were booming along in the late seventies and early eighties all these guys were after me to invest in these fancy ventures and deals they had cooked up," Red says. "I told 'em, 'Not me. Not this time. I *learned* my lesson. This time, I'm heavily invested in cash.' A lot of those dudes went belly-up, but Kemmie and I have been all right."

By late July of 1959 things were not all right. For three months, Red had been paying rent for his office, the salaries of his employees, and all the bills at home without taking in ten cents, and he was out of money. As broke as he'd been twenty years earlier when he'd contemplated mugging a drunk.

The situation was so bad he didn't have the money to pay for hot dogs and soda for Robyn's birthday party, but he couldn't bring himself to tell that to his daughter. Kemmie was on the verge of canceling the party altogether when one of her dearest friends, Grace Carothers, a woman in her sixties whom the family called Mamma Grace, said, "Kemmie, we can't do that to the girl. It isn't right. I'll just give her the party as my birthday present to her. The kids don't even have to know about your money problems."

Then, the day after Robyn's party, three jobs came in at once, two in West Texas and one in South Texas. They were small jobs, but they were just in time. Red decided to take the ones out west and send Coots south. Kemmie was so happy she thought she'd burst. She ran out and bought a bottle of fine champagne, came home and waited for Red to arrive. He barreled through the door, gathering his equipment without even sitting down, and when she offered him one of the glasses to toast their good fortune he said he didn't have time for any of that and dashed back to his car.

Suddenly, Kemmie was all alone, sitting in her kitchen, staring at the spotless floor and the untouched glasses of champagne on the table. "Well, the heck with it," she thought, "I'm gonna celebrate, even if I have to do it all by myself." She hadn't felt like singing for quite some time. Now that was all she wanted to do.

There was one club in Houston, the Keyboard Club, where Kemmie knew she could go alone without fear of Red losing his temper. It was owned by the Adairs' good friends Bob and Lois Larson, and Red would not feel threatened if Kemmie spent the evening there. Before she left, Kemmie made sure to go next door to tell the neighbors where she'd be. She knew Red would call her. It was Friday night, Robyn was staying at a friend's house, and Jimmy was away at college, so no one would be there to answer the phone. Red would be frantic, convinced either the house had burned down or a gang of thugs had abducted her and the kids, and he'd start calling the neighbors.

Kemmie had a wonderful time at the Keyboard Club, playing the piano and singing. Everyone said she'd never sounded better, and though she knew in her heart they were being kind, the compliments made her feel like a young girl again.

When it was time to close, Bob Larson asked her to stick around. He wanted to learn the bridge to "Sophisticated Lady," an extremely difficult passage Kemmie could sing without missing a note. She stayed after closing and taught Bob the bridge, and when they were done he insisted on walking her to her car. You never knew who might be hanging around the club, and it was very dark in the parking lot.

As Kemmie was opening the door to her car, another vehicle, a bright red one, came tearing into the lot with her husband half hanging out the driver's window. He'd driven straight from the second job he'd done that day and was still covered with oil and dirt. "What the hell's going on?" he screamed. "What are you doing out here? I'll talk to you about this when we get home, Kemmie." With that, he roared off. He was so wild with rage he hadn't noticed that the man with her was their old friend Bob Larson, and that his wife Lois was there, too, though in the shadows.

Kemmie took off after Red in her car, finally caught up to him at the Fairbanks Supermarket parking lot and jumped into his car. "I saw that no-good son of a bitch holding the car door for you," he shouted.

"Red, that was Bob Larson," she hollered back. "What exactly do you think *was* going on, because you know Lois was standing about twenty feet away. In fact, I'm going to make you call Bob and apologize when we get home."

When Red got off the phone, he saw Kemmie throwing his clothes into a suitcase. "What the hell are you doing that for?" he asked. He was calm now, convinced of her innocence.

"What am I doing this for?" she replied. "What am I doing this for? All the time, Red, you go out with this old buddy and that old friend, doing just as you damn well please, and now, when our company finally lands a job, when we're finally in business for real and I want to go out and celebrate at the Keyboard Club, which you well know isn't any wilder than our neighbor's kitchen, you throw a fit. It isn't fair, Red. I have a right to a life, too."

Kemmie didn't make Red leave, but the problems didn't leave either. With no one to share the job of child rearing, she had devoted herself to her children totally, protecting them, sheltering them ("Don't mess with Kemmie's Cubs" was one of her favorite sayings), doing everything for them to the point where, as young adults, they would have difficulty accepting responsibility for themselves.

When things did go wrong while Jimmy and Robyn were growing up, Red wouldn't talk about them with her. She was always home. She cooked and cleaned and sewed and taxied and PTA'd until she felt like one of the beaters on an electric mixing bowl, and Red thought it was wonderful. That was what a *real* mother did. His mother hadn't been able to do these things because of her health but, by God, Kemmie was different. With someone like her in your home, how could there be problems? So every time she said there was a difficulty, he'd say there wasn't and storm out.

As the years went by and the problems grew, she felt more and more like a single-handed sailor on a stormy sea. In spite of her devotion to her children, in spite of giving them all the attention in the world, things had not turned out the way they did on the Ozzie and Harriet show. Jimmy had begun partying too much and Robyn was talking about quitting school. Dealing with it by herself was making her nuts. Why wouldn't Red talk about these things with her? she wondered. He was so smart, so clever, so aware of what was going on around him, surely he had to see that she wasn't inventing anything.

One day in 1961 it all came to a head when Red walked out of the house while she was in the middle of a sentence. "I'm goin' down to the office," he said, which was his way of concluding the conversation. The burden of dealing with everything at home was by this time making it hard for Kemmie to sleep, and she felt that if she and her husband didn't communicate she'd become truly sick. She got into her car, a brand new Cadillac Red had bought for her as a present to smooth things over, drove to his office, and parked behind his new Lincoln. She rarely came to the office, but she was desperate and had determined once and for all to make him sit and listen to what was bothering her.

She climbed out of her Caddy, took a deep breath and went inside. "Hey, Kemmie," Red said when she came through the door. "Whatcha doin' here?" He was smiling at her, glad to see her, as though what had transpired at home had happened in another life, but as soon as she told him why she was there his demeanor changed. He paced around the room, fiddled with the trinkets on his desk, gazed longingly at the traffic going by on the street. ("I got the door covered," she thought. "Will he try to jump out the window to escape?") "We don't have any problems," he finally said. "Everything's fine and that's that."

Kemmie, who knew things were not fine, walked from Red's office to the parking lot and got back into her car. "I can't stand any more of this," she said aloud. "I've had enough!" With that, she yanked the gearshift lever into drive, took aim at Red's car in front of hers, and floored the accelerator.

Kemmie's Cadillac was one of those models with big chrome bullets sticking out of the grill, and when it hit Red's Lincoln it nearly tore the rear end of his car off. The crash could be heard for blocks. Windows popped open and heads peered out all up and down the street. Red came racing out of his office, reached in the Caddy's window and grabbed the keys out of the ignition. He could see Kemmie wasn't hurt, and had reacted from his years of experience racing stock cars, where the first thing you do after a crash, once you determine the driver isn't hurt, is shut the machine down so it won't catch fire. The two of them looked at each other for a minute without saying a word. Then Red handed her back the keys and Kemmie drove home.

She sat in the living room for hours, until it was dark, terrified that Red would come home and kill her, even though he had never lifted a hand toward her in violence in all the years they'd been together. This time, though, might be different. This time she had trashed his car, which was the next thing to attacking his manhood. When Red came home, however, he was calm. He sat across from her and cleared his throat. "I know what happened," he said. "I know why you did it." At last, she thought. At last he's going to talk to me and we can get all the stuff that's been bothering me out into the open.

"What happened is that the gearshift position for drive on your new Cadillac is where reverse used to be on your old Oldsmobile. You put it in drive thinking you were putting it into reverse."

He knew better. He knew deep down, from having lost too many races to her, she was a slicker driver than that, but he had sat in his office all afternoon figuring out an excuse for what she'd done because he couldn't bring himself to admit she'd rammed his car on purpose. Then *she* knew, as clearly as if he'd screamed it at her, why he could never say what he understood perfectly in his heart. "If he doesn't say it," she thought, "he thinks it will be as though none of it is true, as though none of it has ever happened, as if our lives are nothing like the life he had when he was young."

KEMMIE

I went into this bad, bad place inside my head. I wound up talking to a psychiatrist. I wound up in the hospital. I remember it was 1963 because I was going to that psychiatrist's office when Kennedy was shot. I talked to that psychiatrist for three months telling him all the stuff I did. Brownies and cub scouts and music lessons and dancing school. Carpooling and PTA-ing and running up to the kids' schools for every committee they had. One day, that doctor smiled at me and said, "Kemmie, do you really think you did all that just for your children?" I thought about that a lot and I knew that wasn't all there was to it. You see, at the time I never thought I was part of the problem at all. I never thought that maybe I'd done *too* much for them and hadn't let them do enough for themselves. I thought all the problems were Red's fault for not being at home all the time. I figured if only the kids saw a typical nuclear family — mom, dad, dinner at six all together, Sunday drive in the country — then everything would be perfect. I didn't know then there were no perfect families. I know that now. And I know that if Red *had* stayed home he never would have become who he became. Luckily, I couldn't change him. I couldn't make him into something he wasn't.

WEST TEXAS — 1965

About the same time he heard the roar of the blowout, Red could see the men, thirty or forty of them, crowded together half a mile from the well. He was running flat out in his new Cadillac, having driven straight from the Houston airport, where the car had been parked for almost a month. That was how long Adair had been out of the country, first at a burning well off the coast of Nigeria, and then at a blowout in Indonesia.

He was dog tired, not only from fighting the wells, but from dealing with the human drama that swirled around them. In Nigeria, the Biafran civil war was in progress. Nigerian military gunboats, searching for rebels, patrolled the inland waterways around Port Harcourt where the oil company had its camp. One of these gunboats thought it saw rebel activity near the camp and opened fire, tearing half the roof off the hut where Red was sleeping. Then, after Adair put the well fire out and was installing new blowout preventers on the wellhead, he had to stop work in order to prevent a riot by Nigerian workers who came offshore daily by barge. The Nigerians demanded that the oil company give them all the food on the rig to take back to port. The oil company at first refused, but changed its mind when Adair pointed out that a few thousand dollars' worth of food was cheaper by far than any further trouble on the platform.

In Indonesia he ran into a similar problem. Twelve thousand five hundred feet of pipe casing had blown clear out of the hole at a well in the middle of the jungle there, in country so hot and humid you could work up a drenching sweat bending over to tie your shoes. Bad welds had caused the blowout, which was covering everything within a hundred yards of the wellhead with distillate and shaking branches right off the trees with its noise. Red had flown into this jungle outpost at night, landing on a dirt strip in a small, twin-engine plane. "Don't walk around barefoot, Red," the oil-company pilot told him. "They have some badass snakes over here that killed a guy just last week."

The next morning Red stood by the blowing well, one eye on the sky, the other on the oil company's drilling crew. There were thunderheads building off to the west, so he'd have to move carefully as he got the site cleaned of debris and the well capped. More than once he'd seen a lightning bolt strike near a blowing well and turn the place into an enormous hole in the ground.

The drilling crew was potentially almost as explosive. They were a bunch of good ol' boys from Texas and Louisiana who loved to fight under the best of circumstances and whose fuses had been shortened considerably by the jungle weather and the noise of the well. Local rebels had been showing up periodically at the location asking for supplies, and the well hands were ready to go to war.

"Those bastards show up again, we're gonna kick some ass," they told Red.

"How about we kick some ass right here and now," Red said, "and get all this pipe and other crap pulled back away from the well so I can cap the damn thing and go home?"

With that, Adair, who was now in charge of the location, organized the roughnecks and drillers into a cleanup brigade, but no sooner had the dozers begun dragging debris from the well than an old Dodge four-by-four came bouncing down the rutted jungle road and skidded to a stop in front of them. There were two men in civilian clothes inside the truck, along with another man in a military officer's uniform. The rebel officer got out, walked over to the drilling crew's tool pusher, and handed him a list of the supplies he wanted.

"Here's what they want," the tool pusher said to Red, showing him the list. The drilling crew had left their jobs and were milling about, mumbling curses, spitting tobacco juice into the mud.

"There's thirty of us and only three of them, Red," one roughneck said. "Don't give 'em nothin'. We can take 'em."

Adair looked at the drilling crew and then at the list. It was for food, considerably more than was needed to feed three men. Instinct told him there was at least a platoon of rebel soldiers in the area, if not a whole battalion. "I told you men before, all I'm fighting is that blowout. After I leave, you can do what the hell you like. Now get back to work." He turned to the tool pusher. "Give them everything on the list," he said. "And smile when you do it."

It took six trips with the four-by-four for the rebels to get everything they wanted from the drilling camp. When they were through, the officer in charge, a colonel who had gone to school at Dartmouth, came to personally thank Red Adair, about whom he'd heard many fascinating stories. They had a drink of the colonel's best cognac and spoke about the importance of good relations between the oil companies and what would surely be the region's new government. Red gave the colonel a small American-flag pin. The colonel gave Red a tiny wooden carving of a tiger. The colonel had 150 men with him.

They'd paged Red at the Houston airport and told him about the West Texas well. Boots and Coots were both out of the country on other jobs, so Red said he'd drive straight to the blowout and get it. He drove four hundred miles in just over four hours and was fatigued to the bone when he spun the big red Cadillac onto the location in a cloud of dust. He hopped out, opened the trunk, and began handing Zippo cigarette lighters — the ones with "Red Adair Company" and a picture of a burning well engraved on them — to all the men there. Then he shook hands with every roughneck and driller on the site, and every truck driver, cowboy, and rancher who'd come to see the blowing well.

It was a bad one, an extremely high-pressure well making gas and oil, that had blown out with such force its back pressure was forcing gas up through the ranchers' water wells for miles around. Even the gopher holes in the vicinity of the location were pressurized. You could see little puffs of gas spurting out of them all across the prairie. At any second, the entire landscape could have exploded, but Red never even looked at the well. Not yet. He was going to need some of these men as helpers, so he stood calmly on the trembling ground, telling them about where he'd recently traveled, laughing about how loud he had to yell for them to hear him, reassuring them simply by being there, inspiring them with his confidence.

"All right, men, this is what we're going to do here," Red said, finally turning his attention to the well. In his slow, deep drawl, he outlined his battle plan, and now all of these men felt they were part of it. Every one of them, even those who hours earlier had run in terror from the blowing well, was ready and willing to follow him and do whatever he asked. They would help him clear the area around the well, bring in the equipment he needed to rig up, even walk with him toward the terrifying roar of the wellhead, because when it was over, all of them were going to be able to say they'd been on a job with Red Adair.

There were two ways Red could cap this well, two ways for him to get the new blowout preventer dead center over the flow to control it. He could either lower it down from above with a crane, or pull the blowout preventer across the flow using steel cables. These cables would be attached to winches mounted on the front of three trucks placed around the wellhead. Red chose the latter method to save time, since there wasn't a crane on the location. He showed the men in each of the trucks the hand signals he would use to direct their winching so that he could maneuver the preventer. He explained to them how critical their job was, since each of them had to maintain tension on his line throughout the operation. Because of the power of the flow, if one of them pulled the preventer even a few inches in the wrong direction, the result would be catastrophic. Red told these men not to do anything unless he signaled.

Red stood in the cellar of the rig now, next to the blowing well, his arms and legs vibrating from the noise. His ears were protected in the usual way with vaseline-soaked cotton, but still he was suffering from sharp darts of pain that radiated from his ears along his jawbone and down the back of his neck. The force of the flow was so great it sucked most of the air around the wellhead up with it, so that he was only able to take shallow, rapid breaths. Both his hands were on the four-foot-high preventer that swung in the air at eye level in front of him, suspended from the three cables.

The cellar was twelve feet deep and filled with a mixture of water and oil. Red was standing over this bubbling fluid on boards, three inches thick by fifteen feet long, that he'd placed across the cellar. The ends of the boards rested on the edges of the massive concrete pillars that supported the derrick. From his vantage point, Red had a good view of the three trucks positioned fifty to seventy-five yards from him, though he had to squint through a stinging mist of distillate that spumed from the flow.

The tension on the cable from the preventer to one of the trucks was so great it had lifted the truck's front wheels a foot off the ground. Red could see this but wasn't worried. He had the blowout preventer almost over the flow, and as long as the cable remained taut, there was no danger. But the truck driver didn't know that. Though he'd received no distress signal from Adair, he was worried that his vehicle was causing Red trouble, and climbed from his truck to help. He jumped onto his front bumper to push the front wheels back down on the ground, and when the wheels hit, the truck's cable went slack. The preventer shifted abruptly, tipping at an angle that diverted the flow from the wellhead downward into the cellar. The power of this flow was so intense it emptied the cellar as fast as a blast from an air compressor would empty a thimble full of water. Three thousand cubic feet of fluid was blown skyward, as were the dozen or so fifteen-foot-long boards, and Red Adair was catapulted twenty feet into the air with them like a matchstick.

If Red had fallen into the cellar they might never have found him, because that's where the boards landed, along with all the water and oil. But once again, Red was lucky. He came to rest on his seat, on top of one of the concrete pillars, conscious, but temporarily blinded by the chemicals in the fluid.

It took half an hour and continuous flushing of his eyes with water before Red was able to see clearly. Probably, it's a good thing so much time passed, because the conversation Red eventually had with the wayward truck driver, while forceful, was nothing compared to what he might have done to the man if he'd been able to reach him right away. On his second attempt, Red pulled the preventer into place without incident and by nightfall of his second day in West Texas he had capped the well, diverting the surging gas and oil into flow lines attached to the valves he installed at the wellhead. After dinner, he refused several offers of lodging for the night, saying he'd rather get on the road for Houston.

As a full moon rose over the prairie, he drove east at high speed, continuously shifting his position behind the wheel. Landing on the concrete pillar had aggravated the old injury he suffered at the well in California back in 1953, and the Cadillac's deeply cushioned seat did little to alleviate his pain. It would be nice to stay home for a while, but his instincts told him he probably wouldn't get more than a couple of days' rest before another job came in.

He was traveling so much now, working at locations in so many different parts of the world, that distinctions between day and night, heat and cold, wet weather and dry, no longer had any meaning. One country blurred into the next. The civil wars and wrangling for control of oil fields all seemed to blend together into a single, never-ending confrontation.

He sighed. It was tough always being away from his family. He had missed being with them for years and years, but that was the way it had to be. That was what he told them. Life was black and white as far as he was concerned. Either he worked the way he did and they all got to eat good food, live in nice houses, and drive fancy cars, or he spent his days in a place like the Southern Pacific Railroad shop and it was back to beans, small rented apartments, and rusty old wrecks.

On the dashboard in front of him was a slip of white paper. It had been stuck under the windshield wiper of the Cadillac when he picked the car up at the airport at dawn, the previous day, but he'd been in such a hurry he hadn't bothered to read it. Now he held the paper up, switched on the Caddy's interior light so that he could make out the handwriting. "Keep up the good work," the note said. The note was signed by his old friend from the oil patch George Bush, then head of the Zapata Offshore Corporation.

CHAPTER SEVENTEEN

I'm not sayin' Red Adair's in a class by himself, but the one he's in, it sure wouldn't take very long to call the roll.

Bum Phillips,
Ex-coach, Houston Oilers

Red always loved boats. When he was a teenager, and he and his friends went down to Galveston Bay on weekends, he would sit and watch them for hours. Trawlers, sailboats, cabin cruisers, freighters, it didn't make any difference to him. Every one of them filled him with a sense of freedom and exhilaration. He promised himself that someday he'd own one, even if it were only a six-foot dinghy.

A few years after he quit racing stock cars he finally got his first boat, and though it wasn't a six-foot dinghy, it wasn't much more. It was little more than a rowboat, the kind you might rent at a small, freshwater lake. It came with a twenty-horsepower Buccaneer motor and another five-horse Buccaneer kicker for trolling, and had two speeds — slow and slower. Red took it down to the bay, and watching him creep through the water, one hand on the outboard's control handle, the other scratching his head, you could tell this craft was not going to last very long. Red Adair did not come off a raging well fire to mosey up and down inlets at four or five miles an hour.

Before long, he'd ditched the rowboat and gotten himself a Century Coronado twenty-one-foot speedboat that would run fifty miles an hour. Soon, the Century was gone and in its place was a forty-one-foot Chris Craft cruiser Red christened *Blow Out*, the name of almost every one of his boats from then on. It was big and comfortable, perfect for entertaining friends and business associates, and Kemmie loved it, but Red was not about to treat his boats any differently than he dealt with his cars. "Nice boat," he said to Jimmy one morning, "but way too slow."

Out came the original motors and in went two turbo-charged 427-cubic-inch Chevrolets. Now the cruiser would run almost fifty miles an hour, an unheard of speed for a boat of that design in the early 1960s. Then he bought a bigger cruiser, the fifty-three-foot *Blowout II*, and sold the first one to a doctor in Louisiana who had no idea what he was getting himself into and promptly ran the Chris Craft up on the beach at Lake Pontchartrain.

BETTY DEMONTROND

During those days, Red kept his boat tied up next to ours at the Lakewood Yacht Club. You couldn't miss it. Everybody but Red Adair had a boat with a white hull. Red had the hull of his sport fisherman painted black with red flames on the gunwales so it looked like fire was pouring over the side. On the forward deck it had the most horns I'd ever seen on a yacht in my life. They were big air horns that played several tunes. I'd heard about Red, and I wanted to meet him — meet the man who owned that outrageous boat. One day my husband and I were up at the swimming pool and we heard all those air horns cut loose at once. It sounded like a Rock Island locomotive was coming through the middle of the yacht club. Our son, Lea, was five years old at the time, and we thought, oh no, Lea's gotten onto Red's boat and is pulling all the horns, so we raced down around the harbor and sure enough it was Lea, but it was Red who was letting him operate the horns. Lea said, "Mom, Dad, I want you to meet my friend Red Adair." So there was my five-year-old son introducing me to a man I'd wanted so much to meet.

LEA DEMONTROND

Red was like a hero to me, and when I was a little kid I invited him to my birthday party. He told me he would be there, so I told everybody else he would be there too. It was real funny, because when everybody started showing up for the party the fathers of the kids were bringing them instead of their mothers. Mama kept telling me that Red was a busy man and that he probably wouldn't be able to make it. I told her over and over again that she was wrong. Red said he was going to be there, and that was that. All of a sudden this big red car shows up and two guys jump out with their arms full of gifts. Red was out of town and couldn't make it, but he did the next best thing and had his men show up. It was the most exciting day of my life. Somehow, I knew he wouldn't forget my birthday.

222

But what impressed Betty most wasn't Red's flamboyance. "He knew I did a lot of charity work in Houston, and one day he called my husband and said, 'George, I wish you'd stop by my office, because I have a check for one of Betty's charities.' So George went over and picked up the check and looked at it. It was for $25,000 made payable to Betty DeMontrond. George said, 'Red, you made the check out to my wife.' Red said, 'Well, I know Betty works with Texas Children's Hospital and she'll know what to do with the money.' George said, 'But Red, you can't deduct it from your income taxes if you don't make it out to the charity.'"

What impressed Betty was that Red Adair wasn't *looking* for a tax write-off. He really and truly didn't care about that at all. All he wanted to do was help children.

Red turned out to be even better at the controls of a boat than he was behind the wheel of a car. He is still one of the few people on the Gulf Coast who can easily jump on a sixty-foot cruiser and run it himself with no crew. To this day, he will think nothing of hopping on a boat that size, going out on Galveston Bay, continuing into the gulf, out alone on the sea, where he can ride the swells and think. Many a surprised dock master along the Texas coast tells of watching a fifty-five- or sixty-foot cruiser with only one man aboard pull up to his dock, whip right up to it without so much as an audible thump, and shut down, like the boat was a Volkswagen pulling into an empty three-car garage. The single-hander on board reaches over and throws him the lines, hops ashore, says, "How ya doin', my name's Red Adair. Could you gas up my boat for me while I get me somethin' to eat?," slips a $50 bill into the man's hand as a tip, and jogs off toward the restaurant.

The fifty-three-foot boat was great for entertaining, but Red wanted something to go along with it, something with a little more snap, so he bought *Blowout Junior,* an eighteen-foot Chris Craft ski boat with a bored-out Chevy V-8 motor that would do sixty miles an hour. A couple more small cruisers followed, then another big one, and then finally, early in 1965, he figured he'd monkeyed around long enough, gave Kemmie the keys to the cruiser, bought himself an old Stevens inboard drag boat that would do ninety-eight miles an hour through the quarter mile with no problem, and went racing.

For the next ten years, boat racing was the leitmotif of Red's life. Work always came first, before everything else. As much as Red loved winning, he'd jump out of his boat in the middle of a race if his crew radioed that a well somewhere had caught fire. But when the well was dead, boat racing was the activity that kept his adrenaline pumping, the place he could keep on competing after he'd beaten a string of fires or blowouts. Give him a twenty-foot racing hull with a 530-horsepower motor and turn him loose; one hundred miles an hour or more through the water suited his psyche to perfection.

Kemmie realized this, and though she was mindful of the fact that race boats flipped over on a regular basis and drivers were killed, she recognized her husband's need for constant action, for always living on the edge. Forget about how bad he was around the office when there was a lull; she'd seen how he was around the house.

Once he decided to try fishing. He took her favorite cane pole down to the creek next to their Jersey Village home and threw in his line. Five minutes went by and no fish bit. He stuck the first pole in the creek bank and got another one; two lines in the water ought to be better than one. Still no luck, still no action. After an hour, Kemmie went down to the creek and couldn't believe her eyes. Red had taken all her poles, then gone to the hardware store and bought a dozen more. He had no fish, but eighteen fishing poles were stuck in the bank, lines tangling below the water's surface. It looked like opening day of the trout season for ghosts and, as she stood there watching Red bait yet another hook, her favorite cane pole pulled loose and went floating off downstream.

"Red, what the hell are you doing?" she hollered.

"These hooks don't seem to be gettin' it, Kemmie," he said. "I was thinkin' of maybe tryin' some of that dynamite I got in the trunk of my car. Make a helluva mess, but I bet you we'd get us some fish."

Then there was yard work. Kemmie shudders when she remembers Red doing yard work. He'd begin by going out to mow the lawn. The first mower wouldn't be cutting fast enough, so he'd try another one. That one wasn't any better, so he'd go to the store and buy a third. Once, she looked out the window and there were six mowers in the yard. And eight holes. Red had decided in the middle of mowing the lawn that he wanted to plant a bush, so he dug a hole, but it wasn't in quite the right place, so he dug another, and another, and another. "How could the same man who worked with absolute precision, neatness, and efficiency in the oil patch create such havoc at home?" she wondered. "Maybe if the house were on fire when he went out to mow the lawn none of this would happen."

So Kemmie understood and supported Red's boat racing, and besides, she found boat-racing people to be more considerate and a whole lot more refined than the stock-car crowd that had trashed her kitchen back in 1953. When the races were held up near her home in Austin or down at Clear Lake, southeast of Houston, where she and Red had a house, she would often make huge picnic lunches for the crew and sit in the stands cheering for Red and, later, for Jimmy, when he began racing too.

It didn't matter to Red where the race was or how long. If he wasn't on a job, he was ready and willing to travel anywhere, any time. He ran marathons — 250 or 500 miles — one-hour races, six-hour races, races on oval circuits, races on rivers, on lakes, on the gulf. If he was free and there wasn't a race scheduled, he'd organize one himself. If no sponsor could be found, he'd dig the prize money out of his own pocket. Sometimes he'd simply be sitting with a couple of buddies in a bar and someone would slap a $100 bill on the table and say, "My boat'll whip your boat from here to Galveston and back," and off they'd go.

As with his cars, Red would buy one boat, make it run as fast as possible, then sell it and buy another that he thought might go even faster. Sometimes his strategy failed. He sold one that was particularly quick to a man who did nothing to further modify it, but changed its name to *Red's Old Boat*. Then he showed up at a boat race and beat Red, who was driving his brand new one.

Once, Red and oil man John Mecom, Jr. (son of Red's old friend, John Mecom, Sr., and at the time owner of the New Orleans Saints football team), along with another Texas oil millionaire, decided to race down the Mississippi River from Baton Rouge to New Orleans as the opening act of a big boat show. They calculated the distance to be about one hundred miles, but didn't figure on all the twists and turns in the river, so three-quarters through the race Red ran out of gas. Mecom stopped to help Red, and when he did a tugboat came by, swamped him, and his boat sank. Red pulled Mecom out of the river while the third racer, who'd swung his boat around in a wide arc, ran *his* boat up onto the riverbank. As night fell, the three of them, worth a combined total of half a billion dollars or so, sat there in the mud, trying to hitch a ride downriver. They never did reach New Orleans, but a man going upriver tossed them a bottle of whiskey, so the night wasn't a total loss. Red was so upset that they'd used his name to sell tickets to the boat show and he hadn't appeared, he donated a large sum of money to a charity in New Orleans.

Red entered boat races all around the country, from Florida to California. His crew — Jimmy, Raymond Henry, and a man named Richard Hatteberg — would tow the race boats, and Red would meet them at the race, flying in from wherever he was fighting a fire.

About the time Red got his first race boat, he got Richard Hatteberg too. Richard had known Red since 1956, when he went to work for Myron Kinley sweeping floors, cleaning perforating guns, and servicing other oil-field equipment. When Red hired him in 1965, Hatteberg was twenty-five, loved boats as much as Red did, and wanted to become an oil-well fire fighter. He started out working on Red's boats and helping out at the warehouse along with Jimmy and Raymond Henry. That was the way the company hierarchy was arranged and it still is.

It's a simple system, really. A man begins his career at the Red Adair Company at the very bottom and if he works hard, keeps his mouth shut, shows some initiative, and fits into the Red Adair satellite system, he moves on up the line. At first, Red will keep a man at his warehouse. If he is satisfied with his performance there, he'll then have the man deliver equipment to a job, and if that stage of employment goes smoothly, Red will let the man work at the location, watching to see how he handles himself around a wild well. Finally, after several years under Red's guidance, a helper may be promoted to a position as assistant fire fighter and eventually, if Red feels the man can handle jobs on his own, to the rank of senior fire fighter.

When he first started his company, Red was the boss, Boots and Coots were the senior fire fighters, and Jimmy, Raymond, and Richard were the grunts. Over the years, dozens of other grunts came and went, many believing they knew what made Red tick and had the goods to be his successor. Very few lasted more than a couple of months. Only six or eight ever rose to the status of fire fighter, and of those, only two from the early days are still with Red. Raymond Henry is one. Richard Hatteberg is the other, though to look at Richard you'd never guess it.

He stands about five-ten or -eleven, is slightly paunchy, has short, reddish blond hair, wears glasses, and has a perpetually benign expression on his face. In a world of snakeskin cowboy boots, jeans, and $600 belt buckles he comes to work with a leather-bound attaché case and prefers loafers, LaCoste shirts, and chinos, sort of like a yacht salesman wandering around at a rodeo. But Richard Hatteberg's looks no more approximate his personality than a mountain lion approximates a duck. Put him in a race boat and he personifies ice-cold aggression, Red's kind of race driver, and runs that boat pedal-to-the-metal from the moment he gets in to the moment he steps out. Put him next to a burning oil well and he turns into a fearlessly efficient machine and, even better, someone who never hesitates to follow Red no matter how tight the situation. In fairness, it must be said that while racing boats came naturally to Richard (Red recognized this immediately and made him his codriver), fighting oil-well fires took a little bit of getting used to.

At Richard's first job, a blowout in Winnfield, Louisiana, Red's crew was backing a joint of drill pipe out of the hole previous to capping the well. They were unscrewing this pipe manually with come-alongs and had the joint guyed off with three lines so that when it came loose it wouldn't go flopping all around. The moment was critical, because when this joint of pipe came out, gas would flow everywhere around the rig, and if rocks or sand came up with it, it could instantly ignite.

"Whatever you do, Richard, don't move, and keep ahold of that come-along so there's tension on your line," Red said. "Don't worry, if the son of a bitch blows up, we'll be the first to know."

The procedure went smoothly, and after it was all over Red started laughing so hard he had to sit down.

"What the hell's so funny?" Richard asked him.

"C'mere," Red said, and led Richard back over to the place he'd been standing with his come-along, where there was a foot-deep gouge dug into the ground. "Richard, you little fart," Red said, "you *were* moving. Your damn feet were moving so fast I couldn't see your boots. If we'd been any longer gettin' that pipe up, you'd'a dug us a new well. But I'll give you this. You may have been runnin', but you weren't goin' anywhere."

RICHARD

Red was a helluva good boat racer, one of the top racers in the country. If that's all he'd been doing, he would have been the best for sure. He'd run against guys with much bigger, faster boats, and he'd beat 'em by outsmarting 'em. He'd run on the same circuit as the giant seven-liter, unlimited-class boats that would do 150 miles an hour. The little boats we had would only go a bit over 100, but they'd corner so much better that on that short course Red could stay with 'em.

One time, an ol' boy named Sonny Vijon, a true Coonass who lived up in North Louisiana, held a boat race up there where you could run anything that you brought with you. The races were called "Run what you brung." Sonny Vijon had him one of those 150-mile-an-hour jobs. Red had his 100-mile-an-hour, eighteen-foot Mandella, and of course there were all sorts of other boats in the race too.

At the green flag, Vijon took off like crazy and left Red way behind, but on the corners, Red just slipped underneath him, went around the buoys on the inside and was about a hundred yards in front when they came out of the turn. Vijon caught Red again in the straight and passed him. Then in the next corner Red did the same thing. This went on for five laps and made Vijon so damn mad he couldn't stand it. Red was just outdriving him and outthinking him and finally, in one corner, Red kicked up a bit of spray and wet that boy down so bad his boat stalled, and Red won the money. When it came down to the money, Red would always go get it. Same as a well: tell him a well can't be capped, and sure as hell he'll go ahead and cap it anyway. Tell him his boat's too slow, you better watch out. He'd come to see you.

Red wasn't a young man either, when he did all that. He was fifty when he started and sixty when he stopped. I remember his last race. It was in Palacios, Texas, which is on the gulf, south and a bit west of Houston. Red was driving an eighteen-foot boat that was putting out 600–700 horsepower. The race was a one-hour marathon, and he won it by covering just under a hundred miles. We had to carry him to his motor home, and after that Kemmie said, "Red, that's enough. That's it." And that *was* it.

See, in a race boat, the seat is bolted in with just enough cushioning so you don't break your tail bone. You're hanging onto the steering wheel, with one foot on the accelerator and the other on a brace so it won't slide off. There's a plate on the back of the boat called a cavitation plate, which changes the angle of the boat in the water, and the control for it is sitting right in front of your crotch.

A hundred miles an hour in a boat is nothing like 100 miles an hour in a car; nothing like 150 miles an hour in a car, unless you're doing 150 over a dried-out riverbed. The whole time you're in a race boat you're pushing and pulling and taking an incredible pounding from the waves and from the other guys' wakes. Guys come out of race boats and they're totally numb, from their neck to their toes, passing blood, with a headache that feels like somebody drove a railroad spike through your ear. We ran a race one time down at Clear Lake, just west of Galveston Bay, down where Red's house was. NASA headquarters is right near there and Red had gotten to hanging around with some of the astronauts. We even experimented with some of the suits they wore, but the suits were no good for our purposes. They were too hot, and you couldn't maneuver fast enough in 'em.

Anyhow, Gordon Cooper, one of the astronauts, wanted to be a race-boat driver, so Red let him fool around a little with one of our boats. Then he was going to be the backup driver at this race on Clear Lake. It was a 250-mile race, and I started driving and went about 200 miles, and we were right in front. The boat was running good, but I just couldn't go any further because I was out of gas.

I came into the pits, crawled out of the boat, and Cooper got in and took off. After a bit, Red looked down at his watch and said, "Where's Cooper?" He was supposed to be back around the course in two minutes and fourteen seconds. That's what I was running, but he wasn't there. We kept looking for him and he finally come around in about three minutes and twenty seconds. Red started jumping around, cussin' and shoutin', 'cause we'd been in front and now we weren't and he does not like to lose. Mrs. Adair, who never ever did anything like that before, even came down out of the stands and said, "Where is that man? What's he doing out there? Can't you get him out of the boat?"

We waved flags at him. We tried everything, but we couldn't get Cooper's attention to get him back in so either Red or I could get back in the boat. Anyway, he didn't come in and we wound up sixth or seventh. When the race was over he said the boat had some water in it, but there was no more water in it than would normally accumulate from spray or turning corners. He said the boat just wouldn't run over 4,600 rpm.

Red didn't say a thing. He just got in that boat and hauled ass around the course. Then I went out with Red, and the two of us got it up to 5,600 rpm. See, Red had to know. It's an obsession with him that every piece of equipment he owns, be it a fire monitor or a race boat, has to work perfectly. That's one of the reasons he's still alive. So if that boat wasn't right he wanted to know it immediately so he could get it fixed. Well, it was right, but Cooper . . . that was the last time he raced with us. I don't think he realized how tough driving a race boat flat out would be.

KEMMIE

They were a whole lot alike, Red and John Wayne, tough guys on the outside, but soft on the inside. I think they got along so well because they recognized a kind of basic decency and integrity in each other. They were both guys who delivered when the chips were down.

BURBANK, CALIFORNIA — 1973

"We gotta go up that hill, Duke," Red said. "You gonna be able to handle it?"

"Hell, Red," said John Wayne, "I told ya' I wanted to come with you on a real fire, didn't I? Don't go gettin' cold feet on me now."

"I ain't gettin' cold feet, Duke," Red said. "Neither one of us gonna get cold anything in this place. I was just wondering about your leg, is all."

"My leg'll be just fine, Big Red," Wayne said. "I'm with ya' all the way. Let's get to it."

The path leading up the hill they had to climb was only about a quarter of a mile long, but in places it was quite steep, and there was thick brush all along the way. Red needed to get to the top to take a better look at the oil well, which had already burned up the rig. The fire was a real humdinger, hotter than hell, but he figured the two of them would be all right because the wind was blowing the flames away from the hilltop.

The Duke looked terrible. He was a sick man, for sure, gaunt, with bad color. Red could see that his leg was giving him a great deal of pain, even though Wayne wasn't complaining. He also knew Wayne had lost his left lung to cancer a number of years earlier. Still, Adair wasn't about to order him to wait down at the bottom of the hill while he went up to check things out. There was an unspoken understanding between them that made that sort of action unthinkable.

The two of them had met in 1967 when Wayne came to Houston to make *Hellfighters*, a film many people have mistakenly assumed is a portrayal of Red Adair's life. In the movie, John Wayne plays Chance Buckman, an oil-well fire fighter, much like Red in theory, but unlike him in fact.

At one point Chance arrives in Malaysia to fight a fire, walks into a bar, and promptly beats the tar out of an Australian driller who has refused to stop drinking the night before beginning work on the well. In reality, Red would never have done that. For one thing, he'd have no need for the driller (the man had probably done enough damage to the well already). For another, Red didn't go around slugging people he didn't want on a location. When he came on the job, he ruled, and if a man was told to leave, he left.

Once, on an offshore location, Red had his fill of engineers and safety men getting in his way. He told all of them to meet him at eight the next morning on the rig's helideck. When the men were all assembled Red said, "Men, this is what I want you to do. As soon as I stop talking, ya'll climb aboard those two choppers there and fly ashore. Then, you stay there until I'm done killing this well." End of meeting. End of problem with engineers and safety men.

When Red wasn't off fighting real well fires, he helped build the filmmakers a number of rip-roaring facsimiles, first down in Baytown, Texas, where the Malaysian fire was staged, and then out in Casper, Wyoming, on a location that in the movie was supposed to be Venezuela. With Three-Finger George driving the bulldozer, Red blew the fires out, too.

John Wayne was extremely impressed with Three-Finger's dexterity, and grateful, too, since none of the actors had any idea how to drive a D-9 Caterpillar and even less inclination to take lessons next to a well fire, even a controlled one. In appreciation, Wayne gave Three-Finger a gold-plated cigarette lighter, which George cherished above everything in the world, save his beautiful young wife. The lighter was inscribed, "To my friend Three-Finger George from Duke Wayne."

Two years later, a man picked that lighter off a bar in Odessa and hid it while Three-Finger was in the men's room, just to give him a hard time. Three-Finger came back from the men's room and saw his lighter was missing. He walked over to the door of the bar and locked it, then turned and faced the twenty or so men in the room. "I'm gonna start down here at the end of the bar," he said, "and commence to kickin' the shit out of one man at a time until my lighter shows up. If I have to whip every son of a bitch in here I'll do it."

"That won't be necessary," said the man who took the lighter. "Here's your lighter. I just found it layin' on the floor."

Red told John Wayne the story about Three-Finger George's lighter as they walked up the hill together. The two of them laughed and began to reminisce about *Hellfighters*. Making the movie had been fun for Red. He'd never been around movie people before and had been interested to see what they were like. He loved watching the stunt men work and got along famously with Robert Arthur, the producer; Vera Miles, who played John Wayne's wife, Madeleine; and Katherine Ross, John Wayne's daughter, Tish, in the movie.

It was meeting Duke Wayne, though, that overshadowed everything else about the movie. Red remembered the night up in Wyoming when they'd been filming the Venezuelan fire. It had been a long day, starting at four A.M., during which the controlled fire had almost gotten out of hand and Red had been forced to take quick action to avert a disaster. That night, he and Kemmie had been drinking with the Duke, Vera Miles, and a couple of the other actors. At one point Wayne had leaned over to him and given Red a conspiratorial wink. "Big Red," he said. "Big Red, you could get killed doing the kind of work you do."

"It's true, Duke," Red had answered. "But damn it, at least I'd be gettin' killed doing something I love instead of being run down on the street by some drunk."

The Duke had nodded. "I know what you mean, Big Red," he'd said, grinning and slapping Adair on the back.

He called Adair "Big Red" from the first time they'd met, in a hotel in Houston. "Big Red," he'd said, pulling out a bottle of Scotch, "let's you and me have us a little drink. You pour." Adair had put a tiny bit of soda in Wayne's eight-ounce glass and filled it the rest of the way with liquor. "Well, in that case I'll just have to pour you one," Wayne said, filling Adair's glass to the brim. "Right to the top, Big Red. Here's to ya."

"Right to the top" became a standing line between them, whether they were working on the set or hanging out in the hotel bar at night. Red remembered how the Duke had shouted it to him when he'd gotten the jeep to roll over. In one scene of *Hellfighters*, a jeep was supposed to go over an embankment, but no matter what the stunt men tried, they couldn't get it to flip properly. Red had shown them that if they attached a cable to the front axle and pulled back on it at the right moment, the jeep could be upended. The cable flipped the jeep perfectly on the first attempt. "Right to the top, Big Red," the Duke yelled to him as the jeep bounced to the bottom of the ravine.

Ever since they'd spent that time together in Wyoming, Wayne had been after Red to take him on a job, but it had never been convenient for both of them until this fire, in a place called Lethal Canyon not far from where Wayne was shooting *Rooster Cogburn*. As usual, the Duke had been working day and night when by all rights he should have been in bed. When he'd finally gotten a little time off, he had come over to join Adair at the burning well instead of taking a rest. Wayne had come barreling up to the location in his Pontiac station wagon. It had a special roof, raised a foot higher than on a standard model, so he could drive the car while wearing his Stetson hat.

"What the hell you waitin' for, Big Red," Wayne had hollered. "We gonna put out that fire or stand around gawkin' at it?"

"Well, Duke," Red said to him now as they started up the long hill, "it's you and me then, right to the top."

They made the crest of the hill with less trouble than Red thought they'd have and were standing there looking over at the wall of flame when the wind shifted and the fire came over them in a rolling, suffocating wave. Within seconds the vegetation around them was smoldering and little brush fires began to ignite.

"Duke, we gotta get off this hill quick," Red said. "You need any help?"

"Hell, no, Big Red," Wayne said. "You got me up here. Now you're gonna get me back down. I got complete faith in you. By the way, your pants are about to catch fire."

Red looked down and saw flames from the burning undergrowth licking around his boots. "It's a damn hot job I got, Duke. What can I tell you," Red said.

"To the bottom, then, without delay," Wayne said. "I'm with you." When they reached the base of the hill twenty minutes later they were walking arm-in-arm, singing.

John Wayne stayed with Red in Lethal Canyon until Adair killed the fire and capped the damaged well. Afterward, whenever they'd speak on the phone, Wayne would tell Red that he really wanted to make a second movie about Red's work and this time get the story right. Red talked to him shortly before Wayne went into the hospital for the last time. "Big Red," he said, "when I get out of that hospital we're going to do it. We're going to make that movie and tell it like it really is. Maybe we'll both get killed, but like you once said, at least we'll be doing what we love."

It wasn't only the way Red went about killing a wild well that John Wayne wanted to get right. As he got to know Red, as he spent evenings sitting around with him listening to Red's stories, Wayne was intrigued by Adair's actual adventures and experiences that were mentioned briefly but never developed in *Hellfighters*.

In the movie, for example, when Chance Buckman's daughter, Tish, is first given a tour of her father's office, she is shown a mask, presented to Chance, she is told, by a witch doctor. Back in 1961 Red in fact spent some time with a witch doctor in the jungles of Sumatra.

The well that blew out there had been originally drilled by the Dutch in an area as remote from civilization as anything ever imagined by Joseph Conrad. The Japanese had taken this well over during World War II, then after the war the Indonesians assumed control. In the camp, deep in the jungle, where Red stayed for forty-five days fighting the well, he could still see bullet holes from the battle for this oil that had gone on during the war. The whole time he was there he ate native food, served wrapped in banana leaves, and slept in a tent, protected from snakes by a covering of fine screen. There were cobras in this jungle, and tigers, too, though you couldn't hear them above the roaring of the well.

The camp was on a river directly across from the well. To reach it you had two choices. You could take the road through the jungle, all the way around to where the river was spanned by a tiny bridge, or you could take the short way, straight across the river in an old wooden dory. Either way, you took your life in your hands. Small communist rebel bands roamed the jungle. A group of these rebels even came into the camp one night and took a couple of truckloads of supplies. They left Red with a handwritten receipt. "This will be good for payment to you when we take over the country," the rebel leader told Red.

"Whatever you say, pardner," Red replied with a broad smile, hoping to hell he'd never see the man again.

On the river, heavily armed bandits in high-powered Chinese junks, capable of thirty to forty miles an hour, preyed on anyone unlucky enough to come their way. And they weren't the only carnivores in the water.

Usually, Red traveled to the well in a jeep, but one day he was in a hurry and used the old wooden boat. When Red reached the far side of the river, one of the rig hands looked at Red and said, "Man, what's wrong with you? Are you nuts?" He then showed Adair three wooden plugs driven into the old boat's bottom. "If one of those had popped, you'd have been in that river in a minute," the man said.

"Didn't anybody tell you about the crocodiles? And the sharks?"
From then on, Red drove to work.

So there Red was, trying to kill a particularly violent well in the midst of communists, bandits, snakes, tigers, sharks, and crocodiles, when one evening the witch doctor and his followers moved into his camp. The witch doctor was dressed all in white, and Red knew he was no man to trifle with. His tribe had a sacred juju tree in the jungle near the oil rig's helipad. One of the pilots got too close to this tree, and the witch doctor's followers turned that chopper over and killed the pilot quicker than the snapping of a crocodile's jaws.

"What the hell we gonna do, Red?" said Coots, who'd accompanied his boss on this job.

"We're gonna invite that witch doctor to stay just as long as he pleases," said Red. "And his men can stay too." Which is exactly what they did, eating the oil company's food and sitting around with Red and his men at night, talking to them in a language Red never heard before or since.

When the job was over, there was, as usual, a party, in this case more of a ceremonial tribal dinner. At this dinner the witch doctor made a lengthy speech claiming that through his spiritual powers Red had been brought to this place, and that only through him had Red been able to control the well. Through an interpreter, Red in turn thanked the witch doctor for intervening in his behalf, and told him he never would have been able to kill this well without his help.

Witch doctors, bandits, crocodiles, and saboteurs. There'd been a hint of those in *Hellfighters*, but nothing like the real article. Nothing like Butch Davenport and The Wild Bunch. They were a band of modern-day desperados who wanted to get into Red's line of work and tried to do it by first blowing up wells and then attempting to get hired to kill them. The FBI in Wyoming had suspected foul play on those wells and called Red in to examine them. Red could immediately see that the explosions on the wells had come from outside the well bore, not inside, the way it normally happened. Because of Red's knowledge of explosives, Davenport and his men had been caught, convicted, and sent to jail.

There had been sabotaged foreign wells for Red to deal with as well. In the mid-1960s a major oil company dispatched him to Libya, where some of their wells had been blown up. The company had a hunch that the Egyptians had sabotaged these wells, but they weren't sure and wanted the whole situation kept quiet. Red's equipment was flown to the desert in C-130 transport planes that landed right beside the desert encampment where Red stayed so as not to attract attention at any airport. At this camp, a radio taken from a B-25 bomber that crashed in the desert during World War II was used to communicate with the Libyan authorities in Ben Gazzi.

Five wells, three to four miles apart, had been blown up with satchel charges, and in addition to the danger from the well fires, Red and Coots had to deal with the desert winds — the fierce sandstorms — that constantly changed the landscape. They had to pay careful attention to the barrels used as markers in the dunes so that they wouldn't become lost as they went from well to well. While they were there, one pickup truck full of rig hands did disappear and was never found.

> *RED*
>
> It was just me and Coots over there. We got all those wells, one after another. It was hotter'n hell, more than 120 degrees, and then on top of the weather those wells were like an inferno, boiling up all around us. You'd be walking through craters of bubbling oil. Raise some hell with your feet. Blistered the skin right off 'em. It took us six weeks to kill all of 'em. We blew 'em out with shaped charges and then capped 'em, but it was harder than I'd figured it would be because the wind would change and blow sideways and the fire would come over us. Bad shit . . . uh-huh.
>
> I remember that job well because it was back when A. J. Foyt won the Indy 500. We went into Ben Gazzi and listened to the race on the radio. I remember that was the time when the Watusi dance was popular, too. I'd seen all the Watusis — the real ones — over in Mozambique doing it, and then when I got back to the States all the kids were doing the same thing.
>
> This, of course, was before Qaddafi took over in Libya, so things were nice and friendly in Tripoli, but it was dirty and awful in Ben Gazzi, so we went back and stayed in the desert. Our camp was a two- or three-hour drive from Ben Gazzi, right across the desert, right across the dunes, and you had to navigate just like if you were crossing the ocean. Got buzzed by Egyptian fighter planes while we were there, too. They didn't bother us none, but they were there. Politics and oil. Ain't no way you're ever going to change that.

CHAPTER EIGHTEEN

I like to stay away from politics in foreign countries. Even here in my own country I don't get involved in politics too much. I've been invited up to see every president since Lyndon Johnson. It's real flattering. It's amazing to me, actually. I mean, when I was young, I never would have thought a president would want to meet somebody like me. But I steer clear of all that stuff. I do my voting and go on my way. I don't talk about it much either. I feel safer and better that way. I know George Bush, but I consider him a friend, not a guy in politics. I remember back to that little town in Algiers when I was doing The Devil's Cigarette Lighter and we were palling around with that mayor who turned out to be the one stealing the explosives. After they got him, I thought, "Hell, I could have been shot. I could have been blown up by a bomb." I was safer in the desert next to the well than I was in that mayor's town.

Red Adair

HOUSTON — MAY 9, 1977

Red was flying to Washington, where the following day he was going to appear before the House of Representatives Ad Hoc Select Committee on the Outer Continental Shelf. This committee had been convened to conduct hearings about offshore drilling off the east coast of the United States in the wake of a blowout on April 22, 1977, on the EKOFISK Bravo oil platform in the North Sea that spilled 8.2 million gallons of oil into the water.

When Bravo let go, a 180-foot-high gout of oil — 49,000 gallons an hour, 650,000 gallons a day — spewed into the ocean, creating an immediate twenty-square-mile oil slick that eventually covered nearly 200 square miles. Fortunately, the rig's 112-man crew was safely evacuated, but high winds and rough seas made cleanup operations very difficult, and only Red's courageous efforts to kill the well prevented an explosion and fire that would have made matters significantly worse.

The House committee requested Adair's presence at their hearings, and though he was flying to Washington to comply, Red would have been far less agitated back on the North Sea. He drove to the airport, parked his car, and walked through the electric doors of the terminal. He was carrying the dark blue, three-piece suit he would wear the next day at the hearing, a suit Robyn had helped him pick out.

"How does it look?" he'd asked her, when he tried it on the day before.

"Daddy, you look absolutely wonderful," she said.

"Well, it still doesn't make me feel any better about gettin' up in front of all those politicians," Red said. "Those guys. You know they're like a pack of hungry wolves jumpin' on fresh meat. They try to confuse people. Twist what you say."

"Daddy, you aren't on trial," Robyn said. "They just want to hear what you think about offshore drilling. You're going to do fine."

As usual, Red made sure to get to the airport two hours before the departure of his flight. One thing you could say about Red, he was never late. He went into the airport bar, sat down, and ordered himself a beer. Politicians, he thought. Politics. Political intrigue. Political tension. There was no escaping it. It hung on you like a bad cold. Then, of course, sometimes you just plain stepped into it, like that time back in '67 when he and Raymond had been down in Bolivia.

They had a bunch of oil wells down there way back in the mountains, in the southern part of the country near Camiri, nine of them that they'd drilled in the same area. Eight had either blown out or cratered, because basically the people who drilled them hadn't known what they were doing.

They'd encountered very high-pressure gas at a shallow depth. Once a driller gets down past that gas pocket, it is possible to make a good well, but it's one of those delicate balances where the situation is touch-and-go until you have drill pipe set through the shallow gas. Today, with more sophisticated drilling methods and equipment on the surface that monitors every minute change in pressure, this wouldn't pose such a problem, but in 1967, in the mountains of Bolivia, they just stuck that old bit in the ground and let it rip, and just as soon as they hit that high-pressure gas, the well turned around on them as though they'd jabbed an angry bull's ass with a hot poker.

It was a wildcat area, the locations cut into the side of a mountain in shallow sand that varied in depth and would have been tricky drilling for even a major oil company with tons of money to spend on the preparation. Red and Raymond had come down to kill one of these blowing wells, and one morning, while they waited for some high-pressure preventers to be shipped over the mountains by helicopter, they went hiking in the mountains.

The two of them followed a trail they found that led from the location, up over a ridge, and down the other side, along a mountain stream that ran through the woods. They stopped from time to time, looking into the stream for interesting rocks. Red enjoyed doing this whenever he had a little free time in a remote location, but he was always careful. In Sumatra, he and a man named Jim Gaston, a construction superintendent for Mobil, had been gathering rocks one day in the river. As they stood on the bank marveling at the beautifully colored stones they'd collected, a platoon of Indonesian soldiers burst out of the jungle and ordered them back to the location. Red and Gaston were almost on top of a camp with 150 guerillas in it. As they made their way back to the well they could hear gunfire, and they were later told that the soldiers had killed every guerilla in the camp.

Now, in the mountains of Bolivia, he and Raymond were brought up short by the sound of voices nearby in the woods. Neither of them understood enough Spanish to make out what was being said, but the voices did not sound friendly. They decided not to press their luck and doubled back to the well. Weeks later in Houston, when Red sat talking in his office to a couple of government officials, he was informed that he and Raymond had almost stumbled into the mountain hideout of Che Guevara and his men, who shortly afterward were captured by Bolivian rangers. If Red and Raymond had walked any closer to Guevara's camp, they would probably have been shot.

Although he had absolutely no interest in being a spy, Red dealt with the government from time to time through the years. Sometimes, before going into a potentially dangerous area, he would check with them to make sure he wasn't taking too great a risk. Even so, he has had several close calls. In 1982, while fighting a fire on Khark Island off the coast of Iran, Red had to flee across the Persian Gulf in the dead of night aboard a high-powered launch pursued by Iranian gunboats. A year later, Red and his crew went to Kuwait to give advice about cleaning up an oil slick created by an offshore rig that was blowing out. They went to Bahrain, took a boat to the rig, and sent their dirty clothes to the laundry. All their pants came back with one leg cut off.

Then there'd been the job he did for the government of Israel, on a platform in the Gulf of Suez, right in the middle of their 1973 war with Egypt. Red sighed, shook his head, and settled deeper into the deeply cushioned chair of the airport's VIP lounge, remembering the intrigue and tension surrounding that one.

GULF OF SUEZ — 1973

At first Red hadn't wanted to do the job at all. It was on a four-well platform drilled by an Italian drilling company right in the middle of the gulf, seven and a half miles from Egypt, seven and a half miles from the Sinai Peninsula, which had been captured by Israel. The Israelis had also captured the platform from Egypt, but when they did, they shot three surface-to-air missiles into it, ripping all four wells to shreds and setting them on fire. Fighting between the two countries had subsided, but the situation was far from peaceful, and Red was afraid for the safety of his crew. Furthermore, he didn't want to jeopardize his relationship with the Arab world, where he did so much of his work, but the U.S. State Department requested that he travel to the Gulf of Suez to cap the wells, so he agreed to try.

There was none of Red's usual flamboyance on this job. This time he would have to operate incognito, or at least as incognito as Red Adair *could* operate on a burning offshore oil platform. He took Richard and Jimmy with him, and all three of them had phony passports: "Mr. Richards," "Mr. James," and, for Red, "Mr. Paul." He ordered tan coveralls, and to be sure that no "red iron" trumpeted his presence at this well, he had his old friend Jerry Morton paint the water pumps he needed gray instead of red.

Jerry Morton owns United Engines, a Detroit Diesel distributorship in Oklahoma City that also fabricates generator packages — portable generator sets running Detroit Diesel engines — and the giant pumping units Red Adair uses to get water on a burning well. Every Detroit Diesel engine sold in the southeastern and south central United States comes from United Engines. In addition to thousands of trucks, boats, and industrial plants, almost every single drilling rig in the oil patch runs on Detroit Diesel power, and over the years Jerry Morton had become an extremely wealthy man. He started out in Shreveport, Louisiana, about the same time Red went to work for Myron Kinley, and he and Red have worked closely together since then.

JERRY MORTON

In the old days, I never saw a purchase order from Red. He'd just call up and say, "I need ten engines," or pumps or whatever, and I'd send 'em wherever in the world Red needed 'em. On one fire in Indonesia, he needed forty-three pumps. It took seven large transport airplanes to ship 'em all over there. Red trusted me to send what he ordered, and if Red ordered it I knew without a doubt I'd get paid.

The first pumps we built for Red were for a fire in Jennings, Louisiana. Red and I were in New Orleans together, and Red got the intelligent idea that instead of risking being blown up every time he tried to extinguish a fire with explosives he'd do it with water. He figured out that if he could surround the column of flame with water coming from four directions, the water would hit that column, run down between the flame and the gas, shut out the air, and put out the fire. The problem was, most people had high-pressure, low-volume pumps, and Red needed low-pressure, high-volume ones.

I went to Milton Williams, who owned the Williams Pipeline Testing Company, because he had some high-volume, low-pressure pumps he used to flood the pipeline before he tested it. Morton gave me an old Peerless centrifugal pump, which we powered with a twin Detroit Diesel. I called Red and told him what I had, and he went to the little old fire department in Jennings, Louisiana, and got some old nozzles for the pump, and we hauled that baby down to the fire. It put up 125 pounds of pressure per square inch, which is all the pressure Red needed, but it also gave him 3,000 gallons of water a minute. That was the first water pump that put out an oil-well fire. Before that, they all had to be shot out with an explosive charge.

RED

Those old Haliburton pumps were so high-pressure that if a rock got in 'em it would blow your line up and you'd be cooked goose. And hell, they wouldn't squirt but fifty feet at most, so just about the time you'd get good and cool going up toward the fire, that water would quit wetting you down and the last fifty feet you'd be dry. That's what got to Old Man Kinley. Hell, we backed some shots in there, and it'd get so hot it would start to sear you. It wasn't any good.

JERRY

You have no idea how hot it is near one of those fires until you try to get near it. On a couple of occasions I've tried to walk down to the fire with Red, and nobody gets all the way down to where he's at. You can go so far . . . you think it's the heat that'll get you, and you feel your skin beginning to blister and all, but the worst thing is the temperature of the air you're breathing. You can't *get* any air. You finally just turn around and run, gasping for some air.

RED

I don't know why I was able to do it. I don't know why. I remember one time I had this Mobil credit card in my pocket and it was so hot that card melted. Ruined my shirt and all. Another time, this safety engineer from OSHA came on a job I was doing for Pacific Gas and Electric in California and told me we couldn't wear our tin hats. He said we had to wear plastic safety hats. That was the rule. I said, "The work we do, it gets too hot for plastic hats." He said, "That's ridiculous." I said, "C'mon and take a walk with me a minute." I took that dude down as close to the fire as he could stand it and stood there with him, and that plastic hat of his began to melt and run down over his ears. He damn near shit in his pants and he said, "Well, I see your point. I guess we'll have to have a special ruling about this."

JERRY

No one ever put a well fire out with water before Red did it on that Jennings job. The beautiful part of it was that from then on he had the ability to control the fire. He could put it out any time he wanted to, go down and restart it, put it out again. This was especially important on gas-well fires, because during the day gas rises, but at night, if the fire is out, the gas settles down and travels along the ground and then it's really dangerous. It can creep inside a building, a car, any enclosure, and increase the potential for an explosion. What Red would do is put the fire out during the day, and at dark relight it.

He never liked to work at night anyway. He found that at night he would look at the fire, then look away and be unable to see anything. He felt it was too dangerous. Also, if it was wet and boggy on the location from all the water and mud and oil, the heat from the fire at night would dry it up. So Red fought the well all day, then relit it and put the fire, his adversary, to work for him at night.

That's why we all hung around bars so much. You could only work in the daylight hours, and nobody knew from one day to the next whether they were going to be alive or in the hospital or whatever, so at night they had fun. Also, you couldn't talk around the well because of the noise, so you go back to your motel or hotel and you have to sit down and talk somewhere, and the nearest place is the bar. You sit down and have some drinks and dinner. What you most of the time are doing is laying out your plans for the next day.

One place we'd always go in New Orleans was the Club 809. It was run by a guy named Sol Owens who always gave us a real good drink. His wife was named Chris and she was gorgeous. Chris had about six of the ugliest barmaids in the world, which made her look all the more beautiful. Sol's dead now. Had a heart attack. But Chris still dances down there.

Anyway, one night in the early sixties we were all in there, and Rush Johnson got up on a table and offered anybody in the room a thousand dollars to shoot Sol Owens so he could have Chris. Well, damn! Sol Owens carried a .44 right there on his hip. I mean he *owns* the joint! Red calmed ol' Sol down and then said to me, "We gotta get Rush outa here or we're all gonna get killed." By this time Rush had passed out, so we had to carry him, but you know, once Red spoke to Sol it was over. He had that kind of respect for Red.

See, you can pay people all the money in the world, and that still doesn't get you loyalty and respect. Red would walk into our place in Oklahoma City and he would walk through there and shake hands with every person working, whether the guy's sweeping the floor or welding or running a department. And it wasn't just a show he was putting on. He'd stop and talk with 'em, exchange ideas, and they were so much in awe not just because he was Red Adair but because what he said made sense. They knew that Red's life, or the lives of his men, were depending on their work. They knew when Red or one of his fire fighters pushed the button on that pump it *had* to start. Immediately.

But you see, the guy who was welding a piece of pipe together knew he was doing it for a man who cared about that welder's work and appreciated it and had communicated that to him personally. So we used to say, When Red called, the clock stopped. It didn't make any difference what time of day or night it was, everybody would argue as to who was going to get on Red's project because they knew

Red would be up there personally working with them. And they'd work around the clock if they knew it was for Red Adair. I'm telling you the truth. They wouldn't do that for anybody else in the world. So when Red ordered those pumps that were going to the Middle East and told us to paint 'em gray, every man in my company on that project hopped to it triple time. We all knew it had to be for some hush-hush deal, but no one asked any questions and no one ever said a word about it outside the shop. All they knew was that's what Red wanted, and that's all they needed to know.

The burning platform in the Gulf of Suez was the first one Red had ever seen with machine guns mounted on it. The guns were placed there by the Israelis, who also had torpedo boats off one side of the rig. The Egyptians had their torpedo boats on the other side. Red took a look at the whole setup and went on back to Tel Aviv, where he met with the Israeli official in charge of the country's oil. Then he called the Italian drilling company, who in turn called the Egyptians. Red's message was the same to both sides in the conflict.

"Listen," he said, "we're neutral in all of this. All we want to do is put those fires out, cap those wells, and get out of here. You want to continue the war after we leave, that's up to you, but while we're out there on that platform, both sides better put away their guns and let us work in peace. Otherwise, me and my men are going home."

Sure enough, both the Israelis and the Egyptians pulled back their torpedo boats, the Israelis took their machine guns off the rig, and nobody bothered Red or his men whatsoever for the entire sixty-three days it took them to kill the four wells on the platform.

WASHINGTON — MAY 10, 1977

At 10:00 A.M., Representative John M. Murphy introduced Red to the committee and, in effect, to millions of American citizens who had only heard of his exploits in the oil patch. "We are indeed fortunate today to have as our lead-off witness Mr. Paul Adair, known as Red Adair, who is the world's expert and most successful in the control and conquering of tragedies that exist not only onshore, but offshore oil and gas blowouts, and catastrophes. It is a pleasure to have you here today, Mr. Adair. You may proceed."

Red had been so nervous since he awoke that he had been unable to eat breakfast. On the way from his hotel to Longworth House Office Building his stomach had felt like he'd eaten a package of sandpaper and his ears would not stop ringing, but the moment he began to speak — the moment it was time for him to deliver — he became as calm as though he were standing before a burning well.

"Thank you, Mr. Chairman," Red said. "I am kind of dumbfounded at being here. I never thought I would be in a place like this in my life — I am just a country boy from Texas. But I will be glad to answer any questions you have. All I can tell you is what I know, and what we do, and what we recommend."

Red was asked what could be done to help control offshore emergencies, and he predicted the development of a multipurpose support vessel whose design would prove similar to the *Tharos*, which would later work alongside the burning Piper Alpha platform in the North Sea. He submitted his design for this vessel — called "Red One" — to the committee for its research into offshore drilling safety.

"I made about ten to fifteen trips to Europe, to Norway, to England, and proposed a semisubmersible — I call it a work platform — that can work on any well, no matter how rough the sea gets," Red said. "With a vessel like this, I believe, we could control blowouts much quicker and much cheaper than they are today. . . . No matter where you drill, eventually you are going to have a blowout. So you have to have means to control it. It would make the job a lot easier for us. I tried to get it here in the States, but we have not gotten it yet. We are still on the verge of getting one. I do hope we will get one. . . . We are drilling farther offshore, and with a flat-bottomed barge it makes the job difficult. In six-foot seas or better, we have to come in. For instance, on one job in Australia we towed the barge for thirty days to do one day's work. I think that speaks for itself, how badly we really need something like this."

Several committee members tried to pin Red down on the issue of blame for offshore disasters, particularly regarding Phillips Petroleum's culpability in the Bravo platform blowout, but Red stuck to his previous statements to the press in which he said that Phillips had done all they could to prevent it. In fact, it was Phillips, Red reminded the committee, who took his suggestions to heart and was going to build the first semisubmersible firefighting vessel (the *SEDCO/Phillips S.S.*).

Representative Breaux from Louisiana asked Red whether the Bravo blowout had resulted from lack of safety equipment or the lack of the proper use of existing equipment.

"I still feel it goes back to the human element," Red told the committee. "No matter what equipment you put on a drilling rig or any platform, if you do not have the personnel that knows how to operate all this equipment, then it will not work. You have to train your men a little better . . . you should have stricter blowout drills, check your blowout equipment more frequently; make sure everything is working; make sure your personnel knows where every control lever is on your drilling rig. Have certain valves [available] on the rig floor if you are in the hole with the drill pipe, so you have something to set on the drill pipe to close it in."

"We do not have much offshore drilling in Arizona," Representative Udall said to Red. "And I do not know much about oil blowouts. I am an authority on political blowouts. Not much on oil. You say generally the cause of these blowouts is human failure. What happened in the North Sea?"

"Well, we really do not know yet," said Red. "They did the normal procedure. The well had been sitting there, and it had some tools lost in the hole, and there was an obstruction in the flow; the well was not up to its full potential. They were getting a drilling rig ready to go on and go to work and rework this well. They pumped mud in it. That well is ten thousand feet deep. After they pumped mud in it and the well was dead, they set a plug in it to five hundred feet. Now, what happened in there nobody knows. When they were taking the Christmas tree off, that leaves the four-inch tubing exposed to the atmosphere. They were in the process of putting the blowout preventer on it when the well started coming in. And at night, like this, the first thing you do when a well comes in, you start shutting off your power, turn your lights off, and what have you. So, the men grabbed a preventer that was lying there and put it on this wellhead. In that kind of haste nobody looks whether it is upside down or not. That is the way it got put on. What happened, we do not know. But we were able to make it work, even though it was upside down."

"We are all proud of you," Representative Udall said. "You did a great job."

But it was when Representative Young asked Red about who should control offshore platforms that the committee got a taste of vintage Red Adair. "I just want to ask you one question," Mr. Young said. "In the bill it purports to put OSHA in control of the safety requirements on a drilling platform, instead of the Coast Guard. In your dealing with blowouts, do you envision that causing you any problems in the future, when you have to work offshore?"

"Well, I do not know how you feel about OSHA, but I know how I feel," Red said. "I will probably step in the mud here, but I do not care. If I am on a blowout out there and I have one of these fellows that has never seen a blowout before, and he comes up and tries to tell me what to do, he has never seen one; so, then I got my suitcase and told them, 'Let this man do the job, and I will go home.' So, the next day I came out, he was gone." At that point the committee's proceedings had to be momentarily halted because of the laughter and cheering.

That night, Barbara Walters, who was then coanchoring the evening news for ABC, told viewers that people in the United States say there aren't any more heroes, that people say children don't have heroes to look up to any more, but that on this day, the Congress of the United States had a chance to see a real hero. Then she showed a clip of Red speaking to the committee.

"I was raised with Daddy fighting oil-well fires, so that didn't mean that much to me," Robyn remembers, "but when he spoke before Congress, and I saw him on TV holding his own, answering every one of those congressmen's questions, I think that's the proudest I ever was of him. I know it was the proudest Mama's ever been of him too. I mean, there he was, up there with all those educated people, and there was no doubt who had control of that conversation. Not for a minute."

CHAPTER NINETEEN

RED

I was off on another job when the Bravo platform, the EKOFISK well, blew out, so I sent Boots over there with Richard to help him. I'm reading about it in the newspaper — about the preventer being on upside down and how the rams wouldn't hold and all — but see, the preventer being on upside down shouldn't make any difference, really. The rams should still close and they should hold, but something obviously was wrong.

Finally, Phillips Petroleum called me and said, "Red, you better get over there and see what the hell's going on." So I got on a plane and got over there, and the press was having a field day with it. They asked me how long it would take, and I said, "If it hangs like it is I ought to be through in four or five hours."

I got out to that platform and right away I saw what was wrong: the blowout preventer rams simply hadn't adjusted the ram so they would close properly. It's like adjusting the brakes on your car, so that the shoes will come up and grab the drum or the pads will grab the disc correctly. The other problem we were having was with the seals holding, like having a leak in your brake line where you have to keep pumping it and the brakes will hold for a minute but then release. Also, there wasn't enough water being pumped up there onto the platform — water protection for the men the oil was falling on.

Boots was pretty upset about me showing up over there. I said, "Boots, Phillips called me and told me to come, and anyway, I *run* this company. I *own* this company. I'm the boss." I told him all he had to do was pick up the phone, and I would have told him what to do.

This was Friday night. On Saturday morning I changed all the packing in the preventer, put in a new seal, and adjusted the rams. I put five thousand pounds of pressure on 'em and held it for five or ten minutes to make sure they held, and they did. Richard and I got underneath the floor and made some more adjustments, and then we pumped seawater into that well and killed it.

That was the beginning of when they were gonna quit, I'm pretty sure. I should have suspected something was up with him right then, and after that, when he went on another job for me over in Iran and didn't call in. I think he had lined up his own company by then. I think he and Coots had talked about it.

Boots and Coots left the company. They weren't fired, they came into my office with a bunch of demands. They wanted this and they wanted that. They wanted a piece of the company. I said, "This is the way it is, and if you want to stay you can, or if you want to leave you can, but there's no way I can meet your demands." In fact, they had a better setup than I did. They didn't have any obligations, any overhead, or insurance payments. They thought all the money I took in was profit. They didn't realize how it really was. It wasn't like when I worked for Old Man Kinley and I had to pay part of their salaries out of the money Kinley paid me. They drew good salaries, they got big bonuses. I could actually put more money in their profit sharing than I could in mine, and they'd have had the whole company anyway later on.

It hurt my feelings when they left the way they did. It pissed me off. They said a whole bunch of ugly things to the press. They started those rumors about me being retired, about me being out of business. Hell, I hired Boots when he didn't have any signs to paint, and I put him to work. I let him drive my race car and I let him drive one of the race boats. Why? Well, you work together, you want to do things together, to get along with a person, and he wanted to do it, so I said sure.

Coots . . . I don't think he ever really wanted to leave, but he went along. He was looking forward to retiring even when he was working for me. He always said he never wanted to work hard forever. We're still pretty close friends, considering. I even see Boots every now and then down at the bay. I guess we all mellow with age.

HOUSTON — JANUARY 1978

On a cold, drizzly, winter day Red sat in his office staring out the window, sixty-two years old, going on sixty-three, and feeling every day of it. He had just returned from a job on an oil well that had also been producing H_2S gas in Drayton Valley, Canada, about one hundred miles west southwest of Edmonton, Alberta. The temperature had been forty-five degrees below zero, so cold that the oil from the blowing well wouldn't run off. It would come out of the ground black, but in the extremely cold air the gas separated out of it and it turned yellow, like dark mustard. As soon as it hit the ground it became yellow wax that piled up four feet deep around the rig. It was like quicksand when you tried to walk through it wearing your cold-weather suit, a slicker suit on top of that, insulated boots, breathing apparatus on your back, and a mask.

This well had been a bad one, making 28 percent hydrogen sulfide — H_2S — a very high concentration, high enough so that breathing it would kill a man in less than thirty seconds. It was too high to filter through a canister attached to the mask, so Red and Richard Hatteberg, who'd gone on the job with him, had worn air tanks on their backs. In addition to all that clothing, they, in effect, were walking around through chest-deep tar wearing scuba gear, only they didn't have the benefit of water to buoy them up.

Luckily, the well had been out in the middle of nowhere, thirty miles from Lodgepole, the nearest town. The H_2S readings there weren't high enough to warrant evacuating the townspeople, but it smelled so bad it felt like you were living inside a rotten egg. It smelled just as bad fifty miles away in Drayton Valley, where Red and Richard stayed at night. Even in Edmonton, one hundred miles away, people were complaining about the gas tarnishing their silverware.

The reason the well had blown out was because the rams on the blowout preventers had stopped working. This happened because instead of using hydraulic fluid in the control lines that operate the rams, someone had used soluble oil, which has a water base, and the lines had frozen. Red wanted to move the drilling rig away from the wellhead to facilitate his work, but the oil company balked when he told them he'd have to cut the drill pipe and drop the drill string — all the joints of pipe and the drilling bit — down into the casing so he could skid the rig off. The oil company hadn't wanted to deal with a subsequent fishing expedition to pull the drill string back out of the hole. They wanted to try to kill the well without doing that, so for eleven days Red and Richard tried steaming the lines, banging on the preventers, pumping in to kill the well, none of which worked.

Finally, the oil company agreed to go along with Red's plan, and he had his special pipe cutter sent up from Houston, a cutter that clamps around the pipe and uses an air motor and a two-inch rotary blade to cut it. This cutter, which goes in circles around and around the pipe, was made from Red's original design he'd used to cut the drill pipe at The Devil's Cigarette Lighter.

Now, to cut the pipe, Red and Richard had to crawl up above the blowout preventers, right under the drilling rig's rotary table, into a three-foot space, dark as an ocean floor. The darkness was due to the rig's weather shield, a quarter-inch steel-plate cover that had been welded over the entire rig and could not be removed. Red brought in high-intensity, gas-proof lights, the kind that are used in mines, and hung them up, but they were not much help. The conditions were so cramped, Red and Richard used up five air tanks apiece just moving their equipment into place.

So there the two of them were, beside a well blowing like crazy, in forty-five-degrees-below-zero weather, with poison gas going all over the place, trying to cut the drill pipe in semidarkness. If they'd been swimming calmly under the sea, looking at beautiful tropical fish, these tanks would have been good for thirty minutes, but as hard as Red and Richard were working, the air in the tanks lasted for only twenty minutes at most. This meant that while they worked they were keeping an eye on the air-tank gauge (which they really couldn't trust, so they had to keep an eye on their watches too), thinking about their escape route, which lay through 200 feet of that chest-deep yellow wax, and knowing full well that the cutter could make a spark at any time and blow the rig up, and that if it did they'd be sitting in what amounted to a giant Dutch oven.

In spite of this, they were making good progress. Richard was running the cutter and Red was behind him, about twenty feet away, feeding him the air hose that ran the cutter. All of a sudden, the hose stopped coming. Richard yanked and yanked and cussed and finally noticed *he* was running out of air. He backed out from under the rig floor, and when he did he saw that Red was gone and someone else was getting set to feed him more hose. What had happened was that the hose that ran from Red's face mask to the air tank on his back had somehow gotten a pinhole in it, the H_2S seeped in, and out he went, unconscious, seconds away from death. Fortunately, someone saw Red fall, immediately dragged him to safety, and got him medical attention.

The next day, against doctor's orders, Red was back on the job. He had a splitting headache and chest pains when he breathed deeply, but he insisted on going to work. He and Richard finished cutting the pipe and began setting up to pull the rig off the hole. It was Christmas Eve and they were about to move the rig when Red said, "Nah, it's too dark, we'll do it in the morning." As they were driving from Drayton Valley the next morning, they felt the ground shake under the three-quarter-ton Ford pickup truck they were driving and a huge mushroom cloud appeared on the horizon. The well was on fire.

They never knew for sure, but Red suspected sabotage, perhaps by local residents who were afraid of problems from the H_2S. All someone would have to have done was put a match to the yellow wax on the ground a hundred yards from the well. The fire would slowly have burned its way to the well, and when it got there, kaboom!

In any case, they now were faced with pulling the rig off a burning well without a shield for the bulldozer or any fire fighting equipment whatsoever. Red drove the dozer and Richard worked on the ground hooking up cables to the rig. At forty-five below zero, there was no way they could be wet down with water, even near the well. The two of them got within four or five feet of the blaze, broiling from the heat on one side of their bodies, freezing from the cold on the other. ("Just keep turning around, Richard," Red said, "and you'll be cooked just right.") They worked frantically, not wanting the rig to melt and fall on the wellhead, which was essential to save, and in only three hours they managed to pull that rig off. It was Christmas Day.

The rig was on the side of a hill. The waxy oil had been running down the hill, and Red had been building little lakes of this oil for over two weeks. Now the whole area was on fire, melting the permafrost, creating three feet of muck on the ground, making it even more miserable to work, but just like at The Devil's Cigarette Lighter, Red was able to back his explosive charge up to the well, blow the fire out, and cap it on New Year's Day.

Cold January rain beat against Red's office window. Sixty-two going on sixty-three, and feeling every day. His chest ached. His hands still didn't feel completely thawed out. The muscles in his legs cramped up and twitched uncontrollably. His eyes burned. Every time he took a deep breath it felt as though someone were trying to stuff an old rope down his throat. But Red was used to feeling this way. He'd been living with physical discomfort so long he actually had no idea what it felt like to live life without it. It was the pain in his heart that made him feel so bad.

On his desk lay a copy of the *Houston Post,* open to a full-page spread devoted to the split between him and Boots and Coots. "Adair team split brewed for years, friends of all say," one headline trumpeted. These friends were not identified by the paper, but Boots and Coots were quoted, and it was obvious they had gone public with what Red regarded as a family disagreement.

Basically, what the article said was that Boots and Coots had left Red's firm to start their own company because they were doing the tough jobs, risking their lives, and they didn't believe they were getting a fair shake, enough of the money that the Red Adair Company was taking in. A "friend" stated that even though Red made "probably three or four million dollars a year," his family "drains a lot of it away."

When Kemmie heard about the story she threw the paper away without reading it and canceled her subscription. She has never read that newspaper since. But Red read the article all the way through, three times. "Friends," he muttered. "Some goddamn friends." No doubt they were the same friends who helped Boots and Coots spread the word that he'd retired, he thought. You'd think after all he'd done in the oil patch people wouldn't believe rumors about him, but he'd already gotten word from London that Iran Oil hadn't called him on a job because they'd been told he was out of business. Friends. Should've brought a whole planeload of the bastards up to Canada with him to see what his retirement looked like. Let 'em all see who the hell was doing the tough jobs. Let 'em crawl in under that rig floor with Richard and watch how expertly he cut the drill pipe under conditions few men would even try to endure.

Red closed his eyes and listened to the wind-driven rain. He remembered another burning H$_2$S well up in Canada in the mid-1960s, another well where it was so cold if you spat it turned to ice before it hit the ground. They'd worn Scott airpacks on their backs on that one too, and asbestos hoods to cover the packs in order to protect them from the fire. Coots had been on that job with him, and so had Jimmy. A piece of steel had fallen from the burning rig and pinned Coots's leg. Coots had pulled and pulled, he and Jimmy had pulled *on* Coots, but his leg had refused to come free. Then the buzzer on Coots's air pack had gone off. He was running out of air, and at the rate he was breathing from all the pulling and twisting, Red knew they had less than two minutes to get him loose from that steel or he would die.

"Go get me an ax, Jimmy," Red said.

"What?" asked his son.

"An ax, goddamn it! Go get me an ax!"

"What the hell you gonna do, Red?" Coots asked him, when Jimmy left.

"I'm gonna chop off your leg," Red told him. "Ain't nothin' else I can do, Coots."

Coots was wearing thick, leather boots with laces halfway up his calf. How he managed to do it, Red never knew, but when Coots saw the ax he yanked his foot clean out of the boot, ripping every single one of those laces to shreds.

"Were you really gonna cut my foot off?" he asked Red afterward.

"You bet your ass I was," Red said. "Which is better, bein' one-footed or bein' dead?"

And Boots. It was funny what you remembered about people you'd spent years and years of your life with. Of all the jobs, hundreds of jobs, they'd done together, all the car races and boat races and all the bars they'd partied in all around the world, he remembered now the time Boots had been with him in Tulsa, Oklahoma, just after he'd started his company in 1959.

He'd bought a brand new, red, '59 Cadillac coupe, and he and Boots and Rush Johnson had driven up to Tulsa to the oil show. Jerry Morton was there, and he'd gotten them all rooms at the Tradewinds Hotel. There'd been a poker game there one night. Red and Boots were in it, Rush and Jerry too, and a guy named Dewey Davis, a superintendent for Penrod Drilling, who raised plum trees on the side. Ol' Dewey only had one arm, his left one. He'd lost the other on a well accident somewhere, and when he played poker he'd open his billfold and lay it right next to his left hand. Then he'd turn those cards over and start pulling out hundreds with his index finger, throwing them in the pot like they were dimes.

It was a no-limit game, and near the end Dewey was trying to buy every pot. It was a lucky night for Red, who'd come to Tulsa nearly broke. On the last hand, with $8,000 on the table, Red had called Dewey with an $1,800 bet and beaten him, three kings to two pairs, nines over sevens. What Red remembered even more than the poker game, though, was what Boots did after the game was over.

They'd played in a room on the second floor and as everybody got ready to walk downstairs to the lobby, Boots had jumped right over the banister. Red looked down after he jumped, expecting to see his friend and new employee unconscious or dead on the floor, but it must have been Boots's lucky night too, because he landed on his back, right in the middle of a plump couch. The image of his round face grinning up at the rest of the poker players was forever imbedded in Red's memory. "Didn't know I could fly, huh, Coach?" Boots said.

It shouldn't have ended the way it did, with them quitting and then saying those things. It should have been like it had been with him and Myron Kinley. Even after the stuff with Kinley's son Jack, he and the old man had stayed the best of friends. They'd respected each other and neither ever said a bad word about the other. That's the way you were supposed to live. He took over from Kinley. Boots and Coots would have taken over from him. Then Jimmy and Raymond and Richard would take over from Boots and Coots. There would be a legacy, a progression, one generation of wild-well men following the next. That would never happen now. He felt something inside him was broken that had nothing to do with his body. He felt tired and lonely. He felt betrayed. When Joy Hamilton, his secretary, peeked in to see why his office was so quiet, she saw him staring out the window. She couldn't see his face, and he wasn't making a sound, but she could tell that he was crying.

CHAPTER TWENTY

I don't use profanity very often. I almost never use the big word, the one that starts with F. But I had a special name for that Mexican well. Once all the politicians got involved, once everyone got in Red's way and started driving him crazy and keeping him from getting finished with it, I quit calling it Ixtoc I. From then on that well was M-F I, and I'm sure y'all know what M-F stands for.

Kemmie Adair

The roughest time of Red Adair's career in the oil patch had nothing to do with anything in his personal life, but was caused by a well known as Ixtoc I, in Campeche Bay, in the southernmost part of the Gulf of Mexico, forty miles north of Ciudad del Carmen on the Yucatan Peninsula. It was a wildcat well — one drilled in an area where no gas or oil production previously existed — and it came in strong. For six or seven months it produced 80,000 barrels of oil a day and 120,000,000 cubic feet of gas, and it showed no signs of slowing down.

The Mexican government was extremely proud of Ixtoc I. It was an indication to the world of the country's oil reserves. It was like saying, "Look at us. Look at the money we have in the bank." The Mexicans, in fact, began borrowing against Ixtoc's oil, incurring a debt that may never be fully paid off. Then, on June 3, 1979, the well blew out, and 80,000 gallons of oil a day began pouring into the Gulf of Mexico. Public outcry was immediate and loud. The press got on the story like locusts on wheat, because in addition to the environmental issues raised by the spill, there were spicy political overtones.

Ixtoc I had been drilled for PEMEX — the Mexican government's oil monopoly — with a rig leased to them by SEDCO Inc., a drilling company owned by William Clements, then Republican governor of Texas. Clements's SEDCO stock had been placed in a blind trust, and the company was being run by his son, B. Gill Clements, but if SEDCO was found negligent, it certainly wouldn't hurt Governor Clements's nemesis, Texas attorney general Mark White, a Democrat considering a run for the governor's office. On top of that was the sensitive issue of Mexican-American relations, which have been a lit fuse in Texas for two hundred years.

"Right off the bat there was this feeling of Mexicans versus Gringos," says Red, "about who was to blame and who'd get the credit for fixing it. Nobody said anything directly, but the feeling was there. I knew it and they knew it. Me, I didn't worry about it. If I worried about those things, I'd never have gotten anywhere in the places I've worked. All I ever did was try to get along with people. All I wanted to do, all I ever wanted to do, is get in there and get my job done." At Ixtoc I, that goal would prove considerably easier said than done.

From the outset, of course, the primary concern for everyone — PEMEX officials, Mexican politicians, Texas politicians, environmentalists, resort owners, and ordinary citizens concerned about oil washing up on the beaches of the Gulf Coast — was the question of how to get the well dead. PEMEX decided the best man to accomplish that was Red Adair. At least that's what they decided at first. Red still had a day or two left to finish up another job, so he sent Raymond Henry down to the gulf to assess the situation and get the well-kill started.

RAYMOND

There were all kinds of stories about how that well blew out, but what I feel really happened was this. They'd drilled down as far as they needed to be. They were at TD (total depth) of that well. Above TD were the zones — the pockets in the formation — that were already producing. They started coming out of the hole with their drill pipe, pulling the pipe out of the hole, up through the drill-pipe casing. Once they had that drill pipe out, they were going to run their production pipe in, all the way to the bottom. When you do that, when you pull your drill pipe out, you have to keep the hole filled — keep mud pumping downhole — so you maintain a hydrostatic balance with the upward pressure of your oil.

Well, they'd had an earlier loss of circulation — an earlier problem where the upward pressure hadn't supported the weight of the mud and the mud had gone south on them — and they'd used up a lot of their mud controlling that, so now they had a shortage of mud. As they pulled up the drill pipe, they were putting mud back in the hole, but it wasn't nearly enough — it wasn't beginning to keep the hole full. When they got to where they were almost out of the hole with their drill pipe, the pressure of the oil came in under 'em and started pushing the pipe out of the hole on its own, and when they called us, that drill pipe was wedged up in the derrick.

When I got down there, it had already caught fire and the drilling pipe had just burnt and it fell into the water. It was a floating type rig, and it was sitting at probably a twenty-degree list. We circled it in a Lear jet — Jesse Echeverria, the guy in charge of drilling for PEMEX was with me — and I saw that the whole drilling package had fallen into the water. There wasn't a whole lot left above the water to work on, to cap the well. I said, "You better start hunting you some drilling rigs 'cause there's gonna be a relief-well problem here, no doubt about it."

Echeverria had 'em circle the Lear a couple more times, and he looked at it and agreed with me. We had divers go down to see what condition the subsea wellhead was in — it was leaning a little bit and there was debris all around it — and then we flew back to town and commenced looking for extra drilling rigs, trying to find some more rigs to drill a relief well — to come in at an angle with a new well and drill into the formation near the well bore. Then we could pump into that relief well and kill it.

That's when all the political bullshit started. We found a rig from Texas and told them where we wanted them to drill us a relief well, but PEMEX was determined to kill the well with a Mexican drilling rig and a Mexican crew, not a rig from the U.S. The Mexicans were sure where the bottom of the well was, and we were sure it was in a different place. So, what you had was two rigs drilling at the same time. It was almost a competition, which it shouldn't have been. Well, in a week or ten days, the rig out of Texas had caught up and passed the PEMEX rig, and that's when the Texas rig began having problems getting drill water, trouble getting mud, trouble getting all the supplies necessary to do their job. The Mexicans kept causing problems for the American rig so the PEMEX rig would get down further.

Then stuff began being ordered that wasn't necessary. They brought in three bargeloads of premixed, eighteen-pound mud — real expensive — when the upward pressure of the well wouldn't support even sea water. They brought in drill pipe that wasn't needed. They sent all kinds of useless equipment, spent 'em a small fortune. See, Echeverria and his right-hand man Espinosa were getting 15 percent of the price of all the material that came down here. There were a whole bunch of guys down there gettin' their pockets full, but none of that had anything to do with us at all. We were drilling a relief well and were out of the picture. Red got a lot of bad publicity because it took so long, but he had no control over the drilling-rig competition (hell, all that did was piss him off) and he had no control over the short-stopping of supplies. None of it was his fault at all. If they'd just listened to him from the beginning like they should've, we'd've gotten that well killed *months* before they finally did.

While the relief well was being drilled, Red actually had the blowing well capped for a short time in late June of 1979, but after several hours pressure inside the casing pipe caused it to burst again, down near the subsea wellhead. Now Ixtoc I was blowing out *under* the water and coming up all around the platform. When it did, the well's hot gas aerated the water, creating a lake of fire a thousand feet across that was too hot to traverse. This meant the divers Red was using to clear debris from the subsea wellhead and prepare it with new blow-out preventers and tie-in lines for his relief well could no longer dive straight down, but had to work instead from a barge 300 yards from the platform.

Still, Red was confident he'd soon have Ixtoc I under control. What he hadn't counted on was that the misfortune of the burst undersea pipe would give rise to the intervention of all manner of so-called wild-well experts. "Red Adair can't kill it his way," they'd say. "But we know how." And in spite of Red's reputation and his record of success, in spite of the fact that he sat down with the man in charge of PEMEX and showed them that the relief-well program he was using had worked dozens of times before and would work on Ixtoc, in spite, even, of the fact that he capped two other offshore wells while all this was going on, PEMEX told Red they were going to try what these new wild-well experts proposed.

Red was beside himself. He would call Kemmie at night and complain bitterly about having to work around a bunch of incompetents, a bunch of corrupt incompetents at that. She would sit and listen to him and sympathize, because she knew Red had no choice. He had to go along with every harebrained idea, even though the only thing these well-killing experiments did was get in his way and slow him down. He couldn't walk off the job; he *wouldn't* walk off the job, not this one, not unless they released him, so he continued supervising the relief-well drilling while the chaos around him increased in tempo.

First came the PEMEX engineers and their "Operation Sombrero" — "Operation Chingadero," Red called it. The sombrero was a giant, inverted, steel funnel, attached to a platform so it could swing out over the well. The engineers theorized the blowing oil would rush into the wide end of the funnel and come out the narrow top, where it would be run through a series of separators. All they'd have to do then, they thought, was run the oil into tanks, flare the gas, and dump the seawater they'd filtered out of the oil overboard into the gulf.

Operation Sombrero cost the Mexican government $50 million. Brown & Root, the Houston contractor on the job, made a lot of money on the project, as did a number of PEMEX executives, but the flow rates of Ixtoc I — the amount of oil coming out of the well — were so high that as soon as the sombrero was put in place it began to vibrate harmonically and had to be removed before it shook itself to pieces.

Then someone at PEMEX got the bright idea of dumping lead balls down the well to plug the hole at the bottom of the well bore.

KEMMIE

I'm no engineer and not mechanically minded in any way at all, but I do have sense enough to know that if there's a great big hole in a pipe way down there underneath the water somewhere, and pressure coming up out of the ground — terrific pressure — when it gets to that hole is gonna be goin' *out* that hole. Anything you drop down the pipe from the top, balls or whatever, when *they* get down to that hole, where there's all that pressure pushing stuff out of the hole, where are those balls gonna go? They're gonna go *out* the hole and lay on the ocean floor. Which is exactly what happened. Red knew it wasn't gonna work. Red knew that sombrero would never work. And then, right in the middle of it, along came those guys called The Wild Bunch from Colorado.

These were terrible people. These were the guys who blew up wells in Wyoming so they could cap 'em. A couple of years after Ixtoc, the FBI flew Red out to Wyoming to testify against these guys. They were bad people . . . *bad* people. When Red got out there FBI men met him at the airport, took him straight to his hotel room, and told him, "We'll come by here and get you at 9 o'clock in the morning and take you straight to the courthouse. Don't leave your room. Anything you want to know you call us."

Well, Red got a telephone call in his hotel room. This man said, "We want to meet you at eight o'clock in the morning in the lobby," and Red said, "OK." He thought it was the same people who had brought him from the airport. But then Red got a hunch he ought to check it out, so he called the FBI agent late that night and the guy said to him, "Uh-uh. Don't go. . . . We did not call you. We did not change it from nine o'clock."

How they knew about when Red was supposed to be picked up I do not know. All he was testifying to was that those wells had been blown up, but these guys did not want him to testify at all. So Red stayed in his room, and he did testify, and those guys were convicted of blowing up those wells, and they went to jail. Red never said he was nervous about testifying, but I'm sure he was. I'd have been. These folks were terrible.

RED

Butch Davenport, the head of that Wild Bunch, was gonna come down to Mexico and do the job at Ixtoc. He told the newspapers he was the only guy who could kill it. He said the reason it hadn't been killed was because my methods were obsolete. He told the newspapers he was going to put two telephone poles right down the well and it would be all over. Telephone poles. Can you believe that? Hell, I'd never even *heard* of this guy before, this expert wild-well man, but the Mexicans talked to him. They talked to him for quite a while.

They talked to everybody. The shit I had to put up with. I told them to watch out, be careful about what they tried, because that well was blowing so hard under the water it was pulling stuff back into it. I told them not to pull any foolish stunts, because that flow would pull someone right in. After we rigged it all up for the Mexicans to pump those lead balls in and we'd turned the well over to them, I went to Europe on another job for a while. While I was there, that flow pulled a diver right into it . . . pulled him right into the well and killed him before anyone knew what had happened. I wasn't there but I heard about it. It also pulled one of the undersea remote control vehicles in.

Meanwhile, Red Adair was being chopped into little pieces by the press. Red was in trouble, they said. Red had met his match. "Futile attempts to cap the blowing well by Houston oil-well troubleshooter Red Adair," or phrases nearly identical to that, became standard in articles about Ixtoc I. One article claimed the well couldn't be capped and that Red had quit his efforts to kill the well.

"Hell, no, we haven't given up," Red told the *Houston Post*. "I don't ever give up. . . . Red Adair and his company have not quit. We're more involved now and we're damn well sure we'll have this thing under control by doing it our way."

Then, in August 1979, oil began washing up on Texas beaches and the publicity got even worse. Now PEMEX and SEDCO were being blamed for ruining the environment, and in addition the press was implicating Red because the well was taking so long to kill. PE-MEX said it was SEDCO's fault. SEDCO said it was PEMEX's fault. Lawsuits were threatened by Attorney General White against SEDCO, by the AFL-CIO against SEDCO, PEMEX, and the Mexican drilling contractor who leased SEDCO's rig, by Gulf Coast businesses and hotels against those same three defendants, and finally, months later, by SEDCO itself against the Mexican government.

Red claimed that it wasn't clear whether the oil on the beaches was from Ixtoc, that the oil that washed up was of a different specific gravity from Ixtoc's, and that tankers in the gulf were using the blow-out as a convenient cover to wash out their holds. Whether he was right or not, Red's reputation was suddenly as sullied as the white Gulf Coast sand. Now, even the mention of the word Ixtoc sent Red's blood pressure through the roof.

RAYMOND

It sure as hell wasn't Red's fault. It wasn't SEDCO's fault either. It was just their rig that drilled the hole. The SEDCO people on board the rig told the Mexicans they had to circulate [drilling mud] and to stop pulling the drill pipe, but the Mexican superintendent on board said, "No, by God, I'm the man in charge and we're going to do it my way," and they did it his way and it blew out.

But Clements made the statement that there's been oil on the Galveston beaches since way before we ever drilled in the Gulf of Mexico and a little oil won't hurt nothin', which made it sound like he was insensitive to the environmental issues. So then Mark White piped up and said Clements doesn't care about our Texas coastline and it was his drilling rig that caused the problem. They never proved it *was* Ixtoc oil on the beaches. There was a tanker collision in the gulf during the same time, and the oil on the beaches may have been from that. Whatever it was, it was not a good deal for Red Adair.

Before it was killed, Ixtoc I dumped more than 100 million gallons of oil into the Gulf of Mexico. At the time, it was the world's worst oil spill ever. Later, PEMEX got a new president. Echeverria and Espinosa disappeared, perhaps to Brazil, perhaps to Spain or Portugal, no one knows for sure. Other PEMEX executives were sent to jail.

When they finally did kill Ixtoc, they did it Red's way, with a relief well placed where he told them to place it, using a system of undersea valves that he designed. But that wasn't until the spring of 1980, by which time the media had spread the word that Red Adair, the famed oil-well fire fighter, had finally failed.

The blow to Red's reputation couldn't have come at a worse time, though the full effects would take a couple of years to be felt. From the time Boots and Coots left Red's company in late 1977 until 1983, the oil field boomed, and both the Red Adair Company and Boots and Coots, Inc., prospered. Then, in the mid-1980s, the bottom fell out of the oil industry.

There was some drilling, but not much, and when wells did blow out, Boots and Coots got most of the calls. Red Adair was rich, they told the oil companies. He didn't need the work. They were hungry. They'd do the job for less. Besides, Red was too old to fight wild wells and his men couldn't cut it. They, Boots and Coots, would do a better job.

The men who'd been around the oil patch for years and years knew better. They knew that Red may have slowed down, but that nobody could size up a wild well and kill it quicker than he could. They knew, too, that his men — Jimmy, Richard Hatteberg, Raymond Henry, and now Brian Krause and Danny Clayton — were top fire fighters. They knew that if Red trained them they had to be, that if they weren't he'd never send them to kill a well, that if they didn't have what it takes to work on a wild well Red would have let them go. If nothing else, Red's ego would not let a man come on a location wearing the famous red coveralls unless he could perform up to Red's standards. "Remember one thing," Adair always told his men. "Red coveralls never run."

But few of the old-time oil-field hands were left. Wildcatters like John Mecom, Sr., and Jim West were dead. Rush Johnson was dead. And those from the old days who weren't dead had retired. True, there were a few, such as Armand Hammer, who remained, but the oil business wasn't the same anymore. It was run by lawyers and accountants now — bean counters, Red called them — bottom-liners, who only wanted to hear how cheaply you'd work. To them, Red Adair was a character from a story they'd heard when they were kids.

The oil-field crunch went on and on. Two years, three, four . . . Red came to the office, went down to the bay and took out his boat, went up and visited Kemmie, but he was like a robot going through a series of programmed motions. He became depressed; Robyn, Kemmie, and Jimmy worried about him all the time. He had his minor heart attack, and they worried even more.

"If only he would walk out of that office and not go back," Kemmie thought. "If only he'd quit fighting wild wells and take it easy, go off somewhere with me on the boat." But she knew it was futile to try to talk him into it. It was a waste of time. He was like one of the idle drilling rigs rusting in the South Texas sun down in Sabine Pass, going nowhere, waiting, waiting, waiting for a chance to work again.

Sporadically, jobs came in, and when they did he would perk up and begin planning his attack, drawing furiously on his yellow pads, making sure his men knew just what to do when they reached the well. Then there'd be another lull, and he'd become even sadder than before.

On top of everything else, he'd cosigned on a loan of several hundred thousand dollars for an old friend, the man had gone under, and Red was being sued by the bank for the money. Red didn't care about that. He honestly didn't give a damn about the money. What broke his heart was that his friend of thirty years refused to talk to him, refused to return his phone calls, treated him as though he had ceased to exist. All the guy had to do was say, "Red, I blew it. I lost the damn money and I'm sorry," and that would have been enough. That would have been the end of it. That was always enough. Red Adair was *that* kind of friend. Had the man forgotten? Didn't he know that Red placed friendship far above dollar bills? Wasn't there anybody left alive from the old days who remembered what kind of man Red Adair was?

Paul Wayne, his grandson, would come up to the office to visit him and catch Red staring out the window, not quite crying, but almost. "Grandpa," he'd say. "What's wrong?"

Red would jump in his chair and compose himself immediately. "Nothin', nothin'," he'd say. "C'mon, let's take a ride over to the warehouse and see how those pumps are doin'." The pumps, the row after row of red iron, were fine. Paul Wayne knew that because he cleaned and started every one of them every week. Every one of them was ready to go, anywhere in the world, at a moment's notice. Like the man who'd designed them, they too were waiting.

Red dreamed and in his dream he heard the thub, thub, thub, of helicopter rotors, but he couldn't see the chopper; it had disappeared into the poison shroud of hydrogen sulfide mist that covered the rig. It was the Phillips rig offshore, off Great Yarmouth in the North Sea, the one that blew out and killed three men in 1968. The chopper left him on the helipad with two hours' worth of air tanks, two hours to stay alive, before it would return. The wind was good, but if it shifted (and it could out there, faster than a man could tie his shoes), if it shifted wrong and the chopper couldn't land, the rig would be his tomb.

He was alone on the rig, and he felt lonesome, as though he'd been dropped into an abandoned iron city, on a strange planet poisoned in some awful war. The rig was slippery from oil and it was shaking. It was cold and dark, and the poison gas swirled around him in the wind. When he'd done the job, twenty years before, he'd tied into the wellhead by himself, for in fact he'd been alone. He'd tied into the flow line right below the kelly, so they'd been able to pump in and kill the well, but in his dream that didn't happen. In his dream, there was only a hole where the wellhead should have been, and he was sliding toward it, sliding on the slick steel plating of the drilling floor.

He tried to yell but with the mask from the air pack on his face that was impossible. And who would hear him if he yelled? Who could help him? He tried to grab onto something to break his slide, but he kept losing his grip, and he was getting closer and closer to the hole where the column of gas was blowing, where he would die. Then something fell and landed on his shoulder and he jumped and was awake.

He was on an airplane, but for a second he had no idea where it was going. He looked up and saw a British Airways flight attendant with her hand on his shoulder, and then he knew.

"Mr. Adair," she said, "are you all right?"

"Yeah," Red said. "I'm fine. I was having a dream there. Strange how that is. I felt just like I was back at that Great Yarmouth job I did in '68. I thought I was right out on that rig, on the North Sea. Boy, that was somethin'! In the dream I was even cold. I did *that* job in November, but it's always cold out there. Even now, in July."

CHAPTER TWENTY-ONE

THE NORTH SEA — JULY 8, 1988

Gradually the fires on Piper Alpha died down, but the crew of the support vessel *Tharos*, afraid of another massive explosion, pulled back a quarter of a mile from the platform, where they waited for Red Adair. Black smoke still billowed up from the rig, and tongues of flame were visible from time to time, darting out over the water, then disappearing, like a dragon's threat. Now and then, lone pieces of hot metal fell into the water, hissing, sending up a puff of steam. Sometimes they sank, sometimes they joined the flotilla of debris that bobbed in an ever-widening circle in the dark waves around the rig.

All of the thirty-six wells on Piper Alpha were equipped with downhole safety valves, metal flaps inside the production pipe 800 feet below the surface, that look something like a butterfly choke inside the barrel of an automobile's carburetor. These safety valves were connected to a pressure-operated, quarter-inch, stainless steel line running from the metal flap all the way up to the wellhead on the rig floor, and from there to either an air or hydraulic pressure source. As long as pressure is maintained on this downhole safety valve it stays open, but if there is any kind of catastrophe on the surface, anything that happens to break the quarter-inch line — whether someone hits it with a hammer, or it gets too hot, or it is ruptured by an explosive force — then the pressure bleeds off and the safety valve closes in the well.

On Piper Alpha, most of the wells had already shut themselves off, but no one knew this yet. It would be up to Red and his men, Raymond Henry and Brian Krause, to find that out and to determine why several of the wells were still on fire. No one else had any intention of climbing aboard the devastated platform to check it out, certainly not anyone onboard the *Tharos* who had seen Piper Alpha blow up.

Below deck, at one corner of the *Tharos*, is the vessel's saturation diving system equipped with three separate diver compression/decompression chambers — an eight-man chamber and two four-man chambers — where divers can live for as long as a month while working daily at depths up to a thousand feet. There were divers on the vessel, but none of them were going after the members of Piper Alpha's crew hung up in debris below the water's surface or lying almost 500 feet down on the ocean floor. It was far too risky, the *Tharos*'s captain felt; at any moment the remains of Piper Alpha could collapse into the water, pinning a diver beneath hot, sinking steel. Instead, *Tharos*'s ROVs — the remotely operated vehicles — were being used to find and bring back the bodies.

The self-propelled ROVs, equipped with small thrusters, are rectangular in shape and made out of lengths of pipe that look like fat Tinkertoys. The smaller ones, about the size of a standard desk top, are designed only to search beneath the sea, but the larger models, three or four times the size of the small ones, have mechanical arms on them capable of gripping an object and holding it fast. All are mounted with powerful lights and underwater TV cameras.

Now, in the *Tharos*'s below-deck submarine room, two ROV pilots watched the vehicles — the larger ones with arms — on TV screens, maneuvering them with controls similar to those on an airplane as the ROVs probed through the sunken wreckage of Piper Alpha. The submarine room was deathly still, as quiet as the shifting world on the television monitors, even when other members of the *Tharos* crew stopped to stare at the screens. Only when a human form appeared in the eerie beam of the underwater lights was there a sound, a sharp intake of breath, a choked sob. Then the pilots worked glassy eyed, like remote creatures themselves, securing the body in the arms of the ROV and steering it back to the vessel. The pilots worked in shifts, and when their shift was over they ate in silence and went to bed. The ROV worked day and night, unceasingly, retrieving the dead.

"The whole world is watching," Red had told his men before they left Houston, and when he hit the ground in London he knew that he was right. The BBC was there, of course, as were the major American networks, the Cable News Network, wire-service reporters, and dozens of newspaper and magazine journalists. Because of the massive loss of life — more than in any previous oil-field disaster — this job would have more media coverage than Red had ever encountered.

As soon as Red, Raymond, and Brian cleared customs, the

reporters' questions hit them like wind-driven salt, but the fire fighters, whose complete focus was the burning platform, had little time to talk to the press.

Red's first order of business was a meeting in the Occidental office at Aberdeen airport with Oxy's worldwide drilling manager, Leon Daniels, and Glenn Randal, the drilling manager in Aberdeen. Also present were two engineers who'd come over from Bakersfield, California, with Leon Daniels, and a couple of other Occidental executives he hadn't met before. At the meeting Red and his men were briefed on the situation at Piper Alpha. The Occidental people told Red what they knew, which was little more than he'd learned already from the media. Then the Adair crew got on a helicopter for the hour-and-twenty-minute flight to the *Tharos*.

They circled the smoldering rig, and Red could see at once that 80 percent of it was gone, obliterated. He signaled to the pilot to move closer and saw then, through the smoke, that what was left of the platform rested precariously at a 45-degree angle on its heat-warped legs and was covered with twisted, entangled debris that looked like tons and tons of thick, iron spaghetti. "It's not gonna fall," Red said to Raymond and Brian. "Not if it's stood this long. I can tell you that for sure. But it's gonna be a bitch gettin' to those wells."

They landed on the *Tharos*, and Red spoke to the captain, telling him he wanted to move closer to the platform. The captain was at first apprehensive, fearing more explosions could wreck the platform, but once Red assured him the burning wells would prevent that, he pulled the support vessel to within sixty feet of Piper Alpha's remains on the morning of July 9th. Then Red and his men climbed into a six-by-eight-foot basket with a steel-grating floor and four-foot-high wire-mesh sides, and were swung out next to one of the platform's flare booms by *Tharos*'s 350-ton crane.

Piper Alpha had been constructed with heat shields — steel walls running from the top of the platform to the bottom — on three sides. These shields were put in place to keep the intense radiant heat of the flare booms from the crewmen on the rig, but in order for Red and his men to work they would first have to take these heat shields off. Otherwise, there would be no way to connect the *Tharos*'s hydraulic gangway to Piper Alpha. Furthermore, once the heat shields were removed, the thick smoke covering the platform could dissipate in the wind. Next, all the debris would have to be cleared away from the well bay. Only then would the fires be exposed and the men be able to put them out, pump into the well bores, and one by one, kill all of Piper Alpha's wells.

From the basket they saw how the shields could be disconnected from the rig. They saw, too, that there wasn't a flat surface left on the platform and that everything was coated with oil. The heat had twisted and bent all the iron so everything jutted up at angles, slick, sharp, and crooked.

That night Red met with his men in a room below deck on the *Tharos*. On the wall was a chart pinpointing every well on Piper Alpha. While they worked, they would keep records of everything they uncovered so that if Red was wrong and the platform did fall into the ocean, they could return with a team of divers and control them with a subsea kill. If that happened, if the platform collapsed, it would take two to three years to complete the job.

"It's gonna be hell over there," Red said. "We're gonna have to tie ourselves onto that platform with safety ropes, guide the crane in there, and pick that debris off a piece at a time to get to those wells. We'll have the machine shop and the welding shop make us grappling hooks so we can latch onto stuff, and if the wind doesn't get too much worse, we should be all right. We'll get with it first thing in the morning."

It was after midnight, but Red could not sleep. He got dressed, left his small cabin in the crew quarters, below the helideck in the aft portion of the *Tharos*, and went out onto the upper deck. He walked forward, tasting smoke and the bitterness of burnt metal. Even in the semidarkness he had no trouble finding his way along walkways, down stairs, around cranes and booms, equipment bins and lifeboats. He knew every inch of the *Tharos* — the workshops, the diving system, the pollution dispersal equipment, the firefighting apparatus, the hospital. He had helped design it. In the lobby of his warehouse, encased in glass, was a working model of the *SEDCO/ Phillips S.S.* four feet square and three feet high, built in Japan at a cost of $25,000. Red looked at the model all the time, walked around it, demonstrated it to visitors.

The *Tharos* was a near duplicate of the *Phillips S.S.*, the first semisubmersible fire fighting support vessel, which had been Red's idea, his solution to the problem of reaching an offshore platform emergency quickly and efficiently, with every means of assistance possible immediately at hand. If it were up to him, there would be a *Phillips S.S.* or *Tharos* in every body of water where men drilled for oil and gas.

He shook his head. Check, double check, and triple check. Inspect everything five times over, ten times over, if necessary. Always have a hind door. Always have a way to escape. The *Tharos* was close by, but that hadn't done a bit of good for the men of Piper Alpha now lying on the ocean floor. Five of them, found by the ROVs, were being flown at that moment from the *Tharos* back to Aberdeen. They'd decided to airlift the bodies at night so as not to further upset the *Tharos*'s crew.

Red made his way to the submarine room and watched the TV screen silently for a while as the ROVs moved like box-shaped fish over and around pieces of the sunken rig. He sighed and walked back up on deck. It was so sad, he thought. Over the years, during the time he'd worked on rigs in the North Sea — on the Bravo platform near Norway, off Great Yarmouth, here off Scotland — he'd developed a deep affection for the people who lived along the North Sea coast. They were hardworking, honest, courageous people, folks Red related to, folks he respected. It would accomplish nothing for the men who'd died, but he resolved to get the job done on Piper Alpha and get it done as fast as possible. It was the only thing he *could* do.

He walked to one corner of the *Tharos*, where a fire monitor — a red, four-foot, elbow-shaped valve and nozzle assembly controlled by three wheels — faced the Piper platform sixty feet away. He could see the column of smoke and a small arch of fire just above the platform's heat shield. He knew what lay behind that heat shield, precisely what it would be like dealing with the jagged, tangled piles of scrap iron on the tilted, oil-slick deck. He leaned on the monitor and stared at Piper Alpha for a long time, listening to what his instincts told him, not wanting to hear them, but listening just the same, as he always had.

People had called him a daredevil, but he wasn't. He was simply a man whose limits were much greater than most others'. But he was also a man who never tried to do something he couldn't do. The days of flying through a drilling derrick and grabbing hold of a girder with one arm were gone. His presence was absolutely crucial to the completion of this job. His expertise and insight were vital. But it was foolish to think that at seventy-three he could bound from one torn metal protrusion to another on that precipitous, slippery platform.

That was for his young assistants to do now. The time had come for him to admit that to himself. The time had come for change.

"It's gonna be up to you to control that platform," he said to Raymond and Brian at breakfast the next morning. "I'll supervise the operation. I'll make sure the welders and machinists build those hooks just right for you. I'll make sure there's plenty of water on you all of the time. But I'm not gonna be over there on the platform with you. I'll be here on the *Tharos*. We need a man here to make sure everything runs smooth."

> ### BRIAN
>
> It was the first time Mr. Adair ever had to sit back and just watch, which was the hardest thing I think he ever had to do. We were in radio communication, but sometimes that wasn't so good. There were times he had no idea where we were. We were constantly occupied, working our asses off, so we didn't have time to think about the danger, but Mr. Adair worried about us all the time.
>
> See, some of those wells, every two or three hours they'd blow out and burn like hell for fifteen or twenty minutes and then die down, but they'd give a little warning, so we knew which ones were going to do that. We had to keep our eyes open, but we knew what was happening. All he could see was fire and us sliding around on ropes and stuff, directing the crane in and tying onto debris. It was tough on him. He'd be hyper, wanting to know what was going on. He was like a horse wanting to run but you've got him by the reins and won't let him go.

"It's up to us," Raymond and Brian told each other. "Like Red said, the whole world is watching. The whole world wants to know what the Red Adair Company can do, and we're going to show them. We're going to make Red proud."

They worked for weeks, fifteen to sixteen hours a day, clearing debris, starting at one end of the platform where there weren't any fires and working toward the burning wells. The machine shops ran twenty-four hours a day for them, making a grappling hook out of $9\frac{5}{8}$-inch pipe casing that could pull seventy tons, fabricating A-frame supports for them to stand on, building a fifteen-foot square platform out of twelve-inch steel H-beams for them to work from.

Once, when the wind reached seventy-five knots and the seas ran thirty-five feet, they had to stop for three days, but otherwise they never quit. Another time, just after they returned to the *Tharos* for the night, P1, the well they'd been working on, blew out and caught fire. It was the biggest blaze on Piper other than the first ones when the rig blew up. Had they stayed next to it five minutes longer they would have perished.

Right after P1 caught fire, Red met with his two men. "Just between us, we're going to put those fires out and kill those wells," Red said. "I know we will. I've got faith in both of you. But I have to protect Oxy's interests. I owe them that. So I'm gonna give the OK for a drill ship to start drilling a relief well to P1, just in case."

Red did have faith in his men, and it grew daily when he saw the quality of their work. They had determined that there were seven wells on fire, seven that hadn't shut in. On every well, there is a space between the outer cylinder — the well-bore casing — and the inner cylinder — either drill pipe or production pipe. The space between the two cylinders is called the annulus, or the annular space. The downhole safety valve flaps shut over the inner pipe, but does not seal off the annular space, and from that space came the fire of Piper's seven burning wells.

Now, as Raymond and Brian exposed one burning well after another and extinguished it, they could hear the rumble of the drill ship, two hundred yards from the platform, working toward them, breathing down their necks, backing them up, in case they failed.

On the deck of the *Tharos*, Red stood by the fire monitor, rooting for his men. If they succeeded in beating the drill ship, if they put out all the fires and capped the wells before the relief-well operation reached the stage where it would not be economically sensible to abandon it, his team would win. Red would prove to the world that not only he but the men he'd trained, the men who were going to follow him, were still the best wild-well fighters on earth. But as media helicopters circled above him, Red, too, felt hot breath behind him. Already, newspaper headlines were questioning his chances for victory.

"ADAIR PULLS BACK FROM FIERY ALPHA," trumpeted the *Aberdeen Evening Express*. "Flare-up forces Adair to pull out," claimed *The Scotsman*, and "Adair bid to douse rig blaze may fail," stated the London *Times*. "We have not put a finite time scale on Mr. Adair's operation," Gene Grogan, Occidental's vice president in charge of engineering, was quoted in the *Times* article as saying. "But it is not infinite either. It certainly does not look very good."

It was Ixtoc I all over again, only this time Red wasn't being thwarted by politicians and corrupt oil-company officials. Here, at Piper Alpha, it was just a question of whether Red and his crew could do the job, no matter how bad the weather, no matter how treacherous the platform, no matter what.

Then one morning the wind blew right, and Red was able to direct water just where he wanted it on the P1 well. The fire went out. Raymond and Brian grabbed a packer — a sealing device that is secured inside the well bore by expansion — and stuffed it into the well. Quickly they pumped fluid downhole. The fluid went all the way to the bottom, came up around the outside, up through the annulus, and P1 was dead. With P1's fire out, the remaining wells were far easier to reach, and killing them went smoothly. In two weeks, all of them had been controlled.

Raymond and Brian stayed at Piper Alpha until all the wells had been pumped full of cement and permanently sealed. Red went ashore to hold a triumphant press conference in Aberdeen, then flew to Houston. As soon as he returned home, he drove up to spend a few days with Kemmie at the lake. He was filled with mixed emotions. He felt satisfaction because of his team's success. He felt vindicated in the face of those who'd put him down and said he'd lose this one for sure, in the face of those who said he and his company were through. But at the same time he was filled with sorrow for the great loss of life, and it was hard for him to celebrate. There was no victory dinner after the killing of Piper Alpha.

One evening, Red and Kemmie had dinner at her house with two other couples. Their fourteen-year-old granddaughter, Robyn's daughter Sunny Leigh, was there too, along with two of her friends. At first Red was as lively as usual, teasing the teenage girls, telling stories, mixing everyone enormous drinks. Then the girls started playing Uno, and Red took out pictures from the Piper Alpha job to show the grown-ups. He started talking about the camera on the ROV. He was excited about the technology involved. "They'd watch the pictures the ROV sends back to the vessel," he said, "and then they'd see someone and . . ." He stopped in midsentence. "I don't want to talk about this anymore," he said, and went outside.

Kemmie could see him sitting on the dock. She thought about going out with him but changed her mind. She wondered if he was crying, but she decided to leave him alone. He sat there for a long time, close to an hour, then came in to say good night to the guests. He seemed fine now, but Kemmie decided it was a good time to talk to him anyway.

"Red," she said. "Haven't you had enough? Haven't you worked hard enough, helped out enough people, put out enough fires? Do you think maybe you ought to quit completely and take it easy, go boating, travel?"

"Travel?" Red said. "You know, Kemmie, that reminds me. They got these wells blowin' like crazy over in China and they don't know what the hell they're gonna do about 'em, and it ain't for sure yet whether I'm gonna do the job because of the governments' hemmin' and hawin' with one another, but I'm gonna start gettin' my equipment lined up and draw me up some plans because I'm tellin' you, they're gonna need help over there bad. I've never been to China yet. That's a place I'd really like to see."

"I was thinking more about both of us taking a trip, Red," Kemmie said. "Together."

That night Red thought a great deal about what Kemmie had said. He would never quit the oil patch. She knew that as well as he did. But watching how skillfully his men had killed the fires on Piper Alpha had shown him that his company would endure. And though the tragedy on Piper Alpha was too terrible for words, working from the *Tharos*, which he'd helped design, had reminded him of his contributions to the oil patch, of his work and his innovations that had helped prevent countless other Piper Alphas from taking place. "I did become somebody," he thought. "I can rest a little now."

"Kemmie, you're right," he said to her the next morning. "It's about time you and I spent some time together, away from the rat race for just a little while."

At first Kemmie didn't believe it would really come to pass. "It'll be just like always," she thought. "We'll get five miles out of town, the car phone will ring, and Red'll be gone on a job." But sure enough, a few weeks later the two of them left Houston without a hitch and spent three days driving up to Arkansas to visit Jimmy and his wife Candy. On the trip they had so much fun sightseeing that one afternoon Red even forgot to call his office.

That evening Red told Kemmie about his plans to move his office from its location on the Katy Freeway to the building over on Pinemont that serves as the Red Adair Company warehouse. "I want to bring everyone back together," Red told her. "I want to get everybody under one roof like it was in the old days." He was smiling at her, and as she looked at him, she remembered part of a poem she'd written to him way back in 1941 when he'd first begun to realize his dream in the oil patch and was away from home a lot:

Settin' chokes and crackin' jokes
And bailing out some sand.
But gee, my little fellow Red, I wish that I could see,
Just for a while, that grin, that smile,
You summon just for me.

In another year and a half, on December 3, 1989, they would celebrate their fiftieth wedding anniversary. "It has been a long journey," she thought, "but it has definitely been worth it. At last it will come full circle, and we will be back to the way things were when it was just a small company and we were all so close to one another."

They stayed with their son and daughter-in-law several days, then took another three days to drive back to Texas. It was the most time they'd spent alone together since the early days of their marriage. If you'd seen them, as they rolled down the highway, laughing about the old days and the crazy things they'd done, or sitting quietly in some small restaurant off the beaten path, you'd know that Red truly meant it when he returned to his office and announced that he and Kemmie were going traveling again, real soon. "The only difference," he said, "is that next time we're gonna take it real slow. We aren't gonna come home so quick."

EPILOGUE

In Aberdeen, not a day goes by without some reminder of the Piper Alpha tragedy. On October 17, 1988, two of Piper Alpha's accommodation modules were raised from the ocean. The smaller of the two, weighing 180 tons, contained no bodies. The larger, four stories high and weighing 1,100 tons, had seventy-four bodies trapped inside. Of the 167 men who died in the Piper Alpha disaster, 31 are still missing. Occidental divers are looking for them, even now, but it is believed they are buried in the undersea wreckage and will never be recovered.

On January 19, 1989, Lord Cullen, an eminent member of the Scottish bar, convened an official inquiry into the causes of the Piper Alpha explosion. The first phase of this inquiry ended November 1, 1989. The second phase is expected to last at least until January 1990, and any conclusions regarding the exact cause of the explosion or culpability for the Piper Alpha disaster will probably not be made public for several months after that. Thus far, every survivor of Piper Alpha who has appeared as a witness before the inquiry has said he will never go out on an offshore rig again.

On Tuesday, March 28, 1989, in a controlled explosion approved by the British Department of Energy, Piper Alpha's remains were toppled and sank to the bottom of the North Sea.

In the year following the successful capping of the Piper Alpha wells, Red did numerous wild-well control jobs in the United States and South America. He is still waiting, however, to work in China and has not given up the idea of one day returning to kill the burning wells in Iran. He has slowed down a little, but not all that much. In between jobs, and time spent relaxing with Kemmie, he goes out on Galveston Bay in his new boat, a fifty-foot Wellcraft Scarab. It is white, trimmed in red and gold, with three 420-cubic-inch turbocharged Chevrolet engines. It'll run seventy miles an hour.